PRENTICE HALL LITERATURE

Common Core Companion

Grade Eleven

WITHDRAWN

Pearson
Upper Saddle River, New Jersey
Boston, Massachusetts
Chandler, Arizona
Glenview, Illinois

Table of Contents

The instruction and activities in this book are organized around the Common Core State Standards for English and Language Arts.

Reading Standards for Literature   1

Literature 1: Cite strong and thorough textual evidence to support analysis of what the text says explicitly as well as inferences drawn from the text, including determining where the text leaves matters uncertain.

Literature 2: Determine two or more themes or central ideas of a text and analyze their development over the course of the text, including how they interact and build on one another to produce a complex account; provide an objective summary of the text.

Literature 3: Analyze the impact of the author's choices regarding how to develop and relate elements of a story or drama (e.g., where a story is set, how the action is ordered, how the characters are introduced and developed).

Literature 4: Determine the meaning of words and phrases as they are used in the text, including figurative and connotative meanings; analyze the impact of specific word choices on meaning and tone, including words with multiple meanings or language that is particularly fresh, engaging, or beautiful. (Include Shakespeare as well as other authors.)

Literature 5: Analyze how an author's choices concerning how to structure specific parts of a text (e.g., the choice of where to begin or end a story, the choice to provide a comedic or tragic resolution) contribute to its overall structure and meaning as well as its aesthetic impact.

Reading Standards for Informational Texts   89

Writing Standards   184

Writing 1: Write arguments to support claims in an analysis of substantive topics or texts, using valid reasoning and relevant and sufficient evidence.

a. Introduce precise, knowledgeable claim(s), establish the significance of the claim(s), distinguish the claim(s) from alternate or opposing claims, and create an organization that logically sequences claim(s), counterclaims, reasons, and evidence.

b. Develop claim(s) and counterclaims fairly and thoroughly, supplying the most relevant evidence for each while pointing out the strengths and limitations of both in a manner that anticipates the audience's knowledge level, concerns, values, and possible biases.

c. Use words, phrases, and clauses as well as varied syntax to link the major sections of the text, create cohesion, and clarify the relationships between claim(s) and reasons, between reasons and evidence, and between claim(s) and counterclaims.

d. Establish and maintain a formal style and objective tone while attending to the norms and conventions of the discipline in which they are writing.

e. Provide a concluding statement or section that follows from and supports the argument presented.

Writing 2: Write informative/explanatory texts to examine and convey complex ideas, concepts, and information clearly and accurately through the effective selection, organization, and analysis of content.

a. Introduce a topic; organize complex ideas, concepts, and information so that each new element builds on that which precedes it to create a unified whole; include formatting (e.g., headings), graphics (e.g., figures, tables), and multimedia when useful to aiding comprehension.

b. Develop the topic thoroughly by selecting the most significant and relevant facts, extended definitions, concrete details, quotations, or other information and examples appropriate to the audience's knowledge of the topic.

c. Use appropriate and varied transitions and syntax to link the major sections of the text, create cohesion, and clarify the relationships among complex ideas and concepts.

d. Use precise language, domain-specific vocabulary, and techniques such as metaphor, simile, and analogy to manage the complexity of the topic.

e. Establish and maintain a formal style and objective tone while attending to the norms and conventions of the discipline in which they are writing.

f. Provide a concluding statement or section that follows from and supports the information or explanation presented (e.g., articulating implications or the significance of the topic).

Writing 3: Write narratives to develop real or imagined experiences or events using effective technique, well-chosen details, and well-structured event sequences.

a. Engage and orient the reader by setting out a problem, situation, or observation and its significance, establishing one or multiple point(s) of view, and introducing a narrator and/or characters; create a smooth progression of experiences or events.

b. Use narrative techniques, such as dialogue, pacing, description, reflection, and multiple plot lines, to develop experiences, events, and/or characters.

c. Use a variety of techniques to sequence events so that they build on one another to create a coherent whole and build toward a particular tone and outcome (e.g., a sense of mystery, suspense, growth, or resolution).

d. Use precise words and phrases, telling details, and sensory language to convey a vivid picture of the experiences, events, setting, and/or characters.

e. Provide a conclusion that follows from and reflects on what is experienced, observed, or resolved over the course of the narrative.

Writing 4: Produce clear and coherent writing in which the development, organization, and style are appropriate to task, purpose, and audience. (Grade-specific expectations for writing types are defined in standards 1–3.)

Writing 5: Develop and strengthen writing as needed by planning, revising, editing, rewriting, or trying a new approach, focusing on addressing what is most significant for a specific purpose and audience. (Editing for conventions should demonstrate command of Language standards 1–3 up to and including grades 11–12.)

Writing 6: Use technology, including the Internet, to produce, publish, and update individual or shared writing products in response to ongoing feedback, including new arguments or information.

Writing 7: Conduct short as well as more sustained research projects to answer a question (including a self-generated question) or solve a problem; narrow or broaden the inquiry when appropriate; synthesize multiple sources on the subject, demonstrating understanding of the subject under investigation.

Writing 8: Gather relevant information from multiple authoritative print and digital sources, using advanced searches effectively; assess the strengths and limitations of each source in terms of the task, purpose, and audience; integrate information into the text selectively to maintain the flow of ideas, avoiding plagiarism and overreliance on any one source and following a standard format for citation.

Writing 9: Draw evidence from literary or informational texts to support analysis, reflection, and research.

    a. Apply grades 11–12 Reading standards to literature (e.g., "Demonstrate knowledge of eighteenth-, nineteenth- and early-twentieth-century foundational works of American literature, including how two or more texts from the same period treat similar themes or topics").

    b. Apply grades 11–12 Reading standards to literary nonfiction (e.g., "Delineate and evaluate the reasoning in seminal U.S. texts, including the application of constitutional principles and use of legal reasoning [e.g., in U.S. Supreme Court Case majority opinions and dissents] and the premises, purposes, and arguments in works of public advocacy [e.g., *The Federalist*, presidential addresses]").

Writing 10: Write routinely over extended time frames (time for research, reflection, and revision) and shorter time frames (a single sitting or a day or two) for a range of tasks, purposes, and audiences.

Speaking and Listening Standards   277

Speaking and Listening 1: Initiate and participate effectively in a range of collaborative discussions (one-on-one, in groups, and teacher-led) with diverse partners on grades 11–12 topics, texts, and issues, building on others' ideas and expressing their own clearly and persuasively.

    a. Come to discussions prepared, having read and researched material under study; explicitly draw on that preparation by referring to evidence from texts and other research on the topic or issue to stimulate a thoughtful, well-reasoned exchange of ideas.

    b. Work with peers to promote civil, democratic discussions and decision-making, set clear goals and deadlines, and establish individual roles as needed.

    c. Propel conversations by posing and responding to questions that probe reasoning and evidence; ensure a hearing for a full range of positions on a topic or issue; clarify, verify, or challenge ideas and conclusions; and promote divergent and creative perspectives.

d. Respond thoughtfully to diverse perspectives; synthesize comments, claims, and evidence made on all sides of an issue; resolve contradictions when possible; and determine what additional information or research is required to deepen the investigation or complete the task.

Speaking and Listening 2: Integrate multiple sources of information presented in diverse formats and media (e.g., visually, quantitatively, orally) in order to make informed decisions and solve problems, evaluating the credibility and accuracy of each source and noting any discrepancies among the data.

Speaking and Listening 3: Evaluate a speaker's point of view, reasoning, and use of evidence and rhetoric, assessing the stance, premises, links among ideas, word choice, points of emphasis, and tone used.

Speaking and Listening 4: Present information, findings, and supporting evidence, conveying a clear and distinct perspective, such that listeners can follow the line of reasoning, alternative or opposing perspectives are addressed, and the organization, development, substance, and style are appropriate to purpose, audience, and a range of formal and informal tasks.

Speaking and Listening 5: Make strategic use of digital media (e.g., textual, graphical, audio, visual, and interactive elements) in presentations to enhance understanding of findings, reasoning, and evidence and to add interest.

Speaking and Listening 6: Adapt speech to a variety of contexts and tasks, demonstrating a command of formal English when indicated or appropriate. (See grades 11–12 Language standards 1 and 3 for specific expectations.)

Language Standards   313

Language 1: Demonstrate command of the conventions of standard English grammar and usage when writing or speaking.

  a. Apply the understanding that usage is a matter of convention, can change over time, and is sometimes contested.

  b. Resolve issues of complex or contested usage, consulting references (e.g., *Merriam-Webster's Dictionary of English Usage, Garner's Modern American Usage*) as needed.

Language 2: Demonstrate command of the conventions of standard English capitalization, punctuation, and spelling when writing.

  a. Observe hyphenation conventions.

  b. Spell correctly.

Language 3: Apply knowledge of language to understand how language functions in different contexts, to make effective choices for meaning or style, and to comprehend more fully when reading or listening.

  • Vary syntax for effect, consulting references (e.g., Tufte's *Artful Sentences*) for guidance as needed; apply an understanding of syntax to the study of complex texts when reading.

Language 4: Determine or clarify the meaning of unknown and multiple-meaning words and phrases based on grades 11–12 reading and content, choosing flexibly from a range of strategies.

  a. Use context (e.g., the overall meaning of a sentence, paragraph, or text; a word's position or function in a sentence) as a clue to the meaning of a word or phrase.

  b. Identify and correctly use patterns of word changes that indicate different meanings or parts of speech (e.g., *conceive, conception, conceivable*).

  c. Consult general and specialized reference materials (e.g., dictionaries, glossaries, thesauruses), both print and digital, to find the pronunciation of a word or determine or clarify its precise meaning, its part of speech, its etymology, or its standard usage.

Language 5: Demonstrate understanding of figurative language, word relationships, and nuances in word meanings.

a. Interpret figures of speech (e.g., hyperbole, paradox) in context and analyze their role in the text.

b. Analyze nuances in the meaning of words with similar denotations.

Language 6: Acquire and use accurately general academic and domain-specific words and phrases, sufficient for reading, writing, speaking, and listening at the college and career readiness level; demonstrate independence in gathering vocabulary knowledge when considering a word or phrase important to comprehension or expression.

Performance Tasks   338

About the *Common Core Companion*

The Common Core Companion student workbook provides instruction and practice in the Common Core State Standards. The standards are designed to help all students become college and career ready by the end of grade 12. Here is a closer look at this workbook:

Reading Standards

Reading Standards for Literature and Informational Texts are supported with instruction, examples, and multiple copies of worksheets that you can use over the course of the year. These key standards are revisited in the Performance Tasks section of your workbook.

Writing Standards

Full writing workshops are provided for Writing standards 1, 2, 3, and 8. Writing standards 4, 5, 6, 7, 9, and 10 are supported with direct instruction and worksheets that provide targeted practice. In addition, writing standards are revisited in Speaking and Listening activities and in Performance Tasks.

Speaking and Listening Standards

Detailed instruction and practice are provided for each Speaking and Listening standard. Additional opportunities to master these standards are provided in the Performance Tasks.

Language Standards

Explicit instruction and detailed examples support each Language standard. In addition, practice worksheets and graphic organizers provide additional opportunities for students to master these standards.

Performance Tasks

Using the examples in the Common Core framework as a guide, we provide opportunities for you to test your ability to master each reading standard, along with tips for success and rubrics to help you evaluate your work.

Reading Standards for Literature

Literature 1

> **1.** Cite strong and thorough textual evidence to support analysis of what the text says explicitly as well as inferences drawn from the text, including determining where the text leaves matters uncertain.

Explanation

An author creates meaning through the use of details. Some details are **explicit:** they are directly stated. Other details are **implicit:** they give information indirectly. Implicit details act as clues. Readers must apply their own reasoning about these clues to make **inferences** and figure out what is really going on. Sometimes an author chooses to leave matters uncertain, creating **ambiguity.** An ambiguous text can be understood in two or more ways.

Story details provide **textual evidence** to support a reader's inferences and understanding. While noting the concrete details that are explicitly stated, readers should also use their own experience and reasoning to understand details that are implicit or ambiguous.

Examples

- **Explicit details** give readers basic information for understanding a text. Here's an example: "Paint was peeling from the house, and weeds choked the patch that was once a lawn." The details of the peeling paint and choking weeds directly describe the story's setting.

- Understanding **implicit details** involves a collaboration between the author and reader. For example, "Most of the trees were half bare already and dry leaves crackled under Tito's feet. A noisy vee of geese honked overhead. 'Stop complaining,' Tito told them. 'You're lucky to be heading south.'" The author doesn't directly state that it's autumn, but readers can draw these **inferences** from their own experience and from details in the text.

- An author may be purposely vague, giving **ambiguous** details to make a story richer or more interesting. For example, note Mr. Graves's response in this passage: "The owner chattered on, eagerly describing how she had worked for months to decorate this house and insisting that Mr. Graves would never find another one like it. Mr. Graves looked slowly around the living room. 'Indeed,' he said." Mr. Graves's one-word response is ambiguous because a reader might interpret it to mean that he agrees with the owner.

Academic Vocabulary

ambiguity quality of a text that can be interpreted in two or more possible ways
inference conclusion based on the reader's reasoning, experience, and details from the text
textual evidence details from a selection that are used to support a reader's analysis or inference

Apply the Standard

Use the worksheets that follow to help you apply the standard as you read. Several copies of each worksheet have been provided for you to use with a number of different selections.

- Identifying Strong Textual Evidence
- Making Inferences

Name _____ Date _____ Selection _____

Identifying Strong Textual Evidence

Use the organizer to identify strong evidence from the text. Check (√) one of the last three columns to identify what kind of details the text provides.

Quote or Detail from Text	Why It Is Important	Explicit Detail	Implicit Detail	Ambiguous Detail
1.				
2.				
3.				

Name _____ Date _____ Selection _____

Identifying Strong Textual Evidence

Use the organizer to identify strong evidence from the text. Check (√) one of the last three columns to identify what kind of details the text provides.

Quote or Detail from Text	Why It Is Important	Explicit Detail	Implicit Detail	Ambiguous Detail
1.				
2.				
3.				

For use with Literature 1

Name _____ Date _____ Selection _____

Identifying Strong Textual Evidence

Use the organizer to identify strong evidence from the text. Check (√) one of the last three columns to identify what kind of details the text provides.

Quote or Detail from Text	Why It Is Important	Explicit Detail	Implicit Detail	Ambiguous Detail
1.				
2.				
3.				

Name _____ Date _____ Selection _____

Identifying Strong Textual Evidence

Use the organizer to identify strong evidence from the text. Check (√) one of the last three columns to identify what kind of details the text provides.

Quote or Detail from Text	Why It Is Important	Explicit Detail	Implicit Detail	Ambiguous Detail
1.				
2.				
3.				

Name _____ Date _____ Selection _____

Identifying Strong Textual Evidence

Use the organizer to identify strong evidence from the text. Check (√) one of the last three columns to identify what kind of details the text provides.

Quote or Detail from Text	Why It Is Important	Explicit Detail	Implicit Detail	Ambiguous Detail
1.				
2.				
3.				

E

For use with Literature 1

Name _____ Date _____ Selection _____

Identifying Strong Textual Evidence

Use the organizer to identify strong evidence from the text. Check (√) one of the last three columns to identify what kind of details the text provides.

Quote or Detail from Text	Why It Is Important	Explicit Detail	Implicit Detail	Ambiguous Detail
1.				
2.				
3.				

Name _____ Date _____ Selection _____

Making Inferences

Use the organizer to make inferences from the text.

Details from the Text	My Inference or Conclusion
1.	
2.	
3.	
4.	

A

Name _____ Date _____ Selection _____

Making Inferences

Use the organizer to make inferences from the text.

Details from the Text	My Inference or Conclusion
1.	
2.	
3.	
4.	

B

Name _____ Date _____ Selection _____

Making Inferences

Use the organizer to make inferences from the text.

Details from the Text	My Inference or Conclusion
1.	
2.	
3.	
4.	

C

For use with Literature 1

Name _____ Date _____ Selection _____

Making Inferences

Use the organizer to make inferences from the text.

Details from the Text	My Inference or Conclusion
1.	
2.	
3.	
4.	

D

For use with Literature 1

Name _____ Date _____ Selection _____

Making Inferences

Use the organizer to make inferences from the text.

Details from the Text	My Inference or Conclusion
1.	
2.	
3.	
4.	

E

For use with Literature 1

Name _____ Date _____ Selection _____

Making Inferences

Use the organizer to make inferences from the text.

Details from the Text	My Inference or Conclusion
1.	
2.	
3.	
4.	

For use with Literature 1

Literature 2

> 2. Determine two or more themes or central ideas of a text and analyze their development over the course of the text, including how they interact and build on one another to produce a complex account; provide an objective summary of the text.

Explanation

A **theme** is the central idea or message about life that a literary work communicates. Examples of themes that appear throughout literature are the power of love, the danger of greed, and the importance of courage. In some cases, a literary work might have more than one theme. Multiple themes in a text sometimes reinforce each other; in some cases, however, they conflict with or even contradict one another.

A theme may be directly stated, as when a fable concludes with a moral such as, "He who hesitates is lost." In many works, however, themes are implied, not directly stated. To determine the implied theme of a work, the reader needs to identify and analyze elements that the writer emphasizes, such as patterns of events, strong contrasts between or changes in characters, and repeated images. Before determining a work's themes, it helps to **summarize** the text by briefly stating the main topic and ideas and the most important details. You can then analyze your summary to see what it suggests about the themes of the work.

Examples

- **Summary** This summary identifies the main character, conflict, climax, and resolution of a story: In this story, an army private named Marvin is awarded medals and praised for his bravery. Yet the soldier suffers from the guilt of knowing he hasn't acted bravely at all—he was trying to run away when he was wounded. In the end, Marvin confesses his cowardice and returns his medals. His former admirers turn away in disgust, not recognizing the courage it took for Marvin to be honest.

- **Analysis of Themes** The summary above suggests that one theme of the story is the conflict between a person's self-knowledge and others' perceptions of the person. Another theme might be the difference between common notions of heroism and genuine courage. A strong analysis will identify these two themes and examine how they interact. It will also chart their development: For example, the theme of self-knowledge versus others' perceptions might be introduced near the story's beginning, when readers learn the difference between what Marvin actually did and what others think he did. Marvin's guilt when he is awarded the medals might then develop, or reinforce, the theme.

Academic Vocabulary

theme the central idea or message of a literary work

summarize to state in brief and in one's own words the central ideas and key details of a work

Apply the Standard

Use the worksheets that follow to help you apply the standard as you read. Several copies of each worksheet have been provided for you to use with a number of different selections.

- Summarizing a Literary Text
- Analyzing Themes and Central Ideas

Name _____ Date _____ Selection _____

Summarizing a Literary Text

Use the organizer to list the most important elements of a literary text, such as a short story. Then, use that information to write a summary of the text.

Main Character(s)
Central Conflict
Main Points or Events
Climax and Resolution

Summary ....

....

....

....

....

....

....

....

....

....

A

For use with Literature 2

Name _____ Date _____ Selection _____

Summarizing a Literary Text

Use the organizer to list the most important elements of a literary text, such as a short story. Then, use that information to write a summary of the text.

Main Character(s)
Central Conflict
Main Points or Events
Climax and Resolution

Summary ....

....

....

....

....

....

....

....

....

For use with Literature 2

Name _____ Date _____ Selection _____

Summarizing a Literary Text

Use the organizer to list the most important elements of a literary text, such as a short story. Then, use that information to write a summary of the text.

Main Character(s)
Central Conflict
Main Points or Events
Climax and Resolution

Summary ....

....

....

....

....

....

....

....

....

C

Name _____ Date _____ Selection _____

Summarizing a Literary Text

Use the organizer to list the most important elements of a literary text, such as a short story. Then, use that information to write a summary of the text.

Main Character(s)
Central Conflict
Main Points or Events
Climax and Resolution

Summary ....

....

....

....

....

....

....

....

....

....

D

Name _____ Date _____ Selection _____

Summarizing a Literary Text

Use the organizer to list the most important elements of a literary text, such as a short story. Then, use that information to write a summary of the text.

Main Character(s)
Central Conflict
Main Points or Events
Climax and Resolution

Summary ....

....

....

....

....

....

....

....

....

Name _____ Date _____ Selection _____

Summarizing a Literary Text

Use the organizer to list the most important elements of a literary text, such as a short story. Then, use that information to write a summary of the text.

Main Character(s)
Central Conflict
Main Points or Events
Climax and Resolution

Summary ....

....

....

....

....

....

....

....

....

Name _____ Date _____ Selection _____

Analyzing Themes and Central Ideas

Examine your summary of a text to identify two different themes in the text. Use the organizer to state the themes. For each theme, provide details from the text that help convey and develop it.

Theme	Textual Details That Develop the Theme
Theme 1	1. 2. 3.
Theme 2	1. 2. 3.

Name _____ Date _____ Selection _____

Analyzing Themes and Central Ideas

Examine your summary of a text to identify two different themes in the text. Use the organizer to state the themes. For each theme, provide details from the text that help convey and develop it.

Theme	Textual Details That Develop the Theme
Theme 1	1. 2. 3.
Theme 2	1. 2. 3.

Name _____ Date _____ Selection _____

Analyzing Themes and Central Ideas

Examine your summary of a text to identify two different themes in the text. Use the organizer to state the themes. For each theme, provide details from the text that help convey and develop it.

Theme	Textual Details That Develop the Theme
Theme 1	1. 2. 3.
Theme 2	1. 2. 3.

C

Name _____ Date _____ Selection _____

Analyzing Themes and Central Ideas

Examine your summary of a text to identify two different themes in the text. Use the organizer to state the themes. For each theme, provide details from the text that help convey and develop it.

Theme	Textual Details That Develop the Theme
Theme 1	1. 2. 3.
Theme 2	1. 2. 3.

D

Name _____ Date _____ Selection _____

Analyzing Themes and Central Ideas

Examine your summary of a text to identify two different themes in the text. Use the organizer to state the themes. For each theme, provide details from the text that help convey and develop it.

Theme	Textual Details That Develop the Theme
Theme 1	1. 2. 3.
Theme 2	1. 2. 3.

E

Name _____ Date _____ Selection _____

Analyzing Themes and Central Ideas

Examine your summary of a text to identify two different themes in the text. Use the organizer to state the themes. For each theme, provide details from the text that help convey and develop it.

Theme	Textual Details That Develop the Theme
Theme 1	1. 2. 3.
Theme 2	1. 2. 3.

F

Literature 3

> **3.** Analyze the impact of the author's choices regarding how to develop and relate elements of a story or drama (e.g., where a story is set, how the action is ordered, how the characters are introduced and developed).

Explanation

As authors write stories and plays, they make decisions that will have a strong impact on both the work itself and on readers.

- **Setting** The **setting** is the time and place of the action in a story or play. This can include the beliefs and customs of a particular time and place. The setting provides a backdrop for the action. It can also be a force that the characters struggle against and thus, a source of the central conflict. Author's choices about setting help create a work's atmosphere or mood.

- **Plot** The sequence of events in a story or play is the **plot.** Often authors begin a plot by introducing the characters and the conflict, or struggle, between opposing forces. From there, the events in the plot develop the conflict until it rises to a climax and is resolved. Authors choose many variations on this plot structure, however, including starting a story or play in the middle and providing flashbacks to show what happened earlier.

- **Characterization** The way authors choose to introduce and develop the characters is called **characterization.** Authors might choose to tell readers about a character directly, by providing explicit descriptions. Authors may also reveal a character indirectly, through what the character says, thinks, or does or by showing how other characters react to him or her.

Examples

Isaac Bashevis Singer set his story "Zlateh the Goat" in a village during the winter. A poor family must sell their beloved goat, setting the events of the plot in motion. Singer introduces the two main characters: Aaron, the son, who is given the task of bringing Zlateh, the goat, to the butcher. As the two set out on the country road, the setting itself becomes a source of conflict in the story. A terrible blizzard threatens the lives of Aaron and Zlateh, and the pair take shelter by burrowing inside a haystack. Singer uses indirect characterization to show readers Zlateh's strength and warmth. Although she is only a goat, she saves Aaron's life by giving him milk. Singer's choices about the setting, characters, and plot create the story's heartwarming impact.

Academic Vocabulary

characterization the way a writer develops and reveals a character's personality

plot the sequence of events in a story or play, usually involving characters in a conflict

setting the time and place of the action in a story or play

Apply the Standard

Use the worksheets that follow to help you apply the standard as you read. Several copies of each worksheet have been provided for you to use with a number of different selections.

- Analyze Characterization

- Analyzing Setting and Plot

Name _____   Date _____   Selection _____

Analyze Characterization

Use the character wheel to analyze the author's characterization of the main character in a selection.

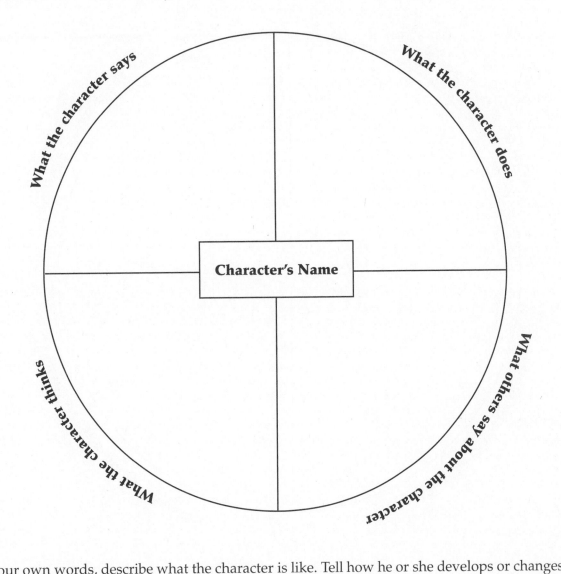

In your own words, describe what the character is like. Tell how he or she develops or changes over the course of the selection. Then, describe how the method used to unveil the character's traits affects your reaction to the story.

....

....

....

....

....

A

Name _____ Date _____ Selection _____

Analyze Characterization

Use the character wheel to analyze the author's characterization of the main character in a selection.

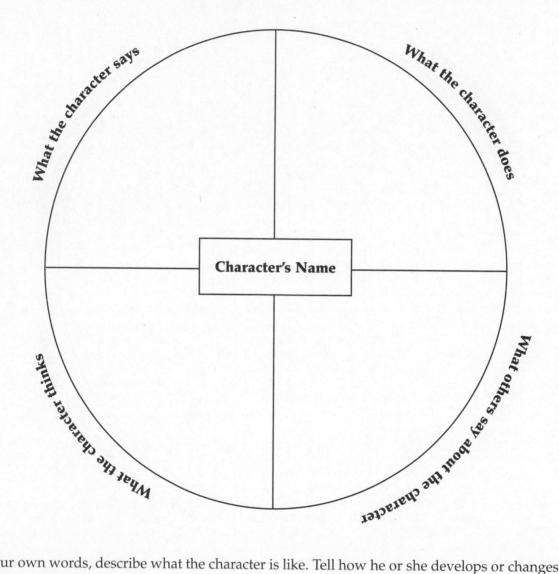

In your own words, describe what the character is like. Tell how he or she develops or changes over the course of the selection. Then, describe how the method used to unveil the character's traits affects your reaction to the story.

....

....

....

....

....

Name _____ Date _____ Selection _____

Analyze Characterization

Use the character wheel to analyze the author's characterization of the main character in a selection.

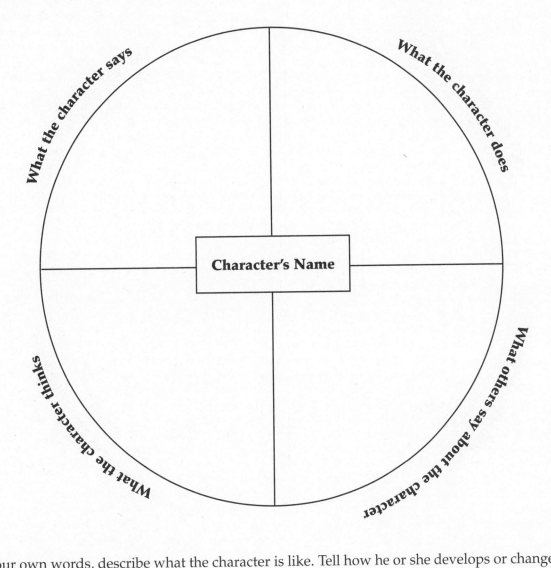

In your own words, describe what the character is like. Tell how he or she develops or changes over the course of the selection. Then, describe how the method used to unveil the character's traits affects your reaction to the story.

....

....

....

....

....

For use with Literature 3

Name _____ Date _____ Selection _____

Analyze Characterization

Use the character wheel to analyze the author's characterization of the main character in a selection.

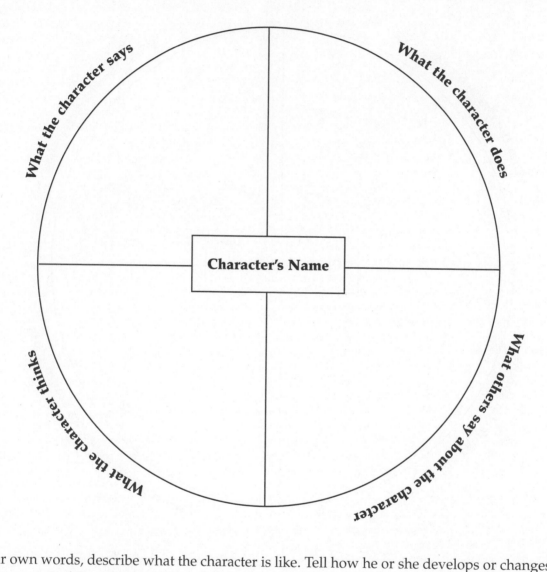

In your own words, describe what the character is like. Tell how he or she develops or changes over the course of the selection. Then, describe how the method used to unveil the character's traits affects your reaction to the story.

....

....

....

....

....

For use with Literature 3

Analyze Characterization

Use the character wheel to analyze the author's characterization of the main character in a selection.

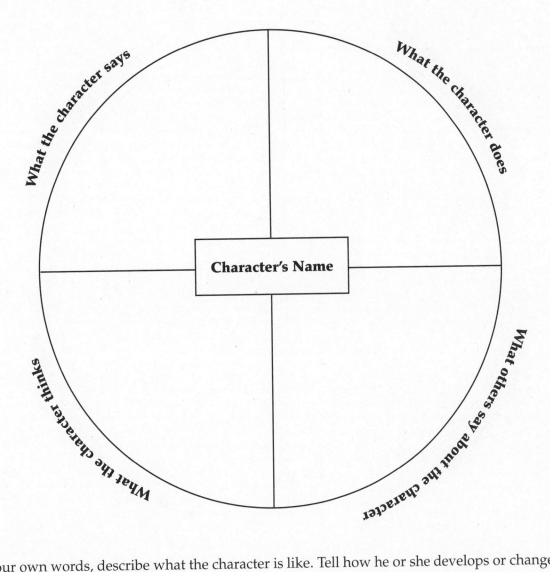

In your own words, describe what the character is like. Tell how he or she develops or changes over the course of the selection. Then, describe how the method used to unveil the character's traits affects your reaction to the story.

....

....

....

....

....

For use with Literature 3

Name _____ Date _____ Selection _____

Analyze Characterization

Use the character wheel to analyze the author's characterization of the main character in a selection.

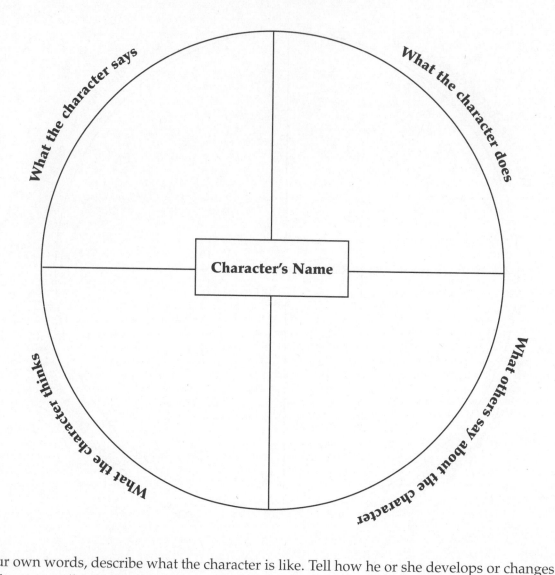

In your own words, describe what the character is like. Tell how he or she develops or changes over the course of the selection. Then, describe how the method used to unveil the character's traits affects your reaction to the story.

....

....

....

....

....

Name _____ Date _____ Selection _____

Analyzing Setting and Plot

Use the graphic organizer to analyze the key elements of the selection.

SETTING:

  Time:

  Place:

PLOT

  3 Key Events:

  1. ....

  2. ....

  3. ....

  Conflict:

  Climax:

  Resolution:

What impact do the author's choices about setting and plot have on the selection and on readers?

....

....

....

....

A

Name _____ Date _____ Selection _____

Analyzing Setting and Plot

Use the graphic organizer to analyze the key elements of the selection.

SETTING:

   Time:

   Place:

PLOT

   3 Key Events:

   1. ....

   2. ....

   3. ....

   Conflict:

   Climax:

   Resolution:

What impact do the author's choices about setting and plot have on the selection and on readers?

....

....

....

....

For use with Literature 3

Name _____ Date _____ Selection _____

Analyzing Setting and Plot

Use the graphic organizer to analyze the key elements of the selection.

SETTING:

  Time:

  Place:

PLOT

  3 Key Events:

  1. ....

  2. ....

  3. ....

  Conflict:

  Climax:

  Resolution:

What impact do the author's choices about setting and plot have on the selection and on readers?

....

....

....

....

Name _____ Date _____ Selection _____

Analyzing Setting and Plot

Use the graphic organizer to analyze the key elements of the selection.

SETTING:
 	
  Time:
 	
  Place:

PLOT
 	
  3 Key Events:
 	
  1. ....
 	
  2. ....
 	
  3. ....
 	
  Conflict:
 	
  Climax:
 	
  Resolution:

What impact do the author's choices about setting and plot have on the selection and on readers?

....

....

....

....

Name _____ Date _____ Selection _____

Analyzing Setting and Plot

Use the graphic organizer to analyze the key elements of the selection.

SETTING:
 	
  Time:
 	
  Place:

PLOT
 	
  3 Key Events:
 	
  1. ....
  2. ....
  3. ....
 	
  Conflict:
 	
  Climax:
 	
  Resolution:

What impact do the author's choices about setting and plot have on the selection and on readers?

....

....

....

....

E

Name _____ Date _____ Selection _____

Analyzing Setting and Plot

Use the graphic organizer to analyze the key elements of the selection.

SETTING:
Time:
Place:
PLOT
3 Key Events:
1. ....
2. ....
3. ....
Conflict:
Climax:
Resolution:

What impact do the author's choices about setting and plot have on the selection and on readers?

....

....

....

....

Literature 4

> **4. Determine the meaning of words and phrases as they are used in the text, including figurative and connotative meanings; analyze the impact of specific word choices on meaning and tone, including words with multiple meanings or language that is particularly fresh, engaging, or beautiful.**

Explanation

Words can express both meaning and feeling. That's why writers choose their words carefully. By analyzing a writer's choice of words, you can figure out both the meaning of a text and its **tone**—the attitude a writer expresses about a subject. To create such effects, writers use

- **Words with Strong Connotations** *Connotation* refers to the associations that a word calls to mind. For example, the words *dignified* and *snobby* are both words that mean "reserved." Yet *dignified* has a positive connotation indicating a seriousness of manner, whereas *snobby* has the negative connotation of being pompous or elitist.

- **Words with Multiple Meanings** Several English words have multiple meanings, such as *grave* which can mean "a burial place" or "deeply serious." Writers sometimes use words with multiple meanings or words with similar sounds for the sake of irony or humor—as they do when making puns. For example, a writer might say, "The reason the baker works is that he *kneads* dough." That is a play on the words *needs* and *kneads*, which sound alike. The word *dough* is informally used to mean money.

- **Figurative Language** Colorful, inventive use of language is called *figurative language*. It is language that is not meant to be interpreted literally. Writers use figurative language to create striking images and comparisons or to state their ideas in new and unusual ways. *Similes* and *metaphors* are two examples of figurative language:

  A **simile** is a comparison of two apparently unlike things that uses the word *like* or *as*. *Mist lay over the field like gauze* is a simile.

  A **metaphor** is a figure of speech in which two apparently unlike things are shown to have a point of similarity. *Death, that long sleep* is a metaphor. It compares death to a long sleep.

Examples

In his famous work *Walden*, Henry David Thoreau uses similes, metaphors, and words with specific connotations to evoke a tone of peace and calm.

- I could not afford to sacrifice the **bloom of the present moment** to any work . . .
- I love a **broad margin to my life**.
- I grew in those seasons **like corn in the night** . . .

Academic Vocabulary

connotation the associations a word calls to mind

figurative language writing or speech that is imaginative and not meant to be taken literally

Apply the Standard

Use the worksheets that follow to help you apply the standard as you read. Several copies of each worksheet have been provided for you to use with different literature selections.

- Understanding Connotations and Multiple-Meaning Words
- Understanding Figurative Language

Name _____   Date _____   Selection _____

Understanding Connotations and Multiple-Meaning Words

Connotations Use this organizer to list words four or phrases from a text you have read that carry strong connotative meanings. Provide the literal (dictionary) meaning for each word or phrase; then describe its connotation.

Word or Phrase from the Text	Literal Meaning	Connotation
1.		
2.		
3.		
4.		

Multiple-Meaning Words Use this organizer to identify four words from the text that can have multiple meanings. In the first column, write the sentence in which the word is used. Then write two meanings for each word. Circle the meaning that is used in the text.

Sentence with Multiple-Meaning Word	Meanings
1.	a) b)
2.	a) b)
3.	a) b)
4.	a) b)

A

For use with Literature 4

Name _____ Date _____ Selection _____

Understanding Connotations and Multiple-Meaning Words

Connotations Use this organizer to list words four or phrases from a text you have read that carry strong connotative meanings. Provide the literal (dictionary) meaning for each word or phrase; then describe its connotation.

Word or Phrase from the Text	Literal Meaning	Connotation
1.		
2.		
3.		
4.		

Multiple-Meaning Words Use this organizer to identify four words from the text that can have multiple meanings. In the first column, write the sentence in which the word is used. Then write two meanings for each word. Circle the meaning that is used in the text.

Sentence with Multiple-Meaning Word	Meanings
1.	a) b)
2.	a) b)
3.	a) b)
4.	a) b)

For use with Literature 4

Name _____ Date _____ Selection _____

Understanding Connotations and Multiple-Meaning Words

Connotations Use this organizer to list words four or phrases from a text you have read that carry strong connotative meanings. Provide the literal (dictionary) meaning for each word or phrase; then describe its connotation.

Word or Phrase from the Text	Literal Meaning	Connotation
1.		
2.		
3.		
4.		

Multiple-Meaning Words Use this organizer to identify four words from the text that can have multiple meanings. In the first column, write the sentence in which the word is used. Then write two meanings for each word. Circle the meaning that is used in the text.

Sentence with Multiple-Meaning Word	Meanings
1.	a) b)
2.	a) b)
3.	a) b)
4.	a) b)

C

For use with Literature 4

Name _____ Date _____ Selection _____

Understanding Connotations and Multiple-Meaning Words

Connotations Use this organizer to list words four or phrases from a text you have read that carry strong connotative meanings. Provide the literal (dictionary) meaning for each word or phrase; then describe its connotation.

Word or Phrase from the Text	Literal Meaning	Connotation
1.		
2.		
3.		
4.		

Multiple-Meaning Words Use this organizer to identify four words from the text that can have multiple meanings. In the first column, write the sentence in which the word is used. Then write two meanings for each word. Circle the meaning that is used in the text.

Sentence with Multiple-Meaning Word	Meanings
1.	a) b)
2.	a) b)
3.	a) b)
4.	a) b)

D

For use with Literature 4

Name _____ Date _____ Selection _____

Understanding Connotations and Multiple-Meaning Words

Connotations Use this organizer to list words four or phrases from a text you have read that carry strong connotative meanings. Provide the literal (dictionary) meaning for each word or phrase; then describe its connotation.

Word or Phrase from the Text	Literal Meaning	Connotation
1.		
2.		
3.		
4.		

Multiple-Meaning Words Use this organizer to identify four words from the text that can have multiple meanings. In the first column, write the sentence in which the word is used. Then write two meanings for each word. Circle the meaning that is used in the text.

Sentence with Multiple-Meaning Word	Meanings
1.	a) b)
2.	a) b)
3.	a) b)
4.	a) b)

E

For use with Literature 4

Name _____ Date _____ Selection _____

Understanding Connotations and Multiple-Meaning Words

Connotations Use this organizer to list words four or phrases from a text you have read that carry strong connotative meanings. Provide the literal (dictionary) meaning for each word or phrase; then describe its connotation.

Word or Phrase from the Text	Literal Meaning	Connotation
1.		
2.		
3.		
4.		

Multiple-Meaning Words Use this organizer to identify four words from the text that can have multiple meanings. In the first column, write the sentence in which the word is used. Then write two meanings for each word. Circle the meaning that is used in the text.

Sentence with Multiple-Meaning Word	Meanings
1.	a) b)
2.	a) b)
3.	a) b)
4.	a) b)

F

For use with Literature 4

Name _____ Date _____ Selection _____

Understanding Figurative Language

Use the left column of the organizer to list examples of figurative language from the text. In the right column, describe or explain the meaning of each figure of speech. Then, at the bottom of the page, write how your examples of figurative language help determine the tone of the selection.

Figurative Language from the Text	What It Means
1.	
2.	
3.	
4.	
5.	

Tone of the Selection

Name _____ Date _____ Selection _____

Understanding Figurative Language

Use the left column of the organizer to list examples of figurative language from the text. In the right column, describe or explain the meaning of each figure of speech. Then, at the bottom of the page, write how your examples of figurative language help determine the tone of the selection.

Figurative Language from the Text	What It Means
1.	
2.	
3.	
4.	
5.	

Tone of the Selection

B

For use with Literature 4

Name _____ Date _____ Selection _____

Understanding Figurative Language

Use the left column of the organizer to list examples of figurative language from the text. In the right column, describe or explain the meaning of each figure of speech. Then, at the bottom of the page, write how your examples of figurative language help determine the tone of the selection.

Figurative Language from the Text	What It Means
1.	
2.	
3.	
4.	
5.	

Tone of the Selection

For use with Literature 4

Name _____ Date _____ Selection _____

Understanding Figurative Language

Use the left column of the organizer to list examples of figurative language from the text. In the right column, describe or explain the meaning of each figure of speech. Then, at the bottom of the page, write how your examples of figurative language help determine the tone of the selection.

Figurative Language from the Text	What It Means
1.	
2.	
3.	
4.	
5.	

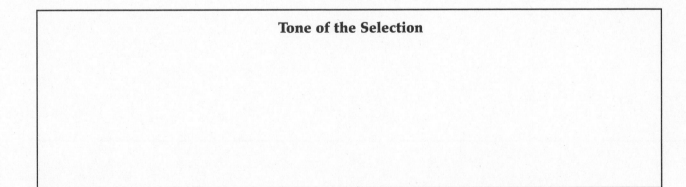

Tone of the Selection

Name _____ Date _____ Selection _____

Understanding Figurative Language

Use the left column of the organizer to list examples of figurative language from the text. In the right column, describe or explain the meaning of each figure of speech. Then, at the bottom of the page, write how your examples of figurative language help determine the tone of the selection.

Figurative Language from the Text	What It Means
1.	
2.	
3.	
4.	
5.	

Tone of the Selection

E

For use with Literature 4

Name _____ Date _____ Selection _____

Understanding Figurative Language

Use the left column of the organizer to list examples of figurative language from the text. In the right column, describe or explain the meaning of each figure of speech. Then, at the bottom of the page, write how your examples of figurative language help determine the tone of the selection.

Figurative Language from the Text	What It Means
1.	
2.	
3.	
4.	
5.	

Tone of the Selection

For use with Literature 4

Literature 5

> 5. **Analyze how an author's choices concerning how to structure specific parts of a text (e.g., the choice of where to begin or end a story, the choice to provide a comedic or tragic resolution) contribute to its overall structure and meaning as well as its aesthetic impact.**

Explanation

Authors must make many choices when they are structuring a work of literature. Each choice affects the overall meaning of the text, as well as its impact on the reader. Manipulating a story's structure is one such technique. Typically, authors arrange the plot, or the series of events in a story, in chronological order—the order in which they take place in time—with events building to a climax, after which the conflict is resolved. However, authors sometimes choose to begin a story in the middle or even at the end. Authors may choose a **tragic resolution,** where the hero dies, or a **comic resolution,** with a happy ending. Analyzing how an author uses structure to contribute to the meaning of a story will help you become a more critical reader, and ultimately, a better writer.

Example

Jack London begins the story "To Build a Fire" at daybreak when a man "turned aside from the main Yukon trail" to follow his own path. This beginning hints at the man's fatal character flaws of overconfidence and ignorance of the Yukon. London develops the plot in chronological order, building suspense with each scene as the cold becomes increasingly bitter. London's use of the limited third-person point of view contributes to the story's sense of doom—the man doesn't realize the severe danger that he is facing, but the reader does. In the story's tragic resolution, the man freezes to death.

Academic Vocabulary

tragic resolution a work of literature that features the downfall or death of the main character

comedic resolution a work of literature that features a happy ending

Apply the Standard

Use the worksheet that follows to help you apply the standard as you read. Several copies of the worksheet have been provided for you to use with different literature selections.

- Analyzing Structure

Name _____ Date _____ Selection _____

Analyzing Structure

Use the graphic organizer to describe the structural elements that appear in a text you have read. Then tell how the author's choices affect the meaning and emotional impact of the text.

Point of View

From what point of view is the story told?

Effect on meaning and emotional impact:

Story Beginning

How does the story begin?

Effect on meaning and emotional impact:

Story Resolution

How is the story resolved?

Effect on meaning and emotional impact:

Flashbacks

Does the story include flashbacks? If so, describe them.

Effect on meaning and emotional impact:

A

For use with Literature 5

Name _____ Date _____ Selection _____

Analyzing Structure

Use the graphic organizer to describe the structural elements that appear in a text you have read. Then tell how the author's choices affect the meaning and emotional impact of the text.

Point of View

From what point of view is the story told?

Effect on meaning and emotional impact:

Story Beginning

How does the story begin?

Effect on meaning and emotional impact:

Story Resolution

How is the story resolved?

Effect on meaning and emotional impact:

Flashbacks

Does the story include flashbacks? If so, describe them.

Effect on meaning and emotional impact:

For use with Literature 5

Name _____ Date _____ Selection _____

Analyzing Structure

Use the graphic organizer to describe the structural elements that appear in a text you have read. Then tell how the author's choices affect the meaning and emotional impact of the text.

Point of View
From what point of view is the story told?
Effect on meaning and emotional impact:
Story Beginning
How does the story begin?
Effect on meaning and emotional impact:
Story Resolution
How is the story resolved?
Effect on meaning and emotional impact:
Flashbacks
Does the story include flashbacks? If so, describe them.
Effect on meaning and emotional impact:

C

Name _____ Date _____ Selection _____

Analyzing Structure

Use the graphic organizer to describe the structural elements that appear in a text you have read. Then tell how the author's choices affect the meaning and emotional impact of the text.

Point of View
From what point of view is the story told?
Effect on meaning and emotional impact:

Story Beginning
How does the story begin?
Effect on meaning and emotional impact:

Story Resolution
How is the story resolved?
Effect on meaning and emotional impact:

Flashbacks
Does the story include flashbacks? If so, describe them.
Effect on meaning and emotional impact:

D

For use with Literature 5

Name _____ Date _____ Selection _____

Analyzing Structure

Use the graphic organizer to describe the structural elements that appear in a text you have read. Then tell how the author's choices affect the meaning and emotional impact of the text.

Point of View

From what point of view is the story told?

Effect on meaning and emotional impact:

Story Beginning

How does the story begin?

Effect on meaning and emotional impact:

Story Resolution

How is the story resolved?

Effect on meaning and emotional impact:

Flashbacks

Does the story include flashbacks? If so, describe them.

Effect on meaning and emotional impact:

Analyzing Structure

Use the graphic organizer to describe the structural elements that appear in a text you have read. Then tell how the author's choices affect the meaning and emotional impact of the text.

Point of View From what point of view is the story told?   Effect on meaning and emotional impact:
Story Beginning How does the story begin?   Effect on meaning and emotional impact:
Story Resolution How is the story resolved?   Effect on meaning and emotional impact:
Flashbacks Does the story include flashbacks? If so, describe them.   Effect on meaning and emotional impact:

Literature 6

> 6. **Analyze a case in which grasping point of view requires distinguishing what is directly stated in a text from what is really meant (e.g., satire, sarcasm, irony, or understatement).**

Explanation

Sometimes what an author means is directly stated in the text. Other times, an author conveys his or her ideas indirectly—by using the literary techniques below. To understand an author's point of view, readers must distinguish between what is stated and what the author really means.

- **Satire** is writing that uses humor to expose and ridicule corruption and folly. Although a satire is often humorous, its main purpose is to correct societal flaws and shortcomings.
- **Irony** is a discrepancy between appearance and reality, between expectation and outcome, or between meaning and intention. With **dramatic irony,** the reader or audience knows or understands something that a character or speaker does not. With **verbal irony,** there is a contrast between what a character says and what is really meant.
- **Sarcasm** is a type of verbal irony in which the tone is particularly mocking or bitter. Sarcasm expresses scorn, contempt, or disapproval for a person or situation.
- **Understatement** is a figure of speech in which the stated meaning says less than what is really meant. It can show humor, bravery, or an unlikely response to a difficult situation.

Examples

- **Satire:** In his poem "The Unknown Citizen," W.H. Auden satirizes the lack of true freedom that exists when people are controlled by bureaucracy. On the surface, the poem provides examples of a happy man: "He was fully sensible to the advantages of the Installment Plan." Yet beneath the surface, readers can see that the man's life is empty.
- **Irony:** In the poem "Richard Cory," Edwin Arlington Robinson portrays a gentleman who seems exceptionally fortunate in life. However, the poem ends in tragic irony: "And Richard Cory, one calm summer night/Went home and put a bullet through his head."
- **Sarcasm:** "A Modest Proposal, Jonathan Swift" shows acute sarcasm: "pretends to sympathize with the British government and its burden (dealing with starving Irish children), while really condemning the government's callous attitude.
- **Understatement:** In *Huckleberry Finn* by Mark Twain, Huck understates his feelings about leaving a horrific scene: "I could a stayed if I wanted to, but I didn't want to."

Academic Vocabulary

satire writing that uses humor to ridicule corruption and folly

irony a contrast between expectation and reality

Apply the Standard

Use the worksheet that follows to help you apply the standard as you read. Several copies of the worksheet have been provided for you to use with different literature selections.

- Distinguishing Meaning

Name _____ Date _____ Selection _____

Distinguishing Meaning

Use the left column of the organizer below to list instances in which an author states something indirectly by using **satire, irony, sarcasm,** or **understatement.** Then, in the right column, explain what the author really means.

Examples from the Text	Actual Meaning

Name _____ Date _____ Selection _____

Distinguishing Meaning

Use the left column of the organizer below to list instances in which an author states something indirectly by using **satire, irony, sarcasm,** or **understatement.** Then, in the right column, explain what the author really means.

Examples from the Text	Actual Meaning

For use with Literature 6

Name _____ Date _____ Selection _____

Distinguishing Meaning

Use the left column of the organizer below to list instances in which an author states something indirectly by using **satire, irony, sarcasm,** or **understatement.** Then, in the right column, explain what the author really means.

Examples from the Text	Actual Meaning

Name _____ Date _____ Selection _____

Distinguishing Meaning

Use the left column of the organizer below to list instances in which an author states something indirectly by using **satire, irony, sarcasm,** or **understatement.** Then, in the right column, explain what the author really means.

Examples from the Text	Actual Meaning

D

Name _____ Date _____ Selection _____

Distinguishing Meaning

Use the left column of the organizer below to list instances in which an author states something indirectly by using **satire, irony, sarcasm,** or **understatement.** Then, in the right column, explain what the author really means.

Examples from the Text	Actual Meaning

Name _____ Date _____ Selection _____

Distinguishing Meaning

Use the left column of the organizer below to list instances in which an author states something indirectly by using **satire, irony, sarcasm,** or **understatement.** Then, in the right column, explain what the author really means.

Examples from the Text	Actual Meaning

Literature 7

> 7. Analyze multiple interpretations of a story, drama, or poem (e.g., recorded or live production of a play or recorded novel or poetry), evaluating how each version interprets the source text. (Include at least one play by Shakespeare and one play by an American dramatist.)

Explanation

Dramas are written to be performed, and stories and poems are often read aloud and sometimes recorded. Each production or reading of a **source text,** or original story, drama, or poem, is an **interpretation** that conveys a particular understanding of the work, emphasizing some elements and downplaying or even adjusting others. To analyze multiple interpretations of a story, drama, or poem, focus on these critical elements:

- **Characterization:** Ask yourself: What methods does each interpretation use to develop the characters? Are the characters portrayed in a way that is faithful to the source text?
- **Setting:** Many interpretations of a play keep the original setting. Sometimes the setting is updated or otherwise changed. Ask yourself: What methods are used to establish the setting? If an interpretation has altered the setting, does the new setting change my understanding of the play?
- **Mood or atmosphere:** Ask yourself: How does this production or recording create a mood or atmosphere? Is the mood appropriate? Is it different from that of the source text?
- **Narrative elements:** Ask yourself: Are any narrative elements from the source text—such as a subplot, character, or scene—left out of this production or recording? Are new narrative elements added? Determine whether these additions or subtractions are justified.
- **Elements of the medium:** Sets, costumes, and lighting are elements of theatrical performances. Vocal expression and sound effects are elements of recordings. Ask yourself: How are these elements used in the interpretation? What do they contribute to its effectiveness?

Examples

- One production of Arthur Miller's play *The Crucible* may strive for historical accuracy. Costumes and sets may evoke colonial New England, and actors may adopt the mannerisms of the Puritans. This interpretation of the drama emphasizes its depiction of real events that unfolded in Salem, Massachusetts in the 1690s.
- In another production, *The Crucible* might be staged without costumes and with minimal sets. Actors might deliver their dialogue using a contemporary style of speech. This interpretation might focus on the social and political themes of the play, which apply even today.

Academic Vocabulary

interpretation a performance of a story, drama, or poem that conveys an understanding of the work

source text an original story, drama, or poem on which an interpretation is based

Apply the Standard

Use the worksheet that follows to help you apply the standard as you read. Several copies of the worksheet have been provided for you to use with different literature selections.

- Analyzing Multiple Interpretations

Name _____ Date _____ Selection _____

Analyzing Multiple Interpretations

Use the graphic organizer to analyze two interpretations of a story, drama, or poem. Explain how the elements in the left-hand column are developed in each interpretation, and evaluate the effectiveness of each element in the two interpretations.

Source Text: ....

	Interpretation 1: Medium .... Performance/ Publication Date .... Contributors .... Publisher	Interpretation 2: Medium .... Performance/ Publication Date .... Contributors .... Publisher	Evaluation
1. Characterization			Interpretation 1: Interpretation 2:
2. Setting			Interpretation 1: Interpretation 2:
3. Mood or Atmosphere			Interpretation 1: Interpretation 2:
4. Narrative Elements			Interpretation 1: Interpretation 2:
5. Elements of the Medium			Interpretation 1: Interpretation 2:

A

Name _____ Date _____ Selection _____

Analyzing Multiple Interpretations

Use the graphic organizer to analyze two interpretations of a story, drama, or poem. Explain how the elements in the left-hand column are developed in each interpretation, and evaluate the effectiveness of each element in the two interpretations.

Source Text: ....

	Interpretation 1: Medium .... Performance/ Publication Date .... Contributors .... Publisher	Interpretation 2: Medium .... Performance/ Publication Date .... Contributors .... Publisher	Evaluation
1. Characterization			Interpretation 1: Interpretation 2:
2. Setting			Interpretation 1: Interpretation 2:
3. Mood or Atmosphere			Interpretation 1: Interpretation 2:
4. Narrative Elements			Interpretation 1: Interpretation 2:
5. Elements of the Medium			Interpretation 1: Interpretation 2:

For use with Literature 7

Name _____ Date _____ Selection _____

Analyzing Multiple Interpretations

Use the graphic organizer to analyze two interpretations of a story, drama, or poem. Explain how the elements in the left-hand column are developed in each interpretation, and evaluate the effectiveness of each element in the two interpretations.

Source Text: ....

	Interpretation 1: Medium .... Performance/ Publication Date .... Contributors .... Publisher	Interpretation 2: Medium .... Performance/ Publication Date .... Contributors .... Publisher	Evaluation
1. Characterization			Interpretation 1: Interpretation 2:
2. Setting			Interpretation 1: Interpretation 2:
3. Mood or Atmosphere			Interpretation 1: Interpretation 2:
4. Narrative Elements			Interpretation 1: Interpretation 2:
5. Elements of the Medium			Interpretation 1: Interpretation 2:

C

Name _____ Date _____ Selection _____

Analyzing Multiple Interpretations

Use the graphic organizer to analyze two interpretations of a story, drama, or poem. Explain how the elements in the left-hand column are developed in each interpretation, and evaluate the effectiveness of each element in the two interpretations.

Source Text: ....

	Interpretation 1: Medium .... Performance/ Publication Date .... Contributors .... Publisher	**Interpretation 2:** Medium .... Performance/ Publication Date .... Contributors .... Publisher	**Evaluation**
1. Characterization			Interpretation 1: Interpretation 2:
2. Setting			Interpretation 1: Interpretation 2:
3. Mood or Atmosphere			Interpretation 1: Interpretation 2:
4. Narrative Elements			Interpretation 1: Interpretation 2:
5. Elements of the Medium			Interpretation 1: Interpretation 2:

D

For use with Literature 7

Name _____ Date _____ Selection _____

Analyzing Multiple Interpretations

Use the graphic organizer to analyze two interpretations of a story, drama, or poem. Explain how the elements in the left-hand column are developed in each interpretation, and evaluate the effectiveness of each element in the two interpretations.

Source Text: ....

	Interpretation 1: Medium .... Performance/ Publication Date .... Contributors .... Publisher	**Interpretation 2:** Medium .... Performance/ Publication Date .... Contributors .... Publisher	**Evaluation**
1. Characterization			Interpretation 1: Interpretation 2:
2. Setting			Interpretation 1: Interpretation 2:
3. Mood or Atmosphere			Interpretation 1: Interpretation 2:
4. Narrative Elements			Interpretation 1: Interpretation 2:
5. Elements of the Medium			Interpretation 1: Interpretation 2:

E

For use with Literature 7

Name _____ Date _____ Selection _____

Analyzing Multiple Interpretations

Use the graphic organizer to analyze two interpretations of a story, drama, or poem. Explain how the elements in the left-hand column are developed in each interpretation, and evaluate the effectiveness of each element in the two interpretations.

Source Text: ....

	Interpretation 1: Medium .... Performance/ Publication Date .... Contributors .... Publisher	Interpretation 2: Medium .... Performance/ Publication Date .... Contributors .... Publisher	Evaluation
1. Characterization			Interpretation 1: Interpretation 2:
2. Setting			Interpretation 1: Interpretation 2:
3. Mood or Atmosphere			Interpretation 1: Interpretation 2:
4. Narrative Elements			Interpretation 1: Interpretation 2:
5. Elements of the Medium			Interpretation 1: Interpretation 2:

F

Literature 9

9. **Demonstrate knowledge of eighteenth-, nineteenth-, and early twentieth-century foundational works of American literature, including how two or more texts from the same period treat similar themes or topics.**

Explanation

Literary works written in a particular **era,** or time period, reflect the historical events and cultural trends of the time. Writers of the time may also influence each other directly, reading each other's works, corresponding, and so on. For these reasons, works from the same era often address similar topics or themes. American Transcendentalist writers such as Henry David Thoreau and Ralph Waldo Emerson wrote works criticizing the materialism of their culture.

The **foundational works** of an era are important literary works that invent, reflect, or challenge the forms and styles defining the era and that address key themes of the time. Foundational works earn an enduring place in the literature of a culture and continue to influence the literature of later eras.

Examples

The first chart below compares themes in works by Emerson and Thoreau, indicating how their ideas reflected their era.

Theme of Thoreau's *Walden*	Theme of Emerson's "Self-Reliance"	Events of the Era
The work advocates self-sufficiency, urging readers to simplify their lives and to make their own choices.	The work advocates self-reliance, urging readers to avoid conformity to society's expectations.	The nation expanded rapidly. Thoreau and Emerson reacted against the new demand for "bigger and faster" by having readers reflect on life's essentials.

Foundational Works of American Literature		
Eighteenth Century	**Nineteenth Century**	**Early Twentieth Century**
• Jonathan Edwards, "Sinners in the Hands of an Angry God" • Patrick Henry, Speech in the Virginia Convention	• Herman Melville, *Moby Dick* • Henry David Thoreau, *Walden* • Mark Twain, *Life on the Mississippi*	• William Carlos Williams, "The Red Wheelbarrow" • Ernest Hemingway, "In Another Country"

Academic Vocabulary

era a period of history marked by a new or distinct order in society, politics, or culture

foundational works represent the significant themes and styles of a literary era and that continues to influence later eras

Apply the Standard

Use the worksheet that follows to help you apply the standard as you read.

- Comparing Foundational Works of an Era

Name _____ Date _____ Selection _____

Comparing Foundational Works of an Era

Use the graphic organizer to compare two foundational literary works of the same era that share a common theme or topic.

Title of text 1: .... **Author:** ....

Title of text 2: .... **Author:** ....

Theme or topic common to both texts:

....

....

	Text 1	Text 2
What main points does the writer make about the theme or topic?		
What details does the writer use to support the theme or main idea?		
What form of writing does the author use to discuss the theme?		
What is unique about the author's approach?		

A

For use with Literature 9

Name _____ Date _____ Selection _____

Comparing Foundational Works of an Era

Use the graphic organizer to compare two foundational literary works of the same era that share a common theme or topic.

Title of text 1: .... **Author:** ....

Title of text 2: .... **Author:** ....

Theme or topic common to both texts:

....

....

	Text 1	Text 2
What main points does the writer make about the theme or topic?		
What details does the writer use to support the theme or main idea?		
What form of writing does the author use to discuss the theme?		
What is unique about the author's approach?		

Name _____ Date _____ Selection _____

Comparing Foundational Works of an Era

Use the graphic organizer to compare two foundational literary works of the same era that share a common theme or topic.

Title of text 1: .... **Author:** ....

Title of text 2: .... **Author:** ....

Theme or topic common to both texts:

....

....

	Text 1	Text 2
What main points does the writer make about the theme or topic?		
What details does the writer use to support the theme or main idea?		
What form of writing does the author use to discuss the theme?		
What is unique about the author's approach?		

C

Name _____ Date _____ Selection _____

Comparing Foundational Works of an Era

Use the graphic organizer to compare two foundational literary works of the same era that share a common theme or topic.

Title of text 1: .... **Author:** ....

Title of text 2: .... **Author:** ....

Theme or topic common to both texts:

....

....

	Text 1	Text 2
What main points does the writer make about the theme or topic?		
What details does the writer use to support the theme or main idea?		
What form of writing does the author use to discuss the theme?		
What is unique about the author's approach?		

D

Name _____ Date _____ Selection _____

Comparing Foundational Works of an Era

Use the graphic organizer to compare two foundational literary works of the same era that share a common theme or topic.

Title of text 1: .... **Author:** ....

Title of text 2: .... **Author:** ....

Theme or topic common to both texts:

....

....

	Text 1	Text 2
What main points does the writer make about the theme or topic?		
What details does the writer use to support the theme or main idea?		
What form of writing does the author use to discuss the theme?		
What is unique about the author's approach?		

E

Name _____ Date _____ Selection _____

Comparing Foundational Works of an Era

Use the graphic organizer to compare two foundational literary works of the same era that share a common theme or topic.

Title of text 1: .... **Author:** ....

Title of text 2: .... **Author:** ....

Theme or topic common to both texts:

....

....

	Text 1	**Text 2**
What main points does the writer make about the theme or topic?		
What details does the writer use to support the theme or main idea?		
What form of writing does the author use to discuss the theme?		
What is unique about the author's approach?		

Literature 10

> **10.** By the end of grade 11, read and comprehend literature, including stories, dramas, and poems in the grades 11-CCR text complexity band proficiently, with scaffolding as needed at the high end of the range.

Explanation

Successful readers are able to independently read and comprehend **complex texts,** works that present difficulties as a result of challenging concepts, organization, language, or sentence structure. Such readers also make an effort to read texts of increasing complexity.

Examples

To determine the complexity of a text, here are some questions that readers ask themselves:

Language	*Subject Matter*
• Is the level of vocabulary high? • Are sentences and paragraphs long? • Does the use of dialect, unfamiliar slang, or older forms of English make the text less accessible? • In drama, are stage directions, scenes, or characters difficult to track or visualize? • In poetry, are the lines or stanzas lengthy?	• Are allusions made to unfamiliar events, places, or people? • Is special background or technical knowledge required for understanding? *Writer's Style* • Does the writer use figurative language? • Does ambiguity, irony, symbolism, or satire make the text difficult to understand?

To master texts of increasing complexity, employ the following Reading Strategies:	
Monitor comprehension	Check your understanding of the text as you read. If you lose the thread of meaning, reread the unclear or confusing passages.
Adjust reading pace	Read difficult, technical, or dense passages more slowly than passages containing simple language or dialogue.
Paraphrase	Clarify confusing passages by restating them in your own words.
Use outside resources	Use reference material to check the meanings of unfamiliar words or acquire important background knowledge.
Visualize	Create mental pictures of characters and events as you read.
Take notes	Take notes on important information and ideas.

Academic Vocabulary

complex texts works with challenging concepts, organization, language, or sentence structure
paraphrase simplify and rephrase a passage in one's own words
visualize create a mental picture of characters or events in a text

Apply the Standard

Use the worksheet that follows to help you apply the standard as you read. Several copies of the worksheet have been provided for you to use with different literature selections.

- • Comprehending Complex Texts

Comprehending Complex Texts

- Use the left-hand column of the graphic organizer to evaluate the complexity of the text that you are reading. For each category, list factors that make the text difficult.

- Use the right-hand column to describe strategies that helped you master each difficulty mentioned in the left-hand column.

Title: .... **Writer:** ....

Things That Make the Text Complex	Helpful Reading Strategies
1. Language	
2. Writer's Style	
3. Subject Matter	
4. Other	

Rating the Text

In your opinion, how complex was the text you read? Rate the complexity of the text on a scale of one to ten, with one being "easy" and ten being "very difficult."

My Rating: ....

Name _____ Date _____ Selection _____

Comprehending Complex Texts

- Use the left-hand column of the graphic organizer to evaluate the complexity of the text that you are reading. For each category, list factors that make the text difficult.

- Use the right-hand column to describe strategies that helped you master each difficulty mentioned in the left-hand column.

Title: .... Writer: ....

Things That Make the Text Complex	Helpful Reading Strategies
1. Language	
2. Writer's Style	
3. Subject Matter	
4. Other	

Rating the Text

In your opinion, how complex was the text you read? Rate the complexity of the text on a scale of one to ten, with one being "easy" and ten being "very difficult."

My Rating: ....

B

Name _____ Date _____ Selection _____

Comprehending Complex Texts

- Use the left-hand column of the graphic organizer to evaluate the complexity of the text that you are reading. For each category, list factors that make the text difficult.

- Use the right-hand column to describe strategies that helped you master each difficulty mentioned in the left-hand column.

Title: .... Writer: ....

Things That Make the Text Complex	Helpful Reading Strategies
1. Language	
2. Writer's Style	
3. Subject Matter	
4. Other	

Rating the Text

In your opinion, how complex was the text you read? Rate the complexity of the text on a scale of one to ten, with one being "easy" and ten being "very difficult."

My Rating: ....

C

Name _____ Date _____ Selection _____

Comprehending Complex Texts

- Use the left-hand column of the graphic organizer to evaluate the complexity of the text that you are reading. For each category, list factors that make the text difficult.

- Use the right-hand column to describe strategies that helped you master each difficulty mentioned in the left-hand column.

Title: .... **Writer:** ....

Things That Make the Text Complex	Helpful Reading Strategies
1. Language	
2. Writer's Style	
3. Subject Matter	
4. Other	

Rating the Text

In your opinion, how complex was the text you read? Rate the complexity of the text on a scale of one to ten, with one being "easy" and ten being "very difficult."

My Rating: ....

D

Name _____ Date _____ Selection _____

Comprehending Complex Texts

- Use the left-hand column of the graphic organizer to evaluate the complexity of the text that you are reading. For each category, list factors that make the text difficult.

- Use the right-hand column to describe strategies that helped you master each difficulty mentioned in the left-hand column.

Title: .... Writer: ....

Things That Make the Text Complex	Helpful Reading Strategies
1. Language	
2. Writer's Style	
3. Subject Matter	
4. Other	

Rating the Text

In your opinion, how complex was the text you read? Rate the complexity of the text on a scale of one to ten, with one being "easy" and ten being "very difficult."

My Rating: ....

Name _____ Date _____ Selection _____

Comprehending Complex Texts

- Use the left-hand column of the graphic organizer to evaluate the complexity of the text that you are reading. For each category, list factors that make the text difficult.

- Use the right-hand column to describe strategies that helped you master each difficulty mentioned in the left-hand column.

Title: _____   Writer: _____

Things That Make the Text Complex	Helpful Reading Strategies
1. Language	
2. Writer's Style	
3. Subject Matter	
4. Other	

Rating the Text

In your opinion, how complex was the text you read? Rate the complexity of the text on a scale of one to ten, with one being "easy" and ten being "very difficult."

My Rating: _____

F

Reading Standards for Informational Text

Informational Text 1

> 1. **Cite strong and thorough textual evidence to support analysis of what the text says explicitly as well as inferences drawn from the text, including determining where the text leaves matters uncertain.**

Explanation

In addition to facts, authors of informational texts sometimes bring unstated beliefs or assumptions to their writing. Readers need to analyze the details in a text to fully understand the author's meaning. Some details are **explicit,** or directly stated. Other details are **implicit,** meaning that they are hinted at. When ideas or attitudes are revealed indirectly, readers must **make inferences.** This involves noticing details that an author provides, spotting where an author's argument rests on assumptions, and drawing logical conclusions.

Ambiguity occurs in an informational text when some element of the work can be interpreted in more than one way. To clarify ambiguity in nonfiction, analyze **textual evidence,** or clues, that reveal the writer's assumptions, such as political opinions and details that overwhelmingly favor one view on a topic or cultural biases favoring certain customs or behavior.

Examples

- Informational texts include **explicit** details that give readers basic facts. Here's an example: "From 1930 to 1936, severe drought caused a period of severe dust storms in the American prairie states. For this reason, the affected region of the U.S. became known as the Dust Bowl."

- Informational texts also contain **implicit,** or unstated, ideas that require readers to "read between the lines" and make their own **inferences,** or conclusions based on textual evidence. For example, in the Dust Bowl essay, the author might provide these details: "Prairie children walked to school with scarves tied over their noses and mouths, and arrived with dark sooty faces when the scarves were removed." These details indirectly state that the level of dust on the prairie was severe and posed serious challenges.

- An **ambiguous** statement can be interpreted in more than one way. For example, consider this statement from the Dust Bowl essay: "The government eventually extended a long arm of aid, instituting programs that saved thousands from hunger." If the author makes this statement without providing further details, it is unclear whether he or she thinks that the "long arm of aid" was generally positive because it saved people from hunger or that, while helpful, it was open to criticism because it arrived "eventually," meaning that it could have helped more people if aid were offered sooner.

Academic Vocabulary

inference conclusion based on details in the text

ambiguity text that can be interpreted in two or more ways

textual evidence details from a selection that support a reader's conclusion

Apply the Standard

Use the worksheets that follow to help you apply the standard as you read. Several copies of each worksheet have been provided for you to use with different informational texts.

- Identifying Strong Textual Evidence
- Making Inferences

Name _____ Date _____ Assignment _____

Identifying Strong Textual Evidence

Use the following graphic organizer to provide strong textual evidence for the central ideas of the selection.

- In the left column, state one of the author's central ideas.

- In the middle column, write quotations from the selection that give textual evidence for the idea.

- In the right column, identify whether the details are explicit, implicit, or ambiguous.

Central Idea	Textual Evidence	Kind of Detail
1.		
2.		
3.		
4.		

A

Name _____ Date _____ Assignment _____

Identifying Strong Textual Evidence

Use the following graphic organizer to provide strong textual evidence for the central ideas of the selection.

- In the left column, state one of the author's central ideas.

- In the middle column, write quotations from the selection that give textual evidence for the idea.

- In the right column, identify whether the details are explicit, implicit, or ambiguous.

Central Idea	Textual Evidence	Kind of Detail
1.		
2.		
3.		
4.		

B

For use with Informational Text 1

Name _____ Date _____ Assignment _____

Identifying Strong Textual Evidence

Use the following graphic organizer to provide strong textual evidence for the central ideas of the selection.

- In the left column, state one of the author's central ideas.

- In the middle column, write quotations from the selection that give textual evidence for the idea.

- In the right column, identify whether the details are explicit, implicit, or ambiguous.

Central Idea	Textual Evidence	Kind of Detail
1.		
2.		
3.		
4.		

C

Name _____ Date _____ Assignment _____

Identifying Strong Textual Evidence

Use the following graphic organizer to provide strong textual evidence for the central ideas of the selection.

- In the left column, state one of the author's central ideas.

- In the middle column, write quotations from the selection that give textual evidence for the idea.

- In the right column, identify whether the details are explicit, implicit, or ambiguous.

Central Idea	Textual Evidence	Kind of Detail
1.		
2.		
3.		
4.		

D

For use with Informational Text 1

Name _____ Date _____ Assignment _____

Identifying Strong Textual Evidence

Use the following graphic organizer to provide strong textual evidence for the central ideas of the selection.

- In the left column, state one of the author's central ideas.

- In the middle column, write quotations from the selection that give textual evidence for the idea.

- In the right column, identify whether the details are explicit, implicit, or ambiguous.

Central Idea	Textual Evidence	Kind of Detail
1.		
2.		
3.		
4.		

E

Name _____ Date _____ Assignment _____

Identifying Strong Textual Evidence

Use the following graphic organizer to provide strong textual evidence for the central ideas of the selection.

- In the left column, state one of the author's central ideas.

- In the middle column, write quotations from the selection that give textual evidence for the idea.

- In the right column, identify whether the details are explicit, implicit, or ambiguous.

Central Idea	Textual Evidence	Kind of Detail
1.		
2.		
3.		
4.		

F

Name _____ Date _____ Assignment _____

Making Inferences

Use the following organizer to make inferences based on the text. In the left column, jot down quotations that suggest ideas without stating them directly. In the right column, write the inferences you can make from these quotations.

Title: .... **Author:** ....

Details from the Text	Inference
1.	
2.	
3.	
4.	

A

Name _____ Date _____ Assignment _____

Making Inferences

Use the following organizer to make inferences based on the text. In the left column, jot down quotations that suggest ideas without stating them directly. In the right column, write the inferences you can make from these quotations.

Title: .... Author: ....

Details from the Text	Inference
1.	
2.	
3.	
4.	

For use with Informational Text 1

Name _____ Date _____ Assignment _____

Making Inferences

Use the following organizer to make inferences based on the text. In the left column, jot down quotations that suggest ideas without stating them directly. In the right column, write the inferences you can make from these quotations.

Title: .... **Author:** ....

Details from the Text	Inference
1.	
2.	
3.	
4.	

For use with Informational Text 1

Name _____ Date _____ Assignment _____

Making Inferences

Use the following organizer to make inferences based on the text. In the left column, jot down quotations that suggest ideas without stating them directly. In the right column, write the inferences you can make from these quotations.

Title: .... Author: ....

Details from the Text	Inference
1.	
2.	
3.	
4.	

Name _____ Date _____ Assignment _____

Making Inferences

Use the following organizer to make inferences based on the text. In the left column, jot down quotations that suggest ideas without stating them directly. In the right column, write the inferences you can make from these quotations.

Title: .... **Author:** ....

Details from the Text	Inference
1.	
2.	
3.	
4.	

E

Name _____ Date _____ Assignment _____

Making Inferences

Use the following organizer to make inferences based on the text. In the left column, jot down quotations that suggest ideas without stating them directly. In the right column, write the inferences you can make from these quotations.

Title: .... **Author:** ....

Details from the Text	Inference
1.	
2.	
3.	
4.	

F

Informational Text 2

> **2. Determine two or more central ideas of a text and analyze their development over the course of the text, including how they interact and build on one another to provide a complex analysis; provide an objective summary of the text.**

Explanation

Informational texts often contain two or more **central ideas,** or essential messages. These ideas support the text's main **topic,** or overall subject or message, and develop and build on one another over the course of the text. As you read, note the central ideas that the author presents and analyze how they interact with one another.

You can improve your comprehension by **summarizing** these central ideas. To write an objective summary, begin by identifying the most important ideas and details of a text. Then, write a brief, focused statement in which you relate the most important ideas and details—without including your own opinions.

Examples

- **Interaction of Central Ideas** An informational article may be written about a single **topic** while also providing two or more **central ideas** about that topic. For example, a text about deforestation of the Amazon rainforests may contain these ideas:

  - With one in ten known species living there, the Amazon contains the richest biodiversity of any rainforest in the world.
  - Rampant deforestation results in severe environmental damage and accelerates global warming.
  - Deforested land used for cattle pasture is worth a fraction of the value of intact forests, which provide sustainable harvests of fruits, timber, and latex.

The author of the Amazon rainforest text would then build on the central ideas listed above to convince readers that the destruction of the Amazon rainforest is harmful. The central ideas interact with one another in the text by showing that deforestation has serious consequences—both ecological and economic.

- **Summarizing** A summary should briefly restate the main points of a text, as in this example:

  Deforestation of the Amazon is particularly harmful because it contains the richest biodiversity of any rainforest on Earth. Destroying the rainforests results in environmental damage, significant economic loss, and a depletion of natural resources.

Academic Vocabulary

topic the chief subject of a text

summary a concise statement that presents the main ideas and most important points in a text

Apply the Standard

Use the worksheets that follow to help you apply the standard as you read. Several copies of each worksheet have been provided for you to use with different informational texts.

- Analyzing Central Ideas
- Summarizing Text

Name _____ Date _____ Assignment _____

Analyzing Central Ideas

Use the following graphic organizer to list the topic of a work and the central ideas that are related to the topic.

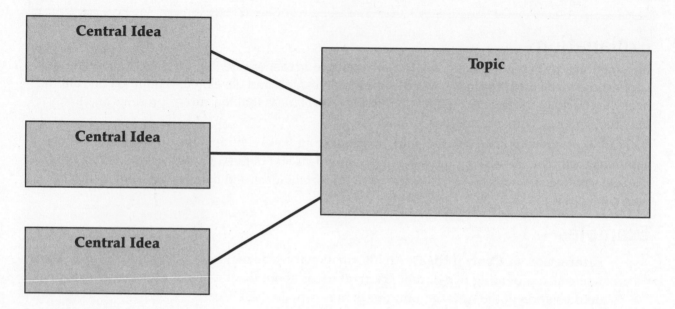

Name _____ Date _____ Assignment _____

Analyzing Central Ideas

Use the following graphic organizer to list the topic of a work and the central ideas that are related to the topic.

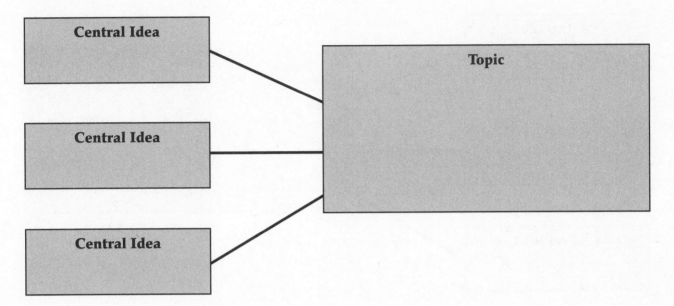

Name _____ Date _____ Assignment _____

Analyzing Central Ideas

Use the following graphic organizer to list the topic of a work and the central ideas that are related to the topic.

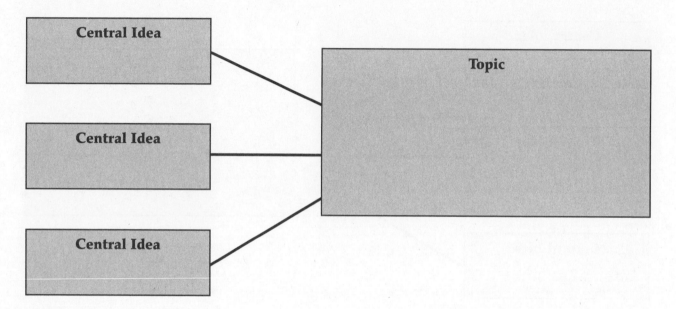

Name _____ Date _____ Assignment _____

Analyzing Central Ideas

Use the following graphic organizer to list the topic of a work and the central ideas that are related to the topic.

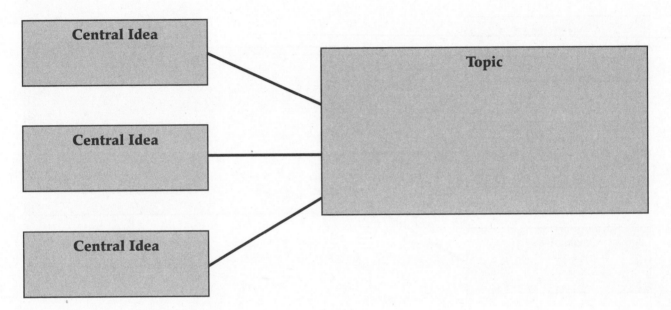

Name _____ Date _____ Assignment _____

Analyzing Central Ideas

Use the following graphic organizer to list the topic of a work and the central ideas that are related to the topic.

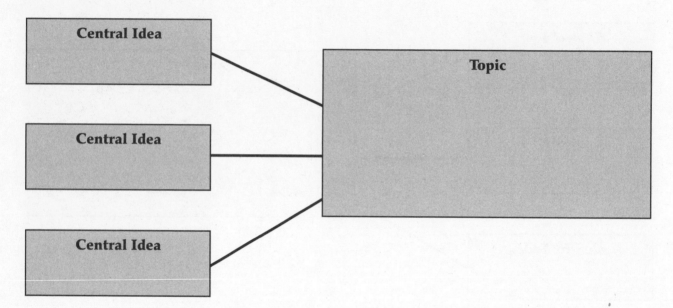

Name _____ Date _____ Assignment _____

Analyzing Central Ideas

Use the following graphic organizer to list the topic of a work and the central ideas that are related to the topic.

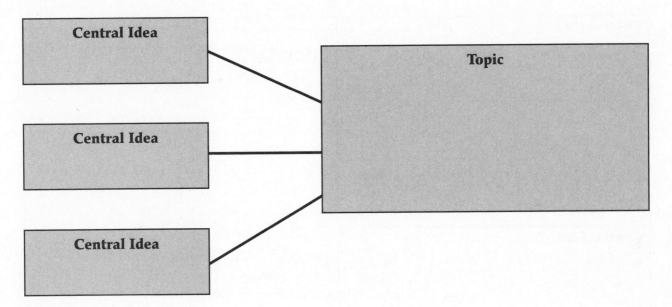

Name _____ Date _____ Assignment _____

Summarizing Text

In the left column of the following graphic organizer, concisely state the central, or essential, ideas of the text. Then, use these ideas to write a summary in the right column.

Central Idea	Summary ....
Central Idea	....
Central Idea	....

A

Name _____ Date _____ Assignment _____

Summarizing Text

In the left column of the following graphic organizer, concisely state the central, or essential, ideas of the text. Then, use these ideas to write a summary in the right column.

Central Idea	Summary
Central Idea	
Central Idea	
Central Idea	

Name _____ Date _____ Assignment _____

Summarizing Text

In the left column of the following graphic organizer, concisely state the central, or essential, ideas of the text. Then, use these ideas to write a summary in the right column.

Central Idea	Summary
Central Idea	
Central Idea	
Central Idea	

C

For use with Informational Text 2

Name _____ Date _____ Assignment _____

Summarizing Text

In the left column of the following graphic organizer, concisely state the central, or essential, ideas of the text. Then, use these ideas to write a summary in the right column.

Central Idea	**Summary** ....
Central Idea	
Central Idea	

Name _____ Date _____ Assignment _____

Summarizing Text

In the left column of the following graphic organizer, concisely state the central, or essential, ideas of the text. Then, use these ideas to write a summary in the right column.

Central Idea	Summary
Central Idea	
Central Idea	

Name _____ Date _____ Assignment _____

Summarizing Text

In the left column of the following graphic organizer, concisely state the central, or essential, ideas of the text. Then, use these ideas to write a summary in the right column.

Central Idea	Summary
Central Idea	
Central Idea	

Informational Text 3

3. **Analyze a complex set of ideas or sequence of events and explain how specific individuals, ideas, or events interact and develop over the course of the text.**

Explanation

Informational text can be densely packed with information and ideas. It may also contain advanced language and technical terms. Its purpose may be to explain a complex set of ideas or **sequence of events.** As a reader, it is your job to comprehend the material no matter how complex it is. To analyze complex text, first take time to read through it. Then go back and **clarify** any advanced concepts with which you are not familiar. To clarify

- reread the text to gather a fuller understanding of its meaning
- use context clues to help you define unfamiliar terms
- read ahead to gather more information
- ask questions or use reference materials to clarify any ideas that remain unclear

Once you have read through the text completely and clarified any unfamiliar terms and ideas, it is time to analyze the text.

To analyze it, examine how individuals, ideas, or events interact or develop over the course of the text. If the text is describing a sequence of events, take notes and list them in order or create a flowchart to identify each event. Then examine how the events are related. Does one event cause another? Are they simply related in chronological order? If the text is describing a complex set of ideas, identify the main ideas and their supporting details. (Outlining the text can help you do so.) Pay attention to how the author develops and interweaves ideas. Examine any graphic elements (for example, charts, photos, diagrams). Consider how the information they relate is connected to the ideas in the body text. Ask yourself: What does the author want me to know? How are ideas connected?

Example

If you were reading "Water on Tap: What You Need to Know," you could use context clues and a dictionary to clarify terms such as *aquifers, contaminants*, and *coagulation*. After reading through the entire text once, you would identify the main ideas and supporting details. The headings in the article help you identify the main ideas, and the subheadings and body text provide important supporting details. Finally, you would examine the diagram and analyze how all the ideas in the article interact.

Academic Vocabulary

clarify to explain or review

sequence of events things, actions, or events that occur in order, one after another

Apply the Standard

Use the worksheet that follows to help you apply the standard as you read. Several copies have been provided for you to use with different informational texts.

- Analyzing Ideas and Events

Name _____ Date _____ Assignment _____

Analyzing Ideas and Events

Use the graphic organizer below to analyze a complex set of ideas or sequence of events in an informational text you have read. Then answer the question at the bottom of the page.

First Reading	
Unfamiliar terms and ideas:	**Strategies I used to clarify them:** ❑ reread ❑ use context clues ❑ read ahead ❑ ask questions/use a reference book

Second Reading	
What does the text describe? ❑ a sequence of events ❑ a complex set of ideas	

Sequence of Events	Set of Ideas

List the events in order:
 	
1st Event:
 	
2nd Event:
 	
3rd Event:
 	
4th Event:
	Outline the main ideas and supporting details:
	
	I.
	  A.
	  B.
	
	II.
	  A.
	  B.
	III.
	  A.
	  B.

How do events or ideas interact and develop over the course of the text?

....

....

....

A

Name _____ Date _____ Assignment _____

Analyzing Ideas and Events

Use the graphic organizer below to analyze a complex set of ideas or sequence of events in an informational text you have read. Then answer the question at the bottom of the page.

First Reading	
Unfamiliar terms and ideas:	**Strategies I used to clarify them:** ❏ reread ❏ use context clues ❏ read ahead ❏ ask questions/use a reference book

Second Reading	
What does the text describe? ❏ a sequence of events ❏ a complex set of ideas	
Sequence of Events	**Set of Ideas**

List the events in order:
 	
1st Event:
 	
2nd Event:
 	
3rd Event:
 	
4th Event:
	Outline the main ideas and supporting details:
	
	I.
	  A.
	  B.
	II.
	  A.
	  B.
	III.
	  A.
	  B.

How do events or ideas interact and develop over the course of the text?

....

....

....

B

For use with Informational Text 3

Name _____ Date _____ Assignment _____

Analyzing Ideas and Events

Use the graphic organizer below to analyze a complex set of ideas or sequence of events in an informational text you have read. Then answer the question at the bottom of the page.

First Reading	
Unfamiliar terms and ideas:	**Strategies I used to clarify them:** ❏ reread ❏ use context clues ❏ read ahead ❏ ask questions/use a reference book

Second Reading	
What does the text describe? ❏ a sequence of events ❏ a complex set of ideas	

Sequence of Events	Set of Ideas

List the events in order:
 	
1st Event:
 	
2nd Event:
 	
3rd Event:
 	
4th Event:
	Outline the main ideas and supporting details:
	
	I.
	  A.
	  B.
	II.
	  A.
	  B.
	III.
	  A.
	  B.

How do events or ideas interact and develop over the course of the text?

....

....

....

C

Name _____ Date _____ Assignment _____

Analyzing Ideas and Events

Use the graphic organizer below to analyze a complex set of ideas or sequence of events in an informational text you have read. Then answer the question at the bottom of the page.

First Reading	
Unfamiliar terms and ideas:	**Strategies I used to clarify them:** ❏ reread ❏ use context clues ❏ read ahead ❏ ask questions/use a reference book

Second Reading	
What does the text describe? ❏ a sequence of events ❏ a complex set of ideas	

Sequence of Events	Set of Ideas

List the events in order:
 	
1st Event:
 	
2nd Event:
 	
3rd Event:
 	
4th Event:
	Outline the main ideas and supporting details:
	I.
	  A.
	  B.
	II.
	  A.
	  B.
	III.
	  A.
	  B.

How do events or ideas interact and develop over the course of the text?

....

....

....

D

For use with Informational Text 3

Name _____ Date _____ Assignment _____

Analyzing Ideas and Events

Use the graphic organizer below to analyze a complex set of ideas or sequence of events in an informational text you have read. Then answer the question at the bottom of the page.

First Reading	
Unfamiliar terms and ideas:	Strategies I used to clarify them: ❑ reread ❑ use context clues ❑ read ahead ❑ ask questions/use a reference book

Second Reading	
What does the text describe? ❑ a sequence of events ❑ a complex set of ideas	
Sequence of Events	**Set of Ideas**

List the events in order:
 	
1st Event:
 	
2nd Event:
 	
3rd Event:
 	
4th Event:
	Outline the main ideas and supporting details:
	
	I.
	   A.
	   B.
	II.
	   A.
	   B.
	III.
	   A.
	   B.

How do events or ideas interact and develop over the course of the text?

....

....

....

E

Name _____ Date _____ Assignment _____

Analyzing Ideas and Events

Use the graphic organizer below to analyze a complex set of ideas or sequence of events in an informational text you have read. Then answer the question at the bottom of the page.

First Reading	
Unfamiliar terms and ideas:	**Strategies I used to clarify them:** ❏ reread ❏ use context clues ❏ read ahead ❏ ask questions/use a reference book

Second Reading
What does the text describe? ❏ a sequence of events ❏ a complex set of ideas

Sequence of Events	Set of Ideas

List the events in order:
 	
1st Event:
 	
2nd Event:
 	
3rd Event:
 	
4th Event:
	Outline the main ideas and supporting details:
	
	I.
	  A.
	  B.
	II.
	  A.
	  B.
	III.
	  A.
	  B.

How do events or ideas interact and develop over the course of the text?

....

....

....

F

For use with Informational Text 3

Informational Text 4

> 4. Determine the meaning of words and phrases as they are used in a text, including figurative, connotative, and technical meanings; analyze how an author uses and refines the meaning of a key term or terms over the course of a text.

Explanation

When reading informational texts, you will come across words and phrases that are new to you or used in unfamiliar ways. To help determine their meanings, think about whether the words and phrases are used figuratively or literally. **Figurative language** is not meant to be interpreted literally. Authors use figurative language to express ideas in a fresh way. Words can also have **connotative meanings,** or emotions and feelings that are associated with them. Connotations can be positive, neutral, or negative. In addition, authors use technical terms specifically related to a subject. Figuring out **technical meanings** is an important part of reading informational text.

Sometimes an author will refine the meaning of a key term over the course of the text. He or she may introduce the term in the opening paragraphs and provide examples or explanations throughout the body text that help you understand its meaning. Take notes on these key terms. Paraphrase them and write out in your own words what you understand them to mean.

Examples

- **Figurative language** goes beyond the literal, word-for-word meaning. For example, you might encounter this sentence in an article about personal finances: "His budget was slippery, and he had trouble sticking to it." The author uses figurative language to explain that the man's budget was not clearly or firmly set.

- **Connotations** of words can be positive, negative, or neutral. If a politician were described as *guarded*, you would form a different opinion than if he or she were described as *secretive*.

- Informational text often includes **technical terms.** In the sentence "Scientists use the satellite data, or information, to help them predict upcoming weather patterns," you can use context clues to figure out the technical phrase *satellite data* ("information coming from devices that circle Earth"). If the text does not provide context clues or a definition, check the meaning of the word in a dictionary.

Academic Vocabulary

connotative meaning the associations related to a word

figurative language writing that is not meant to be interpreted literally

technical meanings word meanings specifically related to a subject

Apply the Standard

Use the worksheets that follow to help you apply the standard as you read. Several copies of each worksheet have been provided for you to use with different informational texts.

- Understanding Connotations, Figurative Language, and Technical Terms
- Analyzing Key Terms

Name _____ Date _____ Assignment _____

Understanding Connotations, Figurative Language, and Technical Terms

Use the graphic organizers below to analyze connotations, figurative language, and technical terms found in informational text.

- In the top organizer, list words from the text that have **connotations** beyond their dictionary meanings. Circle the kind of connotation (*negative, positive,* or *neutral*) and supply the word's meaning.

- In the bottom organizer, list examples of **figurative language** or **technical terms** and explain in your own words what each one means or implies.

Connotations

Words with Connotations	Kind of Connotation (Circle one.)	Meaning of Word
1.	negative positive neutral	
2.	negative positive neutral	
3.	negative positive neutral	
4.	negative positive neutral	

Figurative Language and Technical Terms

Figurative Language / Techical Term	What It Means or Implies
1.	
2.	
3.	
4.	

A

For use with Informational Text 4

Name _____ Date _____ Assignment _____

Understanding Connotations, Figurative Language, and Technical Terms

Use the graphic organizers below to analyze connotations, figurative language, and technical terms found in informational text.

- In the top organizer, list words from the text that have **connotations** beyond their dictionary meanings. Circle the kind of connotation (*negative, positive,* or *neutral*) and supply the word's meaning.

- In the bottom organizer, list examples of **figurative language** or **technical terms** and explain in your own words what each one means or implies.

Connotations

Words with Connotations	Kind of Connotation (Circle one.)	Meaning of Word
1.	negative positive neutral	
2.	negative positive neutral	
3.	negative positive neutral	
4.	negative positive neutral	

Figurative Language and Technical Terms

Figurative Language	What It Means or Implies
1.	
2.	
3.	
4.	

B

For use with Informational Text 4

Name _____ Date _____ Assignment _____

Understanding Connotations, Figurative Language, and Technical Terms

Use the graphic organizers below to analyze connotations, figurative language, and technical terms found in informational text.

- In the top organizer, list words from the text that have **connotations** beyond their dictionary meanings. Circle the kind of connotation (*negative, positive,* or *neutral*) and supply the word's meaning.

- In the bottom organizer, list examples of **figurative language** or **technical terms** and explain in your own words what each one means or implies.

Connotations

Words with Connotations	Kind of Connotation (Circle one.)	Meaning of Word
1.	negative positive neutral	
2.	negative positive neutral	
3.	negative positive neutral	
4.	negative positive neutral	

Figurative Language and Technical Terms

Figurative Language	What It Means or Implies
1.	
2.	
3.	
4.	

Name _____ Date _____ Assignment _____

Understanding Connotations, Figurative Language, and Technical Terms

Use the graphic organizers below to analyze connotations, figurative language, and technical terms found in informational text.

- In the top organizer, list words from the text that have **connotations** beyond their dictionary meanings. Circle the kind of connotation (*negative, positive,* or *neutral*) and supply the word's meaning.

- In the bottom organizer, list examples of **figurative language** or **technical terms** and explain in your own words what each one means or implies.

Connotations

Words with Connotations	Kind of Connotation (Circle one.)	Meaning of Word
1.	negative positive neutral	
2.	negative positive neutral	
3.	negative positive neutral	
4.	negative positive neutral	

Figurative Language and Technical Terms

Figurative Language	What It Means or Implies
1.	
2.	
3.	
4.	

D   For use with Informational Text 4

Name _____ Date _____ Assignment _____

Understanding Connotations, Figurative Language, and Technical Terms

Use the graphic organizers below to analyze connotations, figurative language, and technical terms found in informational text.

- In the top organizer, list words from the text that have **connotations** beyond their dictionary meanings. Circle the kind of connotation (*negative, positive,* or *neutral*) and supply the word's meaning.

- In the bottom organizer, list examples of **figurative language** or **technical terms** and explain in your own words what each one means or implies.

Connotations

Words with Connotations	Kind of Connotation (Circle one.)	Meaning of Word
1.	negative positive neutral	
2.	negative positive neutral	
3.	negative positive neutral	
4.	negative positive neutral	

Figurative Language and Technical Terms

Figurative Language	What It Means or Implies
1.	
2.	
3.	
4.	

E

For use with Informational Text 4

Name _____ Date _____ Assignment _____

Understanding Connotations, Figurative Language, and Technical Terms

Use the graphic organizers below to analyze connotations, figurative language, and technical terms found in informational text.

- In the top organizer, list words from the text that have **connotations** beyond their dictionary meanings. Circle the kind of connotation (*negative*, *positive*, or *neutral*) and supply the word's meaning.

- In the bottom organizer, list examples of **figurative language** or **technical terms** and explain in your own words what each one means or implies.

Connotations

Words with Connotations	Kind of Connotation (Circle one.)	Meaning of Word
1.	negative positive neutral	
2.	negative positive neutral	
3.	negative positive neutral	
4.	negative positive neutral	

Figurative Language and Technical Terms

Figurative Language	What It Means or Implies
1.	
2.	
3.	
4.	

Name _____ Date _____ Assignment _____

Analyzing Key Terms

Use the graphic organizer below to analyze several uses of a key term over the course of the text. Then summarize your understanding of the term.

Key Term	Context Clues
What are textual examples of the key term?	What examples, synonyms, and other context clues helped your understanding of the term?
1.	
2.	
3.	
4.	
Summarize your understanding of the key term after reading the entire text.	

A

Name _____ Date _____ Assignment _____

Analyzing Key Terms

Use the graphic organizer below to analyze several uses of a key term over the course of the text. Then summarize your understanding of the term.

Key Term	Context Clues
What are textual examples of the key term?	What examples, synonyms, and other context clues helped your understanding of the term?
1.	
2.	
3.	
4.	
Summarize your understanding of the key term after reading the entire text.	

Name _____ Date _____ Assignment _____

Analyzing Key Terms

Use the graphic organizer below to analyze several uses of a key term over the course of the text. Then summarize your understanding of the term.

Key Term	Context Clues
What are textual examples of the key term?	What examples, synonyms, and other context clues helped your understanding of the term?
1.	
2.	
3.	
4.	

Summarize your understanding of the key term after reading the entire text.

Name _____ Date _____ Assignment _____

Analyzing Key Terms

Use the graphic organizer below to analyze several uses of a key term over the course of the text. Then summarize your understanding of the term.

Key Term	Context Clues
What are textual examples of the key term?	What examples, synonyms, and other context clues helped your understanding of the term?
1.	
2.	
3.	
4.	

Summarize your understanding of the key term after reading the entire text.

D **For use with Informational Text 4**

Name _____ Date _____ Assignment _____

Analyzing Key Terms

Use the graphic organizer below to analyze several uses of a key term over the course of the text. Then summarize your understanding of the term.

Key Term	Context Clues
What are textual examples of the key term?	What examples, synonyms, and other context clues helped your understanding of the term?
1.	
2.	
3.	
4.	
Summarize your understanding of the key term after reading the entire text.	

E

Name _____ Date _____ Assignment _____

Analyzing Key Terms

Use the graphic organizer below to analyze several uses of a key term over the course of the text. Then summarize your understanding of the term.

Key Term	Context Clues
What are textual examples of the key term?	What examples, synonyms, and other context clues helped your understanding of the term?
1.	
2.	
3.	
4.	

Summarize your understanding of the key term after reading the entire text.

F

Informational Text 5

> 5. **Analyze and evaluate the effectiveness of the structure an author uses in his or her exposition or argument, including whether the structure makes points clear, convincing, and engaging.**

Explanation

Writers deliberately structure, or organize, their ideas in order to make their points clear, convincing, and engaging. The structure of an **exposition** or **argument** can follow several different patterns of organization. Here are four common patterns of organization:

- **Chronological order** Listing steps in a process in the order in which they happen or should be done; telling events in time order

- **Cause-and-effect** Showing how one situation or condition causes or influences another

- **Comparison-and-contrast** Pointing out similarities and differences between items

- **Order of importance** Proceeding from least important point to most important, or from most to least important point

Examples

- *Chronological order:* This structure would be effective for a proposal to clean up a polluted river. The proposal would explain the steps of the plan in the order in which they should occur.

- *Cause-and-effect:* A text about the aftermath of a hurricane might use this structure effectively. The writer would show how the forces of wind and rain caused severely damaging effects.

- *Comparison-and-contrast:* This structure would work well for an argument intended to convince readers that one plan is better than another. The text might compare and contrast the advantages and disadvantages of each plan.

- *Order of importance:* To persuade readers of an idea, a writer might present evidence, or reasons, by order of importance. He or she might start with the least important reason and build to the most important one or present the strongest idea first.

Academic Vocabulary

argument the position that a writer presents, supported by evidence

exposition writing that explains a process or presents information

Apply the Standard

Use the worksheet that follows to help you apply the standard as you read. Several copies have been provided for you to use with different informational texts.

- Analyzing and Evaluating Structure

Name _____ Date _____ Assignment _____

Analyzing and Evaluating Structure

Writers can choose among several types of organization to structure their texts, such as:

chronological order   *comparison and contrast*

cause-and-effect order   *order of importance.*

Use this graphic organizer to analyze and evaluate the structure of the text you are reading.

1. What is the writer's central idea or argument?
2. What type of organization does the writer use?
3. What details from the text show this type of organization?
4. Is this the best type of organization for the text? Explain your answer.

Name _____ Date _____ Assignment _____

Analyzing and Evaluating Structure

Writers can choose among several types of organization to structure their texts, such as:

chronological order   *comparison and contrast*

cause-and-effect order   *order of importance.*

Use this graphic organizer to analyze and evaluate the structure of the text you are reading.

1. What is the writer's central idea or argument?
2. What type of organization does the writer use?
3. What details from the text show this type of organization?
4. Is this the best type of organization for the text? Explain your answer.

B

For use with Informational Text 5

Name _____ Date _____ Assignment _____

Analyzing and Evaluating Structure

Writers can choose among several types of organization to structure their texts, such as:

      chronological order   *comparison and contrast*

      cause-and-effect order   *order of importance.*

Use this graphic organizer to analyze and evaluate the structure of the text you are reading.

1. What is the writer's central idea or argument?
2. What type of organization does the writer use?
3. What details from the text show this type of organization?
4. Is this the best type of organization for the text? Explain your answer.

C

For use with Informational Text 5

Name _____ Date _____ Assignment _____

Analyzing and Evaluating Structure

Writers can choose among several types of organization to structure their texts, such as:

      chronological order   *comparison and contrast*

      cause-and-effect order   *order of importance.*

Use this graphic organizer to analyze and evaluate the structure of the text you are reading.

1. What is the writer's central idea or argument?
2. What type of organization does the writer use?
3. What details from the text show this type of organization?
4. Is this the best type of organization for the text? Explain your answer.

D

For use with Informational Text 5

Name _____ Date _____ Assignment _____

Analyzing and Evaluating Structure

Writers can choose among several types of organization to structure their texts, such as:

chronological order   *comparison and contrast*

cause-and-effect order   *order of importance.*

Use this graphic organizer to analyze and evaluate the structure of the text you are reading.

1. What is the writer's central idea or argument?
2. What type of organization does the writer use?
3. What details from the text show this type of organization?
4. Is this the best type of organization for the text? Explain your answer.

Name _____ Date _____ Assignment _____

Analyzing and Evaluating Structure

Writers can choose among several types of organization to structure their texts, such as:

> *chronological order*   *comparison and contrast*
>
> *cause-and-effect order*   *order of importance.*

Use this graphic organizer to analyze and evaluate the structure of the text you are reading.

1. What is the writer's central idea or argument?
2. What type of organization does the writer use?
3. What details from the text show this type of organization?
4. Is this the best type of organization for the text? Explain your answer.

F

Informational Text 6

> 6. **Determine an author's point of view or purpose in a text in which the rhetoric is particularly effective, analyzing how style and content contribute to the power, persuasiveness, or beauty of the text.**

Explanation

In an informational text, a writer's point of view is his or her position or perspective on an issue. A writer may explicitly state his or her point of view, telling readers exactly what he or she thinks. Other writers may implicitly state their points of view by suggesting them in their arguments. You can determine a writer's point of view by paying attention to the details and to the **rhetoric** he or she uses.

Rhetorical devices are methods that writers use to emphasize their points. The rhetorical devices below add to the beauty, persuasiveness, and power of persuasive arguments.

- *Repetition* is the repeating of a word, phrase, or an idea to add emphasis.

- *Restatement* is the expression of the same idea in different words.

- *Rhetorical questions* are questions with obvious answers, such as, "How long must we endure injustice?"

- *Parallelism* involves repeating similar grammatical structures.

Examples

In his moving "I Have a Dream" speech of 1963, Martin Luther King, Jr., used rhetorical devices to persuade his audience of the injustice of segregation and to encourage them to work to defeat it.

- **Restatement:** Dr. King said Lincoln's Emancipation Proclamation "<u>came as a great beacon light of hope</u> to millions of Negro slaves who had been seared in the flames of withering injustice. It <u>came as a joyous daybreak to end the long night of their captivity</u>."

- **Parallelism:** Dr. King also spoke eloquently about his dream that his four little children will one day live in a nation where they will not "be judged <u>by the color of their skin</u> but <u>by the content of their character</u>."

Academic Vocabulary

rhetoric the art of writing or speaking effectively

Apply the Standard

Use the worksheets that follow to help you apply the standard as you read informational texts. Several copies of each worksheet have been provided for you.

- Determining Point of View

- Analyzing Effective Rhetoric

Name _____ Date _____ Selection _____

Determining Point of View

Use the graphic organizer below to determine the writer's point of view.

- Give details from the text that explicitly or implicitly reveal the writer's point of view.

- Paraphrase the author's viewpoint in your own words.

Title of Selection: ....

Details from the text:

1.

2.

3.

4.

5.

Author's point of view:

Name _____ Date _____ Selection _____

Determining Point of View

Use the graphic organizer below to determine the writer's point of view.

- Give details from the text that explicitly or implicitly reveal the writer's point of view.

- Paraphrase the author's viewpoint in your own words.

Title of Selection: ....

Details from the text:

1.

2.

3.

4.

5.

Author's point of view:

Name _____ Date _____ Selection _____

Determining Point of View

Use the graphic organizer below to determine the writer's point of view.

• Give details from the text that explicitly or implicitly reveal the writer's point of view.

• Paraphrase the author's viewpoint in your own words.

Title of Selection: ....

Details from the text:
1.
2.
3.
4.
5.

Author's point of view:

C

Name _____ Date _____ Selection _____

Determining Point of View

Use the graphic organizer below to determine the writer's point of view.

> • Give details from the text that explicitly or implicitly reveal the writer's point of view.

> • Paraphrase the author's viewpoint in your own words.

Title of Selection: ....

Details from the text:
1.
2.
3.
4.
5.

Author's point of view:

D

Name _____ Date _____ Selection _____

Determining Point of View

Use the graphic organizer below to determine the writer's point of view.

- Give details from the text that explicitly or implicitly reveal the writer's point of view.

- Paraphrase the author's viewpoint in your own words.

Title of Selection: ....

Details from the text:
1.
2.
3.
4.
5.

Author's point of view:

E

Name _____ Date _____ Selection _____

Determining Point of View

Use the graphic organizer below to determine the writer's point of view.

- Give details from the text that explicitly or implicitly reveal the writer's point of view.

- Paraphrase the author's viewpoint in your own words.

Title of Selection: ....

Details from the text:
1.
2.
3.
4.
5.

Author's point of view:

Name _____ Date _____ Selection _____

Analyzing Effective Rhetoric

Use the graphic organizer to analyze the types of rhetorical devices that are used in a text you are reading. (Note that the text you are analyzing may not include examples of each type.) Then answer the question at the bottom of the page.

Title of Selection: ....

Type of Rhetorical Device	Examples from the Text
Repetition:	
Restatement:	
Rhetorical questions:	
Parallelism:	

How does the author's use of these devices contribute to the power, persuasiveness, or beauty of the text?

....

....

....

....

....

A

For use with Informational Text 6

Name _____ Date _____ Selection _____

Analyzing Effective Rhetoric

Use the graphic organizer to analyze the types of rhetorical devices that are used in a text you are reading. (Note that the text you are analyzing may not include examples of each type.) Then answer the question at the bottom of the page.

Title of Selection: ....

Type of Rhetorical Device	Examples from the Text
Repetition:	
Restatement:	
Rhetorical questions:	
Parallelism:	

How does the author's use of these devices contribute to the power, persuasiveness, or beauty of the text?

....

....

....

....

Name _____ Date _____ Selection _____

Analyzing Effective Rhetoric

Use the graphic organizer to analyze the types of rhetorical devices that are used in a text you are reading. (Note that the text you are analyzing may not include examples of each type.) Then answer the question at the bottom of the page.

Title of Selection: ....

Type of Rhetorical Device	Examples from the Text
Repetition:	
Restatement:	
Rhetorical questions:	
Parallelism:	

How does the author's use of these devices contribute to the power, persuasiveness, or beauty of the text?

....
....
....
....

Name _____ Date _____ Selection _____

Analyzing Effective Rhetoric

Use the graphic organizer to analyze the types of rhetorical devices that are used in a text you are reading. (Note that the text you are analyzing may not include examples of each type.) Then answer the question at the bottom of the page.

Title of Selection: ....

Type of Rhetorical Device	Examples from the Text
Repetition:	
Restatement:	
Rhetorical questions:	
Parallelism:	

How does the author's use of these devices contribute to the power, persuasiveness, or beauty of the text?

....

....

....

....

....

D

Name _____ Date _____ Selection _____

Analyzing Effective Rhetoric

Use the graphic organizer to analyze the types of rhetorical devices that are used in a text you are reading. (Note that the text you are analyzing may not include examples of each type.) Then answer the question at the bottom of the page.

Title of Selection: ....

Type of Rhetorical Device	Examples from the Text
Repetition:	
Restatement:	
Rhetorical questions:	
Parallelism:	

How does the author's use of these devices contribute to the power, persuasiveness, or beauty of the text?

....

....

....

....

E

Name _____ Date _____ Selection _____

Analyzing Effective Rhetoric

Use the graphic organizer to analyze the types of rhetorical devices that are used in a text you are reading. (Note that the text you are analyzing may not include examples of each type.) Then answer the question at the bottom of the page.

Title of Selection: ....

Type of Rhetorical Device	Examples from the Text
Repetition:	
Restatement:	
Rhetorical questions:	
Parallelism:	

How does the author's use of these devices contribute to the power, persuasiveness, or beauty of the text?

....

....

....

....

....

Informational Text 7

> 7. **Integrate and evaluate multiple sources of information presented in different media or formats (e.g., visually, quantitatively) as well as in words in order to address a question or solve a problem.**

Explanation

When you investigate a topic, you will find several sources that present information in different formats. Visual formats include photographs, maps, and illustrations. **Quantitative** formats include charts, graphs, and tables. Oral formats include speeches and other types of audio material. Print information includes **primary source** documents—nonfiction works that are firsthand accounts of a specific historical period or event. The documents below are all examples of primary sources:

- Diaries and journals are private, personal records of events. Diaries and journals often provide unique glimpses of real life during notable times. They contain valuable details that only a participant or an eyewitness can supply.

- A letter is a written message addressed to a specific reader or readers.

- A field report is a first-hand record of observations and data written by researchers in the field. Depending on their subjects, writers of field reports may include specialized scientific or technical language and illustrations.

- A government memorandum is a brief official message that summarizes reasons for a particular action and gives instructions on how it is to be performed.

In order to fully address a question or to solve a problem, it helps to integrate and evaluate several sources. Each source or format adds unique content to an in-depth understanding of a subject.

Examples

Several sources can help you address the question, "What was life like for soldiers during the Civil War?" Diaries and letters written by the soldiers themselves can reveal their daily routines and experiences. Graphs and charts can provide statistics on battle casualties. Speeches by President Abraham Lincoln may provide insight into the causes that motivated Union soldiers.

Academic Vocabulary

primary source a first-hand document or recording of an event

quantitative containing data that deals with measurements or amounts

Apply the Standard

Use the worksheet that follows to help you apply the standard as you read informational texts. Several copies of the worksheet have been provided for you.

- Integrating and Evaluating Information

Name _____ Date _____ Selection _____

Integrating and Evaluating Information

Use this organizer to integrate and evaluate information from several sources. First, determine a question or problem that you will address by gathering information. Then select three different sources that present information about the subject in different formats (e.g., map, diary, letter, graph), and answer the questions.

What question or problem will you investigate? ....

....

Evaluating Information	Source 1	Source 2	Source 3
1. In what format is the information presented?			
2. Who is the author and what is the date of the source?			
3. What is the most helpful information the source provides?			

↓

Integrating Information: Think about what you've learned from all three sources. What conclusions can you draw about your topic?

A

Name _____ Date _____ Selection _____

Integrating and Evaluating Information

Use this organizer to integrate and evaluate information from several sources. First, determine a question or problem that you will address by gathering information. Then select three different sources that present information about the subject in different formats (e.g., map, diary, letter, graph), and answer the questions.

What question or problem will you investigate? ....
....

Evaluating Information	Source 1	Source 2	Source 3
1. In what format is the information presented?			
2. Who is the author and what is the date of the source?			
3. What is the most helpful information the source provides?			

Integrating Information: Think about what you've learned from all three sources. What conclusions can you draw about your topic?

For use with Informational Text 7

Name _____ Date _____ Selection _____

Integrating and Evaluating Information

Use this organizer to integrate and evaluate information from several sources. First, determine a question or problem that you will address by gathering information. Then select three different sources that present information about the subject in different formats (e.g., map, diary, letter, graph), and answer the questions.

What question or problem will you investigate? ....

....

Evaluating Information	Source 1	Source 2	Source 3
1. In what format is the information presented?			
2. Who is the author and what is the date of the source?			
3. What is the most helpful information the source provides?			

Integrating Information: Think about what you've learned from all three sources. What conclusions can you draw about your topic?

C

For use with Informational Text 7

Name _____ Date _____ Selection _____

Integrating and Evaluating Information

Use this organizer to integrate and evaluate information from several sources. First, determine a question or problem that you will address by gathering information. Then select three different sources that present information about the subject in different formats (e.g., map, diary, letter, graph), and answer the questions.

What question or problem will you investigate? ....
....

Evaluating Information	Source 1	Source 2	Source 3
1. In what format is the information presented?			
2. Who is the author and what is the date of the source?			
3. What is the most helpful information the source provides?			

Integrating Information: Think about what you've learned from all three sources. What conclusions can you draw about your topic?

D

For use with Informational Text 7

Name _____ Date _____ Selection _____

Integrating and Evaluating Information

Use this organizer to integrate and evaluate information from several sources. First, determine a question or problem that you will address by gathering information. Then select three different sources that present information about the subject in different formats (e.g., map, diary, letter, graph), and answer the questions.

What question or problem will you investigate? ....

....

Evaluating Information	Source 1	Source 2	Source 3
1. In what format is the information presented?			
2. Who is the author and what is the date of the source?			
3. What is the most helpful information the source provides?			

Integrating Information: Think about what you've learned from all three sources. What conclusions can you draw about your topic?

E

For use with Informational Text 7

Name _____ Date _____ Selection _____

Integrating and Evaluating Information

Use this organizer to integrate and evaluate information from several sources. First, determine a question or problem that you will address by gathering information. Then select three different sources that present information about the subject in different formats (e.g., map, diary, letter, graph), and answer the questions.

What question or problem will you investigate? ....

....

Evaluating Information	Source 1	Source 2	Source 3
1. In what format is the information presented?			
2. Who is the author and what is the date of the source?			
3. What is the most helpful information the source provides?			

Integrating Information: Think about what you've learned from all three sources. What conclusions can you draw about your topic?

For use with Informational Text 7

Informational Text 8

> 8. Delineate and evaluate the reasoning in seminal U.S. texts, including the application of constitutional principles and use of legal reasoning (e.g., in U.S. Supreme Court majority opinions and dissents) and the premises, purposes, and arguments in works of public advocacy (e.g., *The Federalist*, presidential addresses).

Explanation

Persuasive writing is writing that presents an argument, or message meant to get readers to think or act in a certain way. Effective persuasion uses the following techniques to convince readers of their **premises:**

- **Appeals to emotion** to influence readers' feelings
- **Appeals to logic,** the use of **reasoning,** to show that an argument is correct
- **Appeals to ethics** to show that a higher principle supports the ideas

Effective writers also use a variety of rhetorical devices to stress their key points: restatement (repeating an idea in a variety of ways), repetition (restating an idea using the same words), parallelism (repeating grammatical structure), rhetorical questions (asking a question with a self-evident answer), and allusions (referring to well-known people, events, or stories).

Writers of political and legal documents may employ several of these appeals and rhetorical devices. Such documents include seminal, or influential, U.S. texts, such as the U.S. Constitution; presidential addresses; and opinions or dissents of the Supreme Court. When you evaluate these documents, look for sound evidence and reasoning that support the writer's message.

Examples

On May 25, 1961, John F. Kennedy delivered a presidential address to Congress in which he argued for the United States to launch a space program that would land U.S. astronauts on the moon. Observe the appeals and rhetorical devices that Kennedy uses in his argument:

- **Appeal to emotion; repetition; parallelism:** "Now it is time to take longer strides—time for a great new American enterprise—time for this nation to take a clearly leading role in space achievement, which in many ways may hold the key to our future on earth."
- **Appeal to logic:** "I believe we possess all the resources and talents necessary. But the facts of the matter are that we have never made the national decisions or marshaled the national resources required for such leadership."
- **Appeal to emotion; repetition:** "For while we cannot guarantee that we shall one day be first, we can guarantee that any failure to make this effort will make us last."

Academic Vocabulary

reasoning the use of logical thinking in order to draw conclusions

premise basis of an argument

Apply the Standard

Use the worksheet that follows to help you apply the standard as you read informational texts. Several copies of the worksheet have been provided for you.

- Evaluating Reasoning

Name _____ Date _____ Selection _____

Evaluating Reasoning

Answer the questions in the graphic organizer to help you evaluate the reasoning in a text that pertains to governmental or legal matters.

Text: .... **Writer:** ....

1. What main arguments or explanations are presented?	
2. What reasoning or evidence supports the writer's argument?	
3. What appeals does the writer make to emotions, logic, or ethics?	
4. What rhetorical devices does the writer use?	
5. What is the writer's main purpose in writing the text?	
6. Overall, would you say the argument is convincing or effective? Why or why not?	

A

Name _____ Date _____ Selection _____

Evaluating Reasoning

Answer the questions in the graphic organizer to help you evaluate the reasoning in a text that pertains to governmental or legal matters.

Text: ....   **Writer:** ....

1. What main arguments or explanations are presented?	
2. What reasoning or evidence supports the writer's argument?	
3. What appeals does the writer make to emotions, logic, or ethics?	
4. What rhetorical devices does the writer use?	
5. What is the writer's main purpose in writing the text?	
6. Overall, would you say the argument is convincing or effective? Why or why not?	

Name _____ Date _____ Selection _____

Evaluating Reasoning

Answer the questions in the graphic organizer to help you evaluate the reasoning in a text that pertains to governmental or legal matters.

Text: .... **Writer:** ....

1. What main arguments or explanations are presented?	
2. What reasoning or evidence supports the writer's argument?	
3. What appeals does the writer make to emotions, logic, or ethics?	
4. What rhetorical devices does the writer use?	
5. What is the writer's main purpose in writing the text?	
6. Overall, would you say the argument is convincing or effective? Why or why not?	

C

For use with Informational Text 8

Name _____ Date _____ Selection _____

Evaluating Reasoning

Answer the questions in the graphic organizer to help you evaluate the reasoning in a text that pertains to governmental or legal matters.

Text: .... **Writer:** ....

1. What main arguments or explanations are presented?	
2. What reasoning or evidence supports the writer's argument?	
3. What appeals does the writer make to emotions, logic, or ethics?	
4. What rhetorical devices does the writer use?	
5. What is the writer's main purpose in writing the text?	
6. Overall, would you say the argument is convincing or effective? Why or why not?	

Name _____ Date _____ Selection _____

Evaluating Reasoning

Answer the questions in the graphic organizer to help you evaluate the reasoning in a text that pertains to governmental or legal matters.

Text: .... **Writer:** ....

1. What main arguments or explanations are presented?	
2. What reasoning or evidence supports the writer's argument?	
3. What appeals does the writer make to emotions, logic, or ethics?	
4. What rhetorical devices does the writer use?	
5. What is the writer's main purpose in writing the text?	
6. Overall, would you say the argument is convincing or effective? Why or why not?	

E

Name _____ Date _____ Selection _____

Evaluating Reasoning

Answer the questions in the graphic organizer to help you evaluate the reasoning in a text that pertains to governmental or legal matters.

Text: .... **Writer:** ....

1. What main arguments or explanations are presented?	
2. What reasoning or evidence supports the writer's argument?	
3. What appeals does the writer make to emotions, logic, or ethics?	
4. What rhetorical devices does the writer use?	
5. What is the writer's main purpose in writing the text?	
6. Overall, would you say the argument is convincing or effective? Why or why not?	

For use with Informational Text 8

Informational Text 9

> **9. Analyze seventeenth-, eighteenth-, and nineteenth-century foundational U.S. documents of historical and literary significance (including The Declaration of Independence, the Preamble to the Constitution, the Bill of Rights, and Lincoln's Second Inaugural Address) for their themes, purposes, and rhetorical features.**

Explanation

Foundational documents are works that helped establish guiding principles for U.S. government, law, and society. Several of these works have literary value as well as historical significance. They include:

- **The Declaration of Independence:** the colonies' declaration of independence from Britain, written in 1776 by Thomas Jefferson
- **The Bill of Rights:** the name for the first ten amendments to the U.S. Constitution, first written by James Madison in 1789. It lists citizens' most important rights, such as freedom of speech.
- **Lincoln's Second Inaugural Address:** Lincoln's speech delivered on March 4, 1865, when the Civil War was nearly at an end. In it, he urges the country to reunite in peace and charity.

When you analyze a foundational document, first determine the author's purpose. Consider the historical context and examine the author's main points to determine the theme, or central message, of the work. Lastly, look for the rhetorical devices that the writer uses to create emphasis and stir emotions, such as:

- **Connotations:** the associations that a word calls to mind
- **Allusions:** references to well-known people, events, or texts
- **Repetition:** repeating a word or phrase
- **Parallelism:** repeating a grammatical structure
- **Appeals to emotion:** appeals to readers' feelings
- **Appeals to logic:** use of reasoning
- **Appeals to ethics:** appeals to readers' principles
- **Figurative language:** language that is not intended to be interpreted literally)

Examples

In order to analyze the Declaration of Independence, it is important to understand the historical context of 1776, when Britain ruled the thirteen colonies. In the opening paragraph, Thomas Jefferson explicitly states that his purpose for writing is to "declare the causes which impel [the colonies] to the separation" from British rule. Jefferson goes on to list the objectionable acts of King George II to the colonies, using parallelism to emphasize them: "He has refused . . ." "He has forbidden . . ." "He has dissolved . . ." The grievances support the theme of the document: that the United States of America must become independent. Jefferson appeals to readers' ethics when he says that all men are created equal and have rights to "life, liberty, and the pursuit of happiness." To reinforce the idea of British unfairness, Jefferson uses negative connotations, such as *abuses, absolute despotism, repeated injuries,* and *absolute tyranny.*

Apply the Standard

Use the worksheet that follows to help you apply the standard as you read informational texts. Several copies of each worksheet have been provided for you.

- Analyzing Historical Documents

Name _____ Date _____ Selection _____

Analyzing Historical Documents

Answer the questions in the graphic organizer to analyze a historical document.

Selection: ....

1. When was the document written? What main historical events were happening at that time?	
2. What is the writer's main purpose?	
3. What key points does the writer make?	
4. What is the theme of the work? (Synthesize the key points you listed in #3.)	
5. What rhetorical devices are employed? Give four examples from the text.	**a.**
	b.
	c.
	d.
6. What makes this document significant? Does it have both historical and literary significance? Explain.	

Name _____ Date _____ Selection _____

Analyzing Historical Documents

Answer the questions in the graphic organizer to analyze a historical document.

Selection: ....

1. When was the document written? What main historical events were happening at that time?	
2. What is the writer's main purpose?	
3. What key points does the writer make?	
4. What is the theme of the work? (Synthesize the key points you listed in #3.)	
5. What rhetorical devices are employed? Give four examples from the text.	**a.**
	b.
	c.
	d.
6. What makes this document significant? Does it have both historical and literary significance? Explain.	

Name _____ Date _____ Selection _____

Analyzing Historical Documents

Answer the questions in the graphic organizer to analyze a historical document.

Selection: ....

1. When was the document written? What main historical events were happening at that time?	
2. What is the writer's main purpose?	
3. What key points does the writer make?	
4. What is the theme of the work? (Synthesize the key points you listed in #3.)	
5. What rhetorical devices are employed? Give four examples from the text.	**a.**
	b.
	c.
	d.
6. What makes this document significant? Does it have both historical and literary significance? Explain.	

Name _____ Date _____ Selection _____

Analyzing Historical Documents

Answer the questions in the graphic organizer to analyze a historical document.

Selection: ....

1. When was the document written? What main historical events were happening at that time?	
2. What is the writer's main purpose?	
3. What key points does the writer make?	
4. What is the theme of the work? (Synthesize the key points you listed in #3.)	
5. What rhetorical devices are employed? Give four examples from the text.	**a.**
	b.
	c.
	d.
6. What makes this document significant? Does it have both historical and literary significance? Explain.	

D

Name _____ Date _____ Selection _____

Analyzing Historical Documents

Answer the questions in the graphic organizer to analyze a historical document.

Selection: ....

1. When was the document written? What main historical events were happening at that time?	
2. What is the writer's main purpose?	
3. What key points does the writer make?	
4. What is the theme of the work? (Synthesize the key points you listed in #3.)	
5. What rhetorical devices are employed? Give four examples from the text.	**a.**
	b.
	c.
	d.
6. What makes this document significant? Does it have both historical and literary significance? Explain.	

E

Name _____ Date _____ Selection _____

Analyzing Historical Documents

Answer the questions in the graphic organizer to analyze a historical document.

Selection: ....

1. When was the document written? What main historical events were happening at that time?	
2. What is the writer's main purpose?	
3. What key points does the writer make?	
4. What is the theme of the work? (Synthesize the key points you listed in #3.)	
5. What rhetorical devices are employed? Give four examples from the text.	**a.**
	b.
	c.
	d.
6. What makes this document significant? Does it have both historical and literary significance? Explain.	

F

For use with Informational Text 9

Informational Text 10

> 10. By the end of grade 11, read and comprehend literary nonfiction in the grades 11–CCR text complexity band proficiently, with scaffolding as needed at the high end of the range.

Explanation

Works of literary nonfiction vary widely in their **complexity,** or how difficult they are to understand. Several factors contribute to the complexity of a text. For example, the level of vocabulary may be difficult, the writer's style may be complicated, and the subject matter itself may be unfamiliar, requiring a special background or technical knowledge. Use reading strategies such as *previewing, monitoring your comprehension, using context clues,* and *paraphrasing* to help you decipher difficult text.

Examples

- **Preview the text:** When you preview the text, you scan it before reading in order to get a basic understanding of what it's about. Pay close attention to the title, subheadings, and boldfaced words since they often give information about the text's main ideas. Once you grasp the topic of the work, activate your own prior knowledge. Review what you already know about the subject and make predictions by asking yourself, "What do I expect to learn more about?"
- **Monitor your comprehension:** Check your understanding of the text as you read. If you lose the thread of meaning, reread the confusing passages. Slow down your reading pace as you reread, and use punctuation cues to break complex sentences into simpler parts. If you still don't understand a passage, read ahead to see if the meaning is clarified.
- **Use context clues:** *Context* is the text around a particular word. When you come upon unfamiliar words, use the following context clues to figure out the meaning: *synonyms* (words that mean the same as the unfamiliar word), *antonyms* (words with opposite meanings), *explanations* (words that give information about the word), and *sentence role* (the way the word is used). For example, a context clue reveals the meaning of *timorous* in this sentence: "A timorous creature, the field mouse flees at the slightest disturbance." The explanation that the field mouse "flees at the slightest disturbance" helps you understand that *timorous* means "easily frightened."
- **Paraphrase:** When you **paraphrase,** you restate a text in your own words. Paraphrasing helps you clarify and remember the most important ideas. Before you paraphrase a line or a passage, reread to clarify the writer's meaning. First, identify the most basic information, then put the ideas and information into your own words. Restate details as simply as you can.

Academic Vocabulary

complexity the degree to which a work is difficult to understand

paraphrase simplify and rephrase a passage in one's own words

Apply the Standard

Use the worksheet that follows to help you apply the standard as you read informational text. Several copies of the worksheet have been provided for you.

- Comprehending Complex Texts

Name _____ Date _____ Selection _____

Comprehending Complex Texts

Explain what makes the literary nonfiction you are reading complex. Then explain how you used reading strategies to understand the difficult parts of the text.

- Use the left-hand column of the graphic organizer to list specific examples of complex text.

- Use the right-hand column to identify reading strategies that you used and how they helped you.

Title: .... **Writer:** ....

What makes this selection complex? ....

....

....

Examples of Complex Text	Helpful Reading Strategies
1.	
2.	
3.	
4.	

A

Name _____ Date _____ Selection _____

Comprehending Complex Texts

Explain what makes the literary nonfiction you are reading complex. Then explain how you used reading strategies to understand the difficult parts of the text.

- Use the left-hand column of the graphic organizer to list specific examples of complex text.

- Use the right-hand column to identify reading strategies that you used and how they helped you.

Title: .... Writer: ....

What makes this selection complex? ....

....

....

Examples of Complex Text	Helpful Reading Strategies
1.	
2.	
3.	
4.	

For use with Informational Text 10

Name _____ Date _____ Selection _____

Comprehending Complex Texts

Explain what makes the literary nonfiction you are reading complex. Then explain how you used reading strategies to understand the difficult parts of the text.

- Use the left-hand column of the graphic organizer to list specific examples of complex text.

- Use the right-hand column to identify reading strategies that you used and how they helped you.

Title: .... Writer: ....

What makes this selection complex? ....

....

....

Examples of Complex Text	Helpful Reading Strategies
1.	
2.	
3.	
4.	

C

Name _____ Date _____ Selection _____

Comprehending Complex Texts

Explain what makes the literary nonfiction you are reading complex. Then explain how you used reading strategies to understand the difficult parts of the text.

- Use the left-hand column of the graphic organizer to list specific examples of complex text.

- Use the right-hand column to identify reading strategies that you used and how they helped you.

Title: ....   **Writer:** ....

What makes this selection complex? ....

....

....

Examples of Complex Text	Helpful Reading Strategies
1.	
2.	
3.	
4.	

D   For use with Informational Text 10

181

Name _____ Date _____ Selection _____

Comprehending Complex Texts

Explain what makes the literary nonfiction you are reading complex. Then explain how you used reading strategies to understand the difficult parts of the text.

- Use the left-hand column of the graphic organizer to list specific examples of complex text.

- Use the right-hand column to identify reading strategies that you used and how they helped you.

Title: .... Writer: ....

What makes this selection complex? ....

....

....

Examples of Complex Text	Helpful Reading Strategies
1.	
2.	
3.	
4.	

E

For use with Informational Text 10

Name _____ Date _____ Selection _____

Comprehending Complex Texts

Explain what makes the literary nonfiction you are reading complex. Then explain how you used reading strategies to understand the difficult parts of the text.

- Use the left-hand column of the graphic organizer to list specific examples of complex text.

- Use the right-hand column to identify reading strategies that you used and how they helped you.

Title: .... **Writer:** ....

What makes this selection complex? ....

....

....

Examples of Complex Text	Helpful Reading Strategies
1.	
2.	
3.	
4.	

Writing Standards

Writing 1

---

1. **Write arguments to support claims in an analysis of substantive topics or texts, using valid reasoning and relevant and sufficient evidence.**

Writing Workshop: Argument

When you develop an **argument** in writing, you present a claim and then support your claim. An argument is not just an assertion or a personal opinion. Sound arguments are reasoned and supported with relevant, sufficient evidence. For example, your essay might present the claim, "To improve student performance, the school year should be extended into the summer." Valid reasoning and evidence that support the claim form the heart of that argument. If your analysis of student performance is clear and your proposal to extend the school year is well-reasoned and supported, your argument will be persuasive.

Assignment

Write an argumentative essay in which you propose a solution to a problem in your school or community. Include these elements:

- ✓ a claim, or brief statement that identifies the problem and offers your solution
- ✓ an analysis of the problem, explaining what caused the problem and who it affects
- ✓ evidence and reasoning to support your claim
- ✓ acknowledgement of opposing claims, pointing out their strengths as well as their limitations
- ✓ effective and coherent organization
- ✓ use of rhetorical technique, including the correct use of academic words and phrases
- ✓ a formal style and objective tone and correct use of language conventions

*Additional Standards

Writing

1. Write arguments to support claims in an analysis of substantive topics or texts, using valid reasoning and relevant and sufficient evidence.

1.a. Introduce precise, knowledgeable claim(s), establish the significance of the claim(s), distinguish the claim(s) from alternate or opposing claims, and create an organization that logically sequences claim(s), counterclaims, reasons, and evidence.

1.b. Develop claim(s) and counterclaims fairly and thoroughly, supplying the most relevant evidence for each while pointing out the strengths and limitations of both in a manner that

anticipates the audience's knowledge level, concerns, values, and possible biases.

1.c. Use words, phrases, and clauses as well as varied syntax to link the major sections of the text, create cohesion, and clarify the relationships between claim(s) and reasons, between reasons and evidence, and between claim(s) and counterclaims.

1.d. Establish and maintain a formal style and objective tone while attending to the norms and conventions of the discipline in which they are writing.

1.e. Provide a concluding statement or section that follows from and supports the argument presented.

4. Produce clear and coherent writing in which the development, organization, and style are appropriate to task, purpose, and audience. (Grade-specific expectations for writing types are defined in standards 1–3.)

5. Develop and strengthen writing as needed by planning, revising, editing, rewriting, or trying a new approach, focusing on addressing what is most significant for a specific purpose and audience.

6. Use technology, including the Internet, to produce, publish, and update individual or shared writing products in response to ongoing feedback, including new arguments or information.

Language

1.a. Apply the understanding that usage is a matter of convention, can change over time, and is sometimes contested.

2. Demonstrate command of the conventions of standard English capitalization, punctuation, and spelling when writing.

6. Acquire and use accurately general academic and domain-specific words and phrases, sufficient for reading, writing, speaking, and listening at the college and career readiness level; demonstrate independence in gathering vocabulary knowledge when considering a word or phrase important to comprehension or expression.

Name _____ Date _____ Assignment _____

Prewriting/Planning Strategies

Choose a topic. Think about any problems you have noticed at your school or in your community. You may want to scan local newspapers to find problems that you had not been aware of before.

Identify your claim. After choosing a topic, decide how you will propose to solve the problem you've identified. If you are not certain how to solve your problem, research to learn more about your topic and about solutions that other people have proposed. Write a sentence that identifies your problem and proposes your solution. That sentence will be your claim.

Define the task, purpose, and audience. At all points of the writing process, consider your **task,** or what specifically you are writing; your **purpose,** or the effect you want your writing to have; and your **audience,** or the people you want to persuade. Will your audience be familiar with the problem you want to solve? Will they agree with you that it's a problem at all?

Problem	Possible problem #1: ....
	Possible problem #2: ....
	Possible problem #3: ....
Solution	Possible problem #1: ....
	Possible problem #2: ....
	Possible problem #3: ....
Task, Purpose, and Audience	❑ Will the topic I've chosen help me achieve my task? ❑ Does my audience see the topic I have chosen as a problem? ❑ Will my solution help me achieve my purpose for writing?
My Claim	....

For use with Writing 1

Name _____ Date _____ Assignment _____

Supporting a Claim

Consider the problem and the solution. Use valid reasoning and relevant, sufficient evidence to demonstrate how your solution will solve the problem you've identified. To support your claim, however, you'll also need to address the problem. Analyze the problem, using evidence to explain what caused it and who it affects. You may need to persuade your audience that what you've identified is, in fact, a problem. For example, if the person reading your essay believes that students in your community are performing well, you will need to include evidence that shows student performance could be improved.

In the chart below, describe the reasoning and evidence you will use to support your claim. Be sure to include:

- what caused the problem and who it effects

- how your solution solves the problem

PROBLEM	SOLUTION
My problem:	My Solution:
What caused the problem:	How the solution solves the problem:
Who the problem affects:	
Reasoning and evidence to support my analysis:	Reasoning and evidence to support my solution:

Name _____ Date _____ Assignment _____

Drafting Strategies

Create a structure for your draft. Plan a strategy for presenting the problem and your solution. Be sure to structure your essay in a way that is both persuasive and easy to follow.

- Evaluate your reasoning and evidence, your analysis of the problem, and your explanation of your solution.

Introduction/Claim ....

....

Analyze the Problem ....

....

    What caused the problem? ....

    ....

    Who does the problem affect? ....

        Evidence A ....

        ....

        Evidence B ....

        ....

Explain the Solution

....

    How does the solution solve the problem? ....

    ....

        Evidence A ....

        ....

        Evidence B...

        ....

    Alternate or opposing solutions ....

    ....

For use with Writing 1

188

Name _____ Date _____ Assignment _____

Develop your claim.

Use the organizer below to develop your claim and to anticipate and respond to counterclaims.

1. Write your claim, using precise wording to identify the problem and propose your solution.

2. Evaluate your claim, being sure to:

• consider both the problem and your proposed solution,

• consider your task, your purpose for writing, and your audience's knowledge of the topic.

3. Anticipate counterclaims and plan your responses. In addition to alternate or opposing solutions, be sure to consider counterclaims related to your analysis of the problem. For example, if you've identified student performance as a problem, a counterclaim may be that students in your community perform at a level above national averages.

My Claim

EVALUATING THE CLAIM	
Problem	**Solution**
❏ Does my claim identify the problem?	❏ Does my claim present a solution?
❏ Will the audience be familiar with the problem?	❏ Does the solution clearly address the problem?
❏ Will the audience recognize that it is a problem?	❏ Is the solution distinguishable from alternate or opposing solutions?

❏ Is my claim suited to my writing task and my purpose for writing?

❏ Does my claim anticipate my audience's knowledge about the issue?

❏ Is my claim supported with valid reasoning and relevant, sufficient evidence?

Counterclaim #1	Counterclaim #2
Alternate or opposing argument about the problem:	Alternate or opposing solution:
Addressing this counterclaim:	Addressing this counterclaim:

For use with Writing 1

Style and Tone

Establish a formal style and an objective tone. A formal style is appropriate for an essay that will be read by a variety of people, such as an essay submitted for a class assignment. A formal style can also help persuade audiences by communicating that you take both the problem you've identified and the solution you've proposed seriously. An objective tone encourages your audience to keep an open mind.

Examples:

Informal Style: A longer school year means that teachers can cover more ground, and students won't spend most of September getting adjusted to being in school again.

Formal Style: A longer school year would allow teachers to include more topics in the curriculum. It would also help students learn by eliminating the readjustment they now face at the beginning of every school year.

Subjective Tone: Some students may complain about giving up their summer vacations. They need to realize that when they grow up, they won't get ridiculously long vacations every year.

Objective Tone: I realize that many students will object to the loss of their traditional summer vacations. However, I believe that it is in their best interests to make this sacrifice.

As you draft your essay, choose words and phrases to maintain a formal style and an objective tone.

Use words, phrases, and clauses to create cohesion. Link the sections of your essay by using transitional words, phrases, and clauses. By including transitions, you help your audience follow your claim, your analysis of the problem, and your explanation of the solution. Here are some examples:

- Linking the problem and its cause(s): *consequently, as a result, therefore*

- Linking the problem and your solution: *in order to, for this reason, because*

- Linking reasoning to evidence: *for example, for instance, specifically*

- Linking your claim to counterclaims: *however, on the other hand, on the contrary*

Appropriate transitional words, phrases, and clauses clarify the relationships between your claim and your reasoning, between your reasons and your evidence, and between the problem and your solution.

- Students in our community are not as well prepared for college and careers as they could be. *For this reason,* our school year should be extended and our traditional summer vacation shortened.

- A longer school year will help improve academic performance in a number of ways. *First of all,* students and teachers will be able to explore complex topics in much greater depth.

- Research indicates that students who spend more time in school perform better academically. *For example,* students in schools that do not have long summer vacations generally earn higher marks.

Name _____ Date _____ Assignment _____

Conclusion

Include a strong conclusion. End your argumentative essay on a strong note. To persuade your audience that your solution should be enacted, include a strong conclusion that follows from and supports your argument. The examples below illustrate different strategies for writing a strong conclusion.

- Return to the problem, placing greater emphasis on the need to solve it: *Student performance in our community is in need of improvement. The problem may not be obvious, but our young people face a future in which they will have to compete with better-prepared graduates. We must take whatever steps we can to ensure that our students are ready for the lives that await them.*

- Describe an added benefit of enacting your solution: *Extending the school year will improve students' academic performance. It may also provide new opportunities for growth and personal development. Students who do not have access to summer activities will now have structure to their days and something productive to do.*

- Call your audience to action: *Summer vacation is a tradition we all treasure. Something more important than that tradition is at stake, however. Our students deserve the best education that we can give them. For their sake, let's extend the school year.*

Use the organizer below to plan and evaluate your conclusion.

Choosing a Strategy	
❏ Return to the problem	❏ Other Strategy:
❏ Describe an added benefit of your solution	....
❏ Call your audience to action	....

My Conclusion:

Evaluating My Conclusion	
❏ Does my conclusion follow from my argument?	❏ Is my conclusion strong? Will it persuade my audience? Explain.
❏ Does it support my claim, reasoning, and evidence?	
❏ Did I maintain a formal style and objective tone?	

For use with Writing 1

191

Name _____ Date _____ Assignment _____

Revising Strategies

Put a checkmark beside each question as you address it in your revision.

	Questions to Ask as You Revise
Writing Task	❑ Have I fulfilled my task? ❑ Does my writing contain the elements of an argumentative essay? ❑ Did I begin with a claim that identifies a problem and proposes a solution? ❑ Did I analyze the problem I identified? ❑ Did I explain the solution I proposed? ❑ Did I address alternative or opposing arguments? ❑ Did I include valid reasoning and relevant, sufficient evidence?
Purpose	❑ Is my argumentative essay persuasive? ❑ Will my audience be persuaded that the problem I've identified needs to be solved? ❑ Will my audience be persuaded that my solution will solve the problem? ❑ What reasons and evidence in my essay helped me achieve my purpose? ❑ Is there enough evidence to support my argument? ❑ Should I add more evidence? If so, list below: .... ❑ Have I provided a strong conclusion that follows from and supports my argument?
Audience	❑ Have I addressed my audience's knowledge of my issue? Have I addressed their concerns? ❑ Is my style of writing and tone suited to my audience? If not, what words and phrases need revision? .... ❑ Will my audience be able to follow my argumentative essay? ❑ What transitions should be added to link sections of my essay, create cohesion, and clarify relationships between ideas? ....

For use with Writing 1

Revising

Revise for academic words and phrases. Academic words and phrases aren't often used in casual conversation. Instead, they're used by teachers and students to describe concepts in language arts, science, social studies, and mathematics. You hear them in classrooms and read them in your textbooks. Some academic words and phrases are "general" because they are used in every subject area.

Sample General Academic Words	
analyze	examine or think about carefully
constitute	be something, or be a part of a larger whole
significant	having an important effect or influence
evaluate	assess the accuracy, validity, or soundness
implement	carry out or fulfill

Domain-specific words and phrases are another type of academic language. They're domain-specific because they are only used in one specific subject area. There are different words and phrases that are used in science, mathematics, language arts, and social studies. The examples below are used in education.

Sample Domain-Specific Words and Phrases	
academic calendar	calendar of important dates for the school year
curriculum	course of study offered at a school
pedagogy	principles and methods of teaching
student-centered classroom	classroom in which students are encouraged to participate
assessment	any method for measuring student progress

Use general academic and domain-specific words and phrases accurately. As you revise your argumentative essay, look for places where you have used general academic and domain-specific words and phrases inaccurately. Also, look for places where you have not used academic language. Rewrite sentences and paragraphs so that academic words and phrases are used accurately.

Original: If the school year is extended, school pedagogy can be enriched. Students will have more time to think about complex material and decide which points of view they think are right.

Revised: If the school year is extended, the **curriculum** offered in our schools can be enriched. Students will have more time to **analyze** complex material and to **evaluate** multiple points of view.

Revision Checklist

❏ Are there sentences or paragraphs in which general academic and domain-specific words and phrases are used inaccurately?

❏ Are there sentences or paragraphs in which general academic and domain-specific words and phrases could be used but are not?

Editing and Proofreading

Review your draft to correct errors in capitalization, spelling, and punctuation.

Focus on Capitalization Review your draft carefully to find and correct capitalization errors. If your argumentative essay includes references to historical periods, special events, and holidays, be sure that you have capitalized their names. The names of seasons are not capitalized.

Incorrect capitalization:	**Correct capitalization**
Veteran's day holiday	Veteran's Day holiday
Summer vacation	summer vacation

Focus on Spelling: An argumentative essay that includes spelling errors loses its authority to convince. Check the spelling of each word. Look for words that you frequently misspell and make sure they are correct. If you have typed your draft on a computer, use the spell-check feature to double-check for errors. Carefully review each suggested change before accepting the spell-check's suggestions. Also note that spell-check features will not catch all errors. Proofread carefully even after running a spell-check.

Focus on Punctuation: Hyphenation Proofread your writing to find and address punctuation errors. In particular, look for places in your writing where you include compound adjectives, compound numbers, and prefixes and suffixes. Be sure you use hyphens correctly.

Rule: Hyphenate compound adjectives and compound numbers. Hyphenate compound adjectives that precede the noun they modify and compound numbers less than one hundred.

a *long-held* tradition; a *much-feared* change; *twenty-three, forty-five*

Rule: Use hyphens with the prefixes *ex-, self-, all-,* and *great-* and with the suffixes *-elect* and *-free.* Also use hyphens with prefixes before proper nouns and adjectives.

self-fulfilling, all-consuming, governor-elect, structure-free

Revision Checklist

❑ Have you reviewed your argumentative essay for names of historical periods, special events, and holidays that should be capitalized?

❑ Have you read each sentence and checked that all of the words are spelled correctly?

❑ Do you have compound numbers or compound adjectives that should be hyphenated?

❑ Do you have prefixes or suffixes that should be used with hyphens?

❑ Have you hyphenated words that should not be hyphenated?

Name _____ Date _____ Assignment _____

Publishing and Presenting

Consider one of the following ways to present your writing:

Send a letter to the editor. Newspaper editorial pages are forums where problems and solutions are discussed. Use your argumentative essay as the basis for a letter to the editor of your local or school newspaper. Shorten your analysis of the problem and your explanation of your solution, and use a business letter format. Send your letter to your local or school newspaper; they may choose to publish it.

Create a blog. Create a blog focusing on the problem you identified in your argumentative essay. Post your analysis of the problem and call for solutions. Use your explanation of your solution as the first comment. Readers of the blog can respond to your solution or post their own solutions. Access to your blog should be limited to your class.

Rubric for Self-Assessment

Find evidence in your writing to address each category. Then, use the rating scale to grade your work. Circle the score that best applies for each category.

Evaluating Your Argument	not very					very
Focus: How clearly has your claim been stated?	1	2	3	4	5	6
Organization: How effectively and coherently have you organized your argument?	1	2	3	4	5	6
Style: How well have you maintained a formal, objective tone throughout your argument?	1	2	3	4	5	6
Support/Elaboration: How valid, sufficient, and suited to your audience is your evidence?	1	2	3	4	5	6
Conventions: How free of errors in grammar, usage, spelling, and punctuation is your argument?	1	2	3	4	5	6

For use with Writing 1

Writing 2

---

2. Write informative/explanatory texts to examine and convey complex ideas, concepts, and information clearly and accurately through the effective selection, organization, and analysis of content.

Writing Workshop: Expository Essay

When you write an **expository essay**, you inform your audience about a topic by defining, presenting steps in a process, comparing or contrasting ideas, outlining a problem and its solution, or explaining causes and effects. In a cause-and-effect essay, you examine the relationship between two or more events, explaining how one event causes or influences another. As with other types of expository writing, the first paragraph of a cause-and-effect essay must present a thesis that clearly identifies the relationship between causes and their effect. It should also analyze both the cause or causes and the effect or effects and fully support that analysis.

Assignment

Write an expository essay that focuses on a cause-and-effect relationship in history, in current events, in your school, in your community, or in the wider world. Include these elements:

✓ a clear statement of the relationship between or among cause(s) and effect(s)

✓ an organization that helps make the cause(s) and effects clear

✓ graphics or multimedia, if they are useful for exploring cause(s) and effect(s)

✓ explanation, sufficient facts, quotations, concrete details, and other development specific to your purpose and audience

✓ appropriate transitional words and phrases

✓ precise language and techniques such as metaphor, simile, and analogy

✓ a logical and effective conclusion

✓ correct use of language conventions and a formal style and an objective tone

*Additional Standards

Writing

2.a. Introduce a topic; organize complex ideas, concepts, and information so that each new element builds on that which precedes it to create a unified whole; include formatting (e.g., headings), graphics (e.g., figures, tables), and multimedia when useful to aiding comprehension.

2.b. Develop the topic thoroughly by selecting

the most significant and relevant facts, extended definitions, concrete details, quotations, or other information and examples appropriate to the audience's knowledge of the topic.

2.c. Use appropriate and varied transitions and syntax to link the major sections of the text, create cohesion, and clarify the relationships among complex ideas and concepts.

2.d. Use precise language, domain-specific vocabulary, and techniques such as metaphor, simile, and analogy to manage the complexity of the topic.

2.e. Establish and maintain a formal style and objective tone while attending to the norms and conventions of the discipline in which students are writing.

2.f. Provide a concluding statement or section that follows from and

supports the information or explanation presented (e.g., articulating implications or the significance of the topic).

Language

1. Demonstrate command of the conventions of standard English grammar and usage when writing or speaking.

2. Demonstrate command of the conventions of standard English capitalization, punctuation, and spelling when writing.

Name _____ Date _____ Assignment _____

Prewriting/Planning Strategies

Examine current events. Scan newspapers and magazines for headlines about events that interest you. Jot down the events, and then generate a list of probable causes and effects. From your list, choose an idea that is narrow enough to analyze in depth. For example, the topic of the Civil Rights Movement is too broad, but discussing the events that led to a particular legal victory during the Civil Rights Movement could be narrow enough.

List and freewrite. Mentally page through topics that interest you in technology, the arts, nature, politics, business, science, or sports. Choose the topic of greatest interest to you and freewrite for three minutes about it. Examine your freewriting for any cause and effects or for ideas that can be discussed in terms of cause and effect. Again choose an idea that is narrow enough to analyze in depth.

Chart causes and effects. Once you have a topic, chart its causes and effects in an organizer. You may have a single cause and effect, one cause with many effects, many causes with one effect, or a cause-and-effect chain. Use the organizer below to show your events or chain of events. Depending on your topic, edit the organizer by eliminating unneeded boxes and drawing connecting arrows as needed.

Cause(s)	Effect(s)

Name _____ Date _____ Assignment _____

Developing a Topic

Explore the cause(s) and effect(s). As you develop your topic, begin by breaking down the cause(s) or effects(s) into explanatory details. The organizer below works best with a single cause or a single effect. Record the cause or effect in the box on the left. Then use the diagram to record main ideas and details related to one or many causes or effects. For example, under "Cause," you might write, "The rise of for-profit colleges." On the major lines of the organizer (the lines that extend up and down at an angle), you might list effects such as "more students able to attend college," "lower costs of education," "more federal loans granted," and "more students defaulting on loans." Then, on the lines that extend from each of the major lines you might write facts and details, such as "22% graduation rate" or "attaining a quick and easy degree."

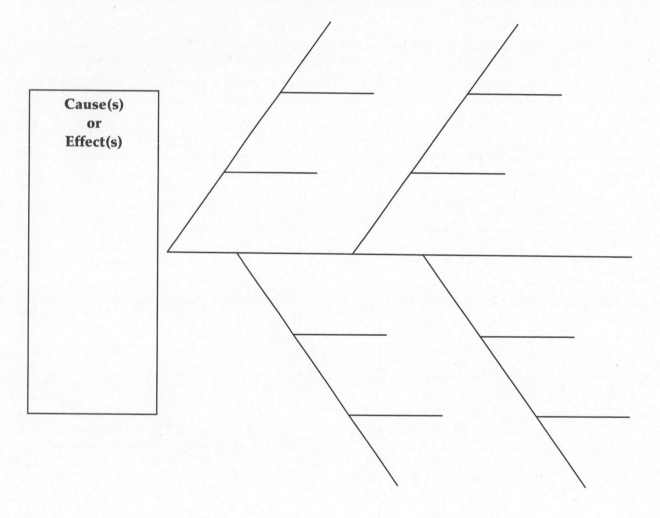

Cause(s)
or
Effect(s)

Organizing Ideas

Develop a structure. Use this organizer to develop major parts of your essay. It will also help as a guide when you begin drafting your essay. You can edit the number of causes and effects in this organizer to suit your topic.

Introduction
Attention-getting opener: **Thesis/Overview statement of cause-and-effect relationship:**
Body Paragraphs

Statement of Cause:
 	
    Detailed analysis, including facts and examples—
 	
Statement of Cause:
 	
    Detailed analysis, including facts and examples—
 	
Statement of Effect:
 	
    Detailed analysis, including facts and examples—
 	
Statement of Effect:
 	
    Detailed analysis, including facts and examples—

Conclusion
Summary statement: **Memorable finish:**

Name _____ Date _____ Assignment _____

Drafting Your Essay

Support your ideas. As you draft your essay, use facts, statistics, quotations, and other examples that will provide a convincing web of support for your major points. Make judgments about how appropriate each piece of evidence is to the audience's knowledge of the topic. Also, consider what kind of information will catch and maintain the audience's interest.

Evidence/Support	What My Audience Already Knows or Needs to Know About the Topic	Ways to Interest My Audience in This Topic

Structure body paragraphs. Use the TRI method to develop body paragraphs.

- **Topic.** Write a sentence that states a fundamental cause or effect that is a focus of your essay. Here is an example: *Text messaging has saved the average person many minutes out of each day.*

- **Restriction.** Write a sentence that restates the topic sentence more concretely: *It is an efficient way to make plans in the shortest possible time.*

- **Illustration.** Illustrate your point through facts, examples, or personal experience: *Mr. Zweigbaum reported having to set up our next troop meeting in less than a minute by texting; if he called each troop member on the phone, it could have taken ten times as long.*

Apply the TRI method with a key cause or effect in your essay. This method will help you get the paragraph started. Then, add supporting evidence to create a fully developed paragraph.

Topic	Restriction	Illustration

Include formatting, graphics, or multimedia. Consider using headings and bulleted points to organize large chunks of information into smaller, more manageable bits. Tables, graphs, charts, and other figures are useful for conveying information in an effective manner. Restrict your use of formatting, graphics, or multimedia to instances when you think that nothing else will work as well. These items cannot substitute for clear writing; they can, however, enhance it.

Using Transitions

Use appropriate and varied transitions. Link the ideas in your writing by using transitional words, phrases, and clauses such as the following:

as a result	*for this reason*	*so that*
because	*if … then*	*therefore*
because of	*since*	*thus*
consequently	*so*	*why*
for		

To help your reader or audience move easily from one paragraph to the next, use repetition to create a link between the end of the previous paragraph and the first sentence of the next paragraph.

Paragraph 1 ends: . . . resulted in the <u>vandalism</u> that took place on the school grounds.

Paragraph 2 begins: Perhaps the main cause for this <u>vandalism</u> was . . .

Adding More Links

Create coherence. Good writing is coherent or easy to follow—a quality that exists when ideas lead smoothly from one to the next. Coherence results from the appropriate use of transitional words and phrases and clear pronoun references. Also, using connecting words that qualify or intensify your major points helps the reader comprehend your message.

Note how each boldfaced word in the paragraph below helps to create coherence, or causes the words to cohere in a unified whole. Note the boldfaced words, and identify which ones are transitional words or phrases, pronouns with clear antecedents, or words that qualify or intensify ideas or other words.

> Experts suggest that **voter** participation decreased during the last national election cycle **for** a number of reasons, **not the least of which** was the lack of a truly **charismatic leader** to exert a strong magnetic pull on **voters. Voters, it appears,** respond to the personality, rather than to the words, of the **candidate: They** want the **personality** that says, "I will get the job done." In the same vein, they prefer the leader who exudes personality over the educated, earnest, **but** dull **candidate. If** the **candidate** is **charismatic, then** there are no worries about the candidate being articulate or **even fully** knowing the issues. **Charisma** alone can guarantee success.

Drafting a Conclusion

Write an effective conclusion. Your cause-and-effect essay should have a formal and effective conclusion. It must support the information and explanation you have provided. To create a strong conclusion, restate your main ideas in a fresh way that re-emphasizes your thesis and the significance of the topic. You might close by giving your reader something to ponder or a final thought that brings a satisfying sense of closure. Another way to conclude your essay might be to direct your reader's attention from the simple causes and effects you have discussed to the more global or far-reaching implications of similar causes and effects. You might also end with a particularly apt quotation that sums up the importance of your topic.

Evaluating Language

Check for precise language. If you are presenting a cause, and your argument is that "text messaging has resulted in accidents," your point may be accurate, but you are not precise. To be precise, you should be more specific and concrete. For example, you might add details such as the following: *Text messaging diverts the driver's attention from the road to his or her mobile device; in 2007, driver distraction was a factor in approximately 1,000 accidents involving drivers who were 16 or 17 years of age.* Get rid of general, imprecise, or overused words and phrases by eliminating clichés, using active verbs whenever possible, and substituting more precise and vivid language for tired modifiers such as *great, really,* or *awesome.*

Check for technological or topic-specific language. Suppose that the cause you are addressing involves the shift to abstract expressionism in art. In that case, unless your audience consists of people who are very knowledgeable about art, you would need to define or explain certain terms for your readers. Similarly, as you integrate words related to abstract impressionism, such as *cubism,* you might need to briefly and concisely explain each term the first time you use it. You could also consider including images or illustrations that might be helpful for your audience.

Replace everyday explanation with literary techniques. A metaphor, a simile, or an analogy can be every bit as powerful in nonfiction writing as it can be in a work of literature. You may also find that such techniques help to keep your audience interested as well as help you to achieve your writing purpose. To create a metaphor, you might suggest "charisma is a nectar" or, for a simile, that "charisma is like a nectar." If you wish, you can also develop that same figure of speech by perhaps noting that people are always drawn to nectar or that they cannot get enough of it. To create an analogy, you might write, "Text messaging is the new drum to which modern communication marches." To extend that analogy even further, you might talk about the ever-increasing tempo and loudness of that drum in daily life.

Evaluating Your Writing Style and Tone

Evaluate your tone. When you write an expository essay, strive for an objective tone. To create an objective tone, make consistent use of the third person. Using *I*, or any other form of the first person, such as *me, my,* and *mine,* or *we, our,* and *ours* will undercut the appearance of objectivity. Similarly, avoid the second person: *you, your,* and *yours* Also avoid casual and personal choices, such as contractions, slang, and chatty or overly-friendly language. Avoid condescension, sarcasm, or anything that might be perceived as glib or disrespectful.

Evaluate your style. While the style of your writing should involve an objective, respectful tone and the use of the third person, you should also adhere to the other conventions of formal writing. This includes using standard English. Avoid fragments except when they create an appropriate effect—such as emphasis. Also avoid using exclamation marks. Aim to create the kinds of varied, balanced, and crafted sentences that reflect a serious purpose and engage a reader's interest.

In the following example, consider why the tone and style choices in bold below are inconsistent with the task, purpose, and the audience. Suggest replacements in the blanks below the example.

(1) The **A-number-one** cause of vandalism is alienation. **(2) Being left out, not belonging, not doing well at school.** Vandals are the outsiders **(3)!** As C. F. Cardinell writes, some **(3) perps (4) don't** develop self-esteem and turn to vandalism as **(5) some kind of (6) weird** release from pressures related to that lack of esteem. The crimes these **kids** commit tend to focus first on the school building and grounds and second on the community. **(7) You rarely see them moving** outside the community. The sprayed paint, broken windows, and turned-over trashcans they leave behind **(8) being like** cries of help from wounded animals.

1. ....
2. ....
3. ....
4. ....
5. ....
6. ....
7. ....
8. ....

Name _____ Date _____ Assignment _____

Revising Strategies

Using the checklist below, put a checkmark beside each question as you address it while revising your essay.

	Questions To Ask as You Revise
Task	❑ Have I written a cause-and-effect essay? ❑ Is there a clear relationship between each cause and each relationship that I present?
Purpose	❑ Have I set forth a clear cause-and-effect relationship beginning with my introduction? ❑ Have I fully developed each cause and effect with sufficient facts, statistics, quotations, concrete details, examples, and other forms of development? ❑ Have I sufficiently explained and supported my major points? ❑ Are all of the details I've included relevent to my explanation? ❑ Have I provided a strong conclusion?
Audience	❑ Will my audience understand the relationship between each cause and effect? ❑ Do I need to add, delete, or adjust any details to suit them better to my audience's interest, knowledge, or experience? ❑ Have I sufficiently explained technical or topic-specific language? ❑ Will my audience think I am objective? ❑ Is my style and tone specific to my audience? ❑ Have I included appropriate graphics, headings, or multimedia as needed to help my audience understand causes and effects? ❑ Have I used transitions, clear pronoun references, and other connectors so that my audience can easily follow my ideas?

For use with Writing 2

Revising

Revise for subject-verb agreement. For a subject and its verb to agree, both must be in either singular or plural form, depending on whether the subject is singular or plural.

Identifying Errors in Subject-Verb Agreement

Agreement errors sometimes occur with compound subjects, subjects joined by *or* or *nor,* or when an indefinite pronoun is the subject of a sentence. In the examples below, the subjects are underlined, and the verbs are italicized.

Compound Subject

Incorrect: Both the <u>owners and neighbors</u> *was outraged* by the vandalism.

Correct: Both the <u>owners and neighbors</u> *were outraged* by the vandalism.

Subject Joined by *Or* or *Nor*

Incorrect: <u>Either a text or an e-mail</u> *are* a good choice for quick communication.

Correct: <u>Either a text or an e-mail</u> *is* a good choice for quick communication.

Indefinite Pronoun as Subject

Incorrect: <u>Everyone</u> *like* the easy-going friendliness of that candidate.

Correct: <u>Everyone</u> *likes* the easy-going friendliness of that candidate.

Fixing Errors

To correct mismatched subjects and verbs, follow these steps:

1. Identify whether the subject in a sentence is singular or plural.

2. Select the matching form of the verb:

For compound subjects joined by *and,* use the plural verb forms.

For singular subjects joined by *or* or *nor,* use the singular verb forms.

When the subject is an indefinite pronoun, use the appropriate verb form. Use the list below for guidance.

Always Singular: *anybody, anyone, anything, each, either, every, everybody, everyone, everything, neither, nobody, no one, nothing, somebody, someone, something*

Always Plural: *both, few, many, others, several*

Singular or Plural: *all, any, more, most, none, some*

Revision Checklist

❑ Have I used the plural form of the verb for compound subjects joined by *and?*

❑ Have I used the singular form of the verb for compound subjects joined by *or* or *nor?*

❑ Have I used the singular form of the verb with subjects that are singular indefinite pronouns?

❑ Have I used the plural form of the verb with subjects that are plural indefinite pronouns?

Editing and Proofreading

Review your draft to correct errors in capitalization, spelling, and punctuation.

Focus on Sentence Clarity: Ensure that your sentences are clear by checking that the subjects agree with the verbs. In addition, read your sentences to be sure that each one expresses a complete thought.

Focus on Capitalization: Review your draft carefully to find and correct capitalization errors. Capitalize all proper adjectives.

> **Incorrect capitalization:** Who was more charismatic: the republican candidate or the democratic candidate?

> **Correct capitalization:** Who was more charismatic: the Republican candidate or the Democratic candidate?

Focus on Spelling: As you read, circle any words that you are not sure how to spell, frequently misspell, or seldom use. Then, use reference resources such as a dictionary or thesaurus to confirm the correct spelling. Follow these steps to find spellings in a dictionary:

- Check the first letters of a word. Think of homophones for that sound.

- Check the other letters. Once you spell the first sound correctly, try sounding out the rest of the word. Look for likely spellings in the dictionary. If you do not find your word, look for more unusual spellings of the sound.

Focus on Punctuation: Commas after Introductory Words, Phrases, and Clauses Proofread your writing to find and address punctuation errors. In particular, look for commas after introductory words, phrases, or clauses. Be sure you use commas correctly.

Rule: Use a comma after an introductory word. *Next, they sprayed paint on the garage.*

Rule: Use a comma after an introductory phrase or phrases. *By moonlight, they set to work. At that hour of the night, there were no witnesses.*

Rule: Use a comma after an introductory clause. *When the police arrived, the vandals had been gone for perhaps four hours.*

Name _____ Date _____ Assignment _____

Publishing and Presenting

Consider one of the following ways to present your writing:

Make an infographic. Turn your essay into a visual display that shows and illustrates the cause-and-effect relationship that you described. Integrate your explanatory text into the display in a way that clearly conveys information and explains the graphics to the reader. Post your infographic on a bulletin board or class Web site.

Give a multimedia presentation. Recreate your essay as a series of slides that illustrate your main ideas. Practice presenting these slides with a detailed oral analysis. Deliver the presentation to the class.

Rubric for Self-Assessment

Find evidence in your writing to address each category listed below. Then, use the rating scale to grade your work. Circle the score that best applies for each category.

Evaluating Your Expository Essay	not very very
Focus: How clearly have you stated the cause-and-effect relationship?	1 2 3 4 5 6
Organization: How effectively have you organized your essay, especially body paragraphs that analyze the cause(s) and effect(s)?	1 2 3 4 5 6
Support/Elaboration: How well is your topic supported by significant and relevant facts, concrete details, and other information appropriate to your audience's knowledge of the topic?	1 2 3 4 5 6
Style: How effectively have you created a formal style and objective tone that are appropriate to your task, purpose, and audience?	1 2 3 4 5 6
Conventions: How free is your essay from errors in grammar, spelling, and punctuation?	1 2 3 4 5 6

For use with Writing 2

Writing 3

> 3. **Write narratives to develop real or imagined experiences or events using effective technique, well-chosen details, and well-structured event sequences.***

Writing Workshop: Narrative

When you write a **narrative,** your goal is to engage your audience through the task of telling a story. Narrative essays tell true stories. Short stories, on the other hand are works of the imagination—even though many of them incorporate realistic elements. The best short stories rely on interesting characters, familiar or new conflicts, well-drawn settings, and methods of moving along the plot, such as effective dialogue, that hold the readers' attention throughout the story. Engaging and memorable short stories also rely on well-chosen details, appropriate pacing, and endings that wrap up loose ends and provide a satisfying sense of closure.

Assignment

Write a realistic or purely imaginative short story. Include these elements:

- ✓ a clear, consistent, single point of view, or clear, effective multiple points of view
- ✓ characters, a setting, and an inciting incident
- ✓ a conflict that precipitates the rising action, leads to the climax, and is resolved in the ending
- ✓ a clear sequence of events that builds toward a particular tone and outcome
- ✓ narrative techniques, including natural dialogue, reflection or interior monologue, multiple plot lines, and appropriate pacing
- ✓ precise words, telling details, and sensory language
- ✓ a satisfying conclusion that follows from the conflict and events of the narrative
- ✓ correct use of language conventions

*Additional Standards

Writing

3.a. Engage and orient the reader by setting out a problem, situation, or observation and its significance, establishing one or multiple point(s) of view, and introducing a narrator and/or characters; create a smooth progression of experiences or events.

3.b. Use narrative techniques, such as dialogue, pacing, description, reflection, and multiple plot lines, to develop experiences, events, and/or characters.

3.c. Use a variety of techniques to sequence events so that they build on one another to create a coherent whole and build toward a particular tone and outcome (e.g, a sense of mystery, suspense, growth, or resolution).

3.d. Use precise words and phrases, telling details, and sensory language to convey a vivid picture of the experiences, events, setting, and/or characters.

3.e. Provide a conclusion that follows from and reflects on what is experienced, observed, or resolved over the course of the narrative.

3.c. Provide a conclusion that follows from and reflects on what is experienced, observed, or resolved over the course of the narrative.

Language

1.a. Use punctuation (commas, parentheses, dashes) to set off nonrestrictive/parenthetical elements.

2. Demonstrate command of the conventions of standard English capitalization, punctuation, and spelling when writing.

Name _____ Date _____ Selection _____

Prewriting/Planning Strategies

Map out plot events. The organization of a story includes several standard elements, which are often presented in a particular order. A plot includes the following:

- **Exposition.** Introduce the characters, setting, and basic situation.

- **Inciting incident.** Introduce the main conflict.

- **Rising action.** Develop the conflict.

- **Climax.** Bring the conflict to a high point of interest or suspense.

- **Falling action.** Wind down the conflict.

- **Resolution.** Provide a general insight or change in the characters.

Jot down two ideas for plots in this story chart.

Plot Line 1			
Exposition (Characters, Setting, Basic Situation)	**Rising Action**	**Climax**	**Resolution**

Plot Line 2			
Exposition (Characters, Setting, Basic Situation)	**Rising Action**	**Climax**	**Resolution**

For use with Writing 3

Name _____ Date _____ Selection _____

Introducing Characters, Conflict, and Setting

Interview the main character. After you choose a plot line, use the chart below to "conduct an interview" with your character. Assume that your character supplies you with rich, full answers.

Name:
Tell me a little about your home, school, and friends.
What's the best thing about being you?
What problems or conflicts are you facing right now?
Tell me more about that problem. Where and when does it happen? Who else is involved?
What else should I know about you?

Name _____ Date _____ Selection _____

Create a setting. Establish a time and a place for your story. Also, determine the environment, such as an ice storm, a breezy day, or blistering sun; silence, soothing or disturbing natural sounds, music, or mechanical noise; darkness or light. Finally, name an overall mood, such as tense, adventurous, thrilling, happy, gloomy, or uncertain.

Time	Place	Environment	Mood

Creating Point of View

Select a point of view. Choose a narrator, the person who will relate the events of your story from start to finish. Use the chart to determine whether the narrator will be named or unnamed and in the story or outside it. Also, decide how the narrator's voice will sound, what person he or she will use (first or third), and how much he or she will or won't know.

Named or unnamed/ Character or not?	Voice and Person	Knows or Doesn't Know—

You also have the choice of telling events from the viewpoint of two or more characters in the story. In this case, the characters take turns relating what is happening or reflecting on events and motives. If you select this option, take special care with transitions so that your reader follows the shift in point of view.

For use with Writing 3

Name _____ Date _____ Selection _____

Organizing the Narrative

Use different techniques. In addition to using chronological or time order, consider integrating one of these techniques:

- **Flashback or foreshadow.** Incorporate a past event, dream, or memory that helped to form the character or contribute to the conflict. Alternatively, or in addition, provide hints of what is to come.

- **Flash-forward.** In the midst of using chronological order, insert a future event into the narrative.

- **Start in the middle.** Start with an event that shows the conflict already under way.

- **Start at the end.** Begin with a final event or the last event in time order; then start at the beginning.

You might also try using multiple plots lines. Try developing a double plot line below.

Plot Line 1: Main Events	Plot Line 2: Main Events
1.	1.
2.	2.
3.	3.
4.	4.
5.	5.

Using Narrative Techniques

Move the plot along with dialogue. Dialogue is one of your best choices for communicating events to the reader. You can and should use it to create rising action and to increase narrative tension.

Follow these guidelines for writing effective dialogue:

- **Make it sound natural.** Recreate the informal, everyday language of real-life conversation by using fragments, including slang and informal word choices, and letting your characters focus on themselves.

- **Incorporate dialect and jargon.** If your characters have a background or come from a region with specific and unique patterns of spoken language, incorporate them. If your characters are NASCAR fans, use the jargon of automobile racing.

- **Vary your speaker tags.** Use a variety of verbs, such as *suggested, whined, howled, reasoned,* and *huffed,* in your speaker tags. Eliminate speaker tags if the identity of the speaker is already clear.

- **Show character differences through word choice.** Distinguish characters through the way they speak. A mother and son who are arguing may use entirely different word choices that typify their generation as well as their point of view.

- **Don't overuse dialogue.** Don't give away the whole story in the dialogue or rely on dialogue to tell everything that happens.

Add interior monologue. Another narrative strategy is revealing the inner thoughts and feelings of a character. In a reflection or interior monologue, a character reacts to events and to other characters, often in an extended fashion. This technique provides insight into the character's mind and motivation and can also move the plot along.

Pace your narrative. Take time with the exposition of your narrative and remember that the action should rise, event by event, and not rush or lurch, to the climax. You should be using about half your story length to build up narrative tension or suspense. Once you reach the climax, you can move more quickly to the resolution.

Build toward a particular tone or outcome. As you build up the tension, aim for a particular tone and keep your ending in mind. Even if you are planning a surprise ending, the surprise cannot be slapped on as a new thought at the end. Instead, you need at least to hint at its possibility through the events that precede it or through your selection of details.

Using Descriptive and Sensory Language

Use sensory language. Sensory details are a key to developing the setting, mood, and tone of your story. They can also help you build suspense. Sensory language should help your reader see and otherwise experience the characters, setting, and action. Keep in mind, however, that too many sensory details can be as disappointing as too few. For example, "the scorching heat" is preferable to "the hot, dry, parching, burning, scorching heat." Similarly, do not aim to engage every sense if the context doesn't work. If, for example, you are describing factory workers in a plant, images that evoke the sound and sights may well be sufficient; there is no need to add how the plant smells or what the conveyor belt feels like.

Use precise, varied, and accurate language. The success of your story hinges in part on the words you choose to bring your characters and their actions to life. Try these techniques for making your story more detailed and descriptive:

- **Observe closely.** Subject each detail you select to scrutiny. For example, ask yourself what the cabin in the woods really looks like, or what you hear or see inside it on a windy, moonless night.

- **Be precise.** Similarly, ask how can you make each verb and noun you select more forceful or more accurate. Replace state-of-being verbs with action verbs, and imprecise verbs such as *run* with precise verbs such as *flee* or *gallop*. Replace abstract and general nouns such as *rest* with more precise or interesting nouns such as *snooze, nap, repose,* or *ease*.

- **Vary descriptive methods.** Description is not just a matter of adding adjectives. Remember that adjective and adverb phrases also modify. Similarly, a participial phrase can tell all the reader needs to know, as in, "Seething with anger, Jacob turned his back to them."

Writing and Evaluating a Conclusion

Resolve the conflict. To end your story, you must bring a satisfying end to the conflict. That is, your ending must arise from the characters and the action that you built to a climax. For example, if you've created a mystery that obsesses your narrator or main character, solve it in your conclusion. If you've created a state of fear or anxiety over a challenge, lift that state of fear at the end of your story.

Evaluate your effect on the reader. You want your reader to know that the conflict is over. To do this, you can end in a big way, such as with an alien world exploding, or in a subtle way, such as with a narrator reflecting on how the experience has receded, over time, into a fading light across the water. No matter how you end, however, your goal is a satisfying sense of closure.

Name _____ Date _____ Selection _____

Revising Strategies

Put a checkmark beside each question as you address it in your revision.

	Questions To Ask as You Revise
Task	❏ Have I written a short story? ❏ Have I included the following elements of a short story: characters, setting, and inciting incident; conflict; rising action; climax; and resolution?
Purpose	❏ Have I created an effective and consistent point of view, or have I effectively and clearly used multiple points of view? ❏ Have I used dialogue to move the plot along? ❏ Have I paced my story to lead slowly to the climax and more quickly from the climax to the resolution? ❏ Have I varied narrative techniques, such as by including reflection or interior monologue, or by incorporating one or more additional plot lines? ❏ Have I sequenced events in an interesting, effective, and clear manner?
Audience	❏ Have I engaged my readers from start to finish? ❏ Have I used precise words, telling details, and sensory language to create interest? ❏ Do I need to add, delete, or adjust any details to make the characters or setting more interesting, more convincing, or more appropriate to the conflict and events? ❏ Do I need to add, delete, or adjust any details to make the events clearer, more interesting, or easier to follow in sequence? ❏ Have I provided my readers with a conclusion that relates clearly to the conflict and follows from the story events?

For use with Writing 3

Developing Your Style

Use punctuation in dialogue. Dialogue conveys the way characters speak. Punctuation can help readers "hear" dialogue. End punctuation—periods, question marks, and exclamation points— affects the tone of a sentence. Other forms of punctuation can also show how a character sounds.

Rule	Example
Use commas to indicate short pauses.	"Okay, so, what do we do next?"
Use an ellipsis to show a longer pause or hesitation. An ellipsis can also show a voice trailing off.	"No . . . I mean, okay, but just this time." "But what about all that work . . . "
Use a dash to indicate a sudden stop, such as an interruption.	"What if we put—."
Use italics to emphasize a word or phrase.	"That's just about the *worst* idea I've ever heard!"
Use apostrophes to show dropped letters in dialect.	"You've been givin' me excuses for too long."

Apply It to Your Writing

To improve dialogue in your story, follow these steps:

1. Read each line aloud. Decide whether the words sound natural. Consider adding punctuation to show natural pauses in your character's voice.

2. Decide whether there is more than one possible reading for each line of dialogue. For important lines, consider adding italics to show which word or words the character emphasizes.

3. Be careful not to overuse special punctuation such as ellipses, dashes, and italics. Limit exclamation points as well; they are most effective when used sparingly. Reread all of the dialogue in your story, paying attention to the balance of punctuation.

Revision Checklist

❑ Have I carefully punctuated dialogue to show how each speaker sounds?

❑ Have I used commas for short pauses, dashes for sudden stops, ellipses for longer pauses or trailing off, italics for emphasis, and apostrophes for dropped letters or sounds?

❑ Have I avoided the overuse of punctuation, especially exclamation points?

Editing and Proofreading

Review your draft to correct errors in capitalization, spelling, and punctuation.

Focus on Capitalization: Review your draft carefully to find and correct capitalization errors. Capitalize the first word in each new bit of dialogue.

Incorrect capitalization: "he's the driver to watch," Zora said.
Correct capitalization: "He's the driver to watch," Zora said.

Capitalize the first word in dialogue that is interrupted by a speaker tag if the words that follow form a complete sentence.

Incorrect capitalization: "Right," Tanya answered, "you should have seen his qualifying run."
Correct capitalization: "Right," Tanya answered, "You should have seen his qualifying run."

Focus on Spelling: For words ending in silent *e*, drop the *e* before adding a suffix that begins with a vowel, such as *-ing, -ed,* or *-ion*. For example, *relates* becomes *relating, related,* or *relation*. Double-check the past tense and past participle of most verbs to be sure you have applied this rule.

Focus on Punctuation: Use punctuation to set off nonrestrictive/parenthetical elements. Proofread your writing to find phrases and clauses that are not essential to the meaning of the sentence. Be sure you have used the correct punctuation before and after these elements.

Rule: Use commas to set off nonrestrictive information.

Diego, who had brought his guitar with him, was not among those chosen to sing.

The house, which had new owners, was not at all as she remembered it.

Rule: Use dashes to set off nonrestrictive information, especially when it interrupts the established train of thought.

Amanda—everyone calls her Mandy—was always the first person I turned to for help.

Thompson Beach—the favorite of locals in our community—is experiencing some serious erosion.

Name _____ Date _____ Selection _____

Publishing and Presenting

Consider one of the following ways to present your writing:

Recite your story. Practice reading your story aloud, experimenting with body language, gestures, and expressions that will help bring the characters, the conflict, and the events to life. Also try out variations in pacing and pauses for dramatic effect. Then deliver the reading to the class.

Videotape a scene. Gather props and a camera, and with classmates, practice and act out a single scene from your story. Post the tape online for others to view.

Rubric for Self-Assessment

Find evidence in your writing to address each category. Then, use the rating scale to grade your work. Circle the score that best applies for each category.

Evaluating Your Narrative	not very very
Focus: How clear and consistent are the point of view, the characters, the setting, the inciting incident, and the conflict?	1 2 3 4 5 6
Organization: How clearly and effectively is the narrative sequenced? How appropriately have you used appropriate pacing, dialogue, and other narrative techniques to help move the plot along and reach a satisfying ending?	1 2 3 4 5 6
Support/Elaboration: How well have you used sufficient details to show the characters, the conflict, and the action?	1 2 3 4 5 6
Style: How well have you engaged the reader with an interesting conflict, precise words that create a vivid picture of the characters and their experiences?	1 2 3 4 5 6
Conventions: How free is your essay from errors in grammar, spelling, and punctuation?	1 2 3 4 5 6

For use with Writing 3

Writing 4

> 4. Produce clear and coherent writing in which the development, organization, and style are appropriate to task, purpose, and audience.

Explanation

Clarity and coherence are important goals for all writers. Because people write for different reasons and readers, producing writing that is appropriate for your specific writing situation—your task, purpose, and audience—is important as well.

Your **task,** or the specific reason you are writing, can be anything from writing an expository essay for an assignment to writing a story for fun. Your **purpose,** or the goal you want your writing to achieve, is related to but different from your task. Persuading people, explaining a topic, and entertaining readers are common purposes for writing. The person or people who will read what you write are your **audience.** Be sure to consider all three of these elements as you develop and organize your writing and select an appropriate style.

- **Development:** Present and build your argument, topic, or narrative by including information, evidence, and details that are appropriate for your specific writing situation. For example, if your task is to write a research report about the causes of the American Civil War, develop your topic by citing the work of well-known historians. If your purpose is to argue that after-school jobs are beneficial for high school students, use examples that are likely to convince your readers.

- **Organization:** Sequence ideas and information—or the events in a narrative— appropriately for your writing situation. For example, if your task is to write an argument supporting healthier choices in your school's cafeteria, you might discuss counterclaims before presenting your strongest argument. If your purpose is to tell an entertaining story about something that happened, you could use flashbacks to introduce background information. Make sure you add transitions to help your audience understand how your ideas, information, evidence, and details are related to one another.

- **Style:** The language and tone in your writing should also be appropriate for your task, purpose, and audience. A research report requires a formal style and an objective tone. An argument about healthy eating needs an objective tone as well, but may be less formal. Use a conversational style for a personal narrative, and include precise details that will appeal to the audience's imagination.

Academic Vocabulary

development the use of information, evidence, and details in writing to present and build an argument, a topic, or a narrative

organization the way ideas, information, and other elements are arranged and connected in writing

style the language and tone used by a writer to communicate clearly and engage readers

Apply the Standard

Use the worksheet that follows to help you apply the standard as you write. Several copies of the worksheet have been provided for you to use with different assignments.

- Writing to a Specific Task, Purpose, and Audience

Name _____ Date _____ Assignment _____

Writing to a Specific Task, Purpose, and Audience

Identify your writing task, purpose, and audience. Then use the organizer to plan appropriate development, organization, and style for your writing. Finally, answer the question at the bottom of the page.

Task: ....

Purpose: ....

Audience: ....

DEVELOPMENT	ORGANIZATION
Argument, topic, or narrative:	**List sequence of ideas or events:**
Ideas for appropriate development:	**List appropriate transitions:**

STYLE
Describe Appropriate Style:
Describe Appropriate Tone:

How appropriate are your development, organization, and style for your writing situation?

....

....

....

Name _____ Date _____ Assignment _____

Writing to a Specific Task, Purpose, and Audience

Identify your writing task, purpose, and audience. Then use the organizer to plan appropriate development, organization, and style for your writing. Finally, answer the question at the bottom of the page.

Task: ....

Purpose: ....

Audience: ....

DEVELOPMENT	ORGANIZATION
Argument, topic, or narrative:	**List sequence of ideas or events:**
Ideas for appropriate development:	**List appropriate transitions:**

STYLE
Describe Appropriate Style:
Describe Appropriate Tone:

How appropriate are your development, organization, and style for your writing situation?

....

....

....

Name _____ Date _____ Assignment _____

Writing to a Specific Task, Purpose, and Audience

Identify your writing task, purpose, and audience. Then use the organizer to plan appropriate development, organization, and style for your writing. Finally, answer the question at the bottom of the page.

Task: ....

Purpose: ....

Audience: ....

DEVELOPMENT	ORGANIZATION
Argument, topic, or narrative:	List sequence of ideas or events:
Ideas for appropriate development:	List appropriate transitions:

STYLE
Describe Appropriate Style:
Describe Appropriate Tone:

How appropriate are your development, organization, and style for your writing situation?

....

....

....

C

Name _____ Date _____ Assignment _____

Writing to a Specific Task, Purpose, and Audience

Identify your writing task, purpose, and audience. Then use the organizer to plan appropriate development, organization, and style for your writing. Finally, answer the question at the bottom of the page.

Task: ....

Purpose: ....

Audience: ....

DEVELOPMENT	ORGANIZATION
Argument, topic, or narrative:	**List sequence of ideas or events:**
Ideas for appropriate development:	**List appropriate transitions:**

STYLE
Describe Appropriate Style:
Describe Appropriate Tone:

How appropriate are your development, organization, and style for your writing situation?

....

....

....

For use with Writing 4

Name _____ Date _____ Assignment _____

Writing to a Specific Task, Purpose, and Audience

Identify your writing task, purpose, and audience. Then use the organizer to plan appropriate development, organization, and style for your writing. Finally, answer the question at the bottom of the page.

Task: ....

Purpose: ....

Audience: ....

DEVELOPMENT	ORGANIZATION
Argument, topic, or narrative:	**List sequence of ideas or events:**
Ideas for appropriate development:	**List appropriate transitions:**

STYLE
Describe Appropriate Style:
Describe Appropriate Tone:

How appropriate are your development, organization, and style for your writing situation?

....

....

....

E

For use with Writing 4

Name _____ Date _____ Assignment _____

Writing to a Specific Task, Purpose, and Audience

Identify your writing task, purpose, and audience. Then use the organizer to plan appropriate development, organization, and style for your writing. Finally, answer the question at the bottom of the page.

Task: ....

Purpose: ....

Audience: ....

DEVELOPMENT	ORGANIZATION
Argument, topic, or narrative:	**List sequence of ideas or events:**
Ideas for appropriate development:	**List appropriate transitions:**

STYLE
Describe Appropriate Style:
Describe Appropriate Tone:

How appropriate are your development, organization, and style for your writing situation?

....

....

....

F

Writing 5

> **5. Develop and strengthen writing as needed by planning, revising, editing, rewriting, or trying a new approach, focusing on addressing what is most significant for a specific purpose and audience.**

Explanation

Writing is a process that starts before you write your introduction and continues after you write your conclusion. The steps that come before and after you write a draft are equally important.

- Before you begin, **develop** your writing by generating ideas and gathering information.
- After completing a draft, **strengthen** your writing by reviewing and making changes.

Develop and strengthen your writing by planning before you write, and **revising** and **editing** after you finish a draft. Keep your focus on addressing your purpose, or goal you want to achieve.

Planning Look for ideas and information that will help you achieve your purpose. For example, if you are planning a research report about the United States in the 1930s, you might choose to focus on the causes of the Great Depression. Researching the stock market crash of 1929 will help you achieve your purpose. Do enough research to explain what caused the Depression.

Revising Review what you have written, focusing on what is most significant for your purpose and audience. For example, if you are revising a letter to the editor of your high school newspaper about adding a foreign language requirement, ask yourself: Have I made my position on this issue clear? Are my reasons persuasive? Have I included enough evidence to convince readers? Be prepared to add, delete, or change ideas, details, sentences, and even whole paragraphs.

Editing After you have revised, edit your writing for errors in grammar, spelling, usage, and punctuation. For example, if you are editing a short story, make sure you have introduced and punctuated dialogue correctly.

If your writing does not address what is most significant for your purpose and audience, rewriting and **trying a new approach** may be necessary. Rewrite your letter to the editor by finding new reasons to support your position. Research a different aspect of the Depression.

Academic Vocabulary

develop present and build an argument, topic, or narrative in writing with information, evidence, and details

editing checking a piece of writing and correcting errors in grammar, spelling, usage, and punctuation

revising reviewing and making changes to a piece of writing to better address its purpose and audience

Apply the Standard

Use the worksheet that follows to help you apply the standard as you write. Several copies of the worksheet have been provided for you to use with different assignments.

- Strengthening Your Writing

Strengthening Your Writing

Revise first and then edit, putting a checkmark beside each question as you address it.

Your Purpose for Writing: ....

Your Audience: ....

	Questions To Ask as You Revise
Focus on addressing your purpose	❑ Do the ideas in my writing help to achieve my purpose? ❑ Do I need to develop new ideas? ❑ Does the information in my writing help to achieve my purpose? ❑ Do I need more information or details?
Focus on addressing your audience	❑ Will my claim, topic, or subject be clear to my audience? ❑ Will my ideas appeal to my audience? ❑ Have I included enough information? ❑ Is my style appropriate for my audience?

How my writing addresses what's most significant for my purpose and audience:

....
....
....
....

What I plan to add, change, or delete:

....
....
....
....

	Questions To Ask as You Edit
Focus on grammar, spelling, and punctuation	❑ Have I used verb tenses consistently? ❑ Are there sentence fragments or run-on sentences? ❑ Have I introduced and punctuated quotations correctly? ❑ Are all of my pronoun references clear? ❑ Have I checked for other errors in grammar, spelling, and punctuation?

Do I need to rewrite or try a new approach to what I've written? ❑ Yes ❑ No

If "yes," describe how you will rewrite or try a new approach.

....
....
....
....
....

A

Strengthening Your Writing

Revise first and then edit, putting a checkmark beside each question as you address it.

Your Purpose for Writing: ....

Your Audience: ....

	Questions To Ask as You Revise
Focus on addressing your purpose	❏ Do the ideas in my writing help to achieve my purpose? ❏ Do I need to develop new ideas? ❏ Does the information in my writing help to achieve my purpose? ❏ Do I need more information or details?
Focus on addressing your audience	❏ Will my claim, topic, or subject be clear to my audience? ❏ Will my ideas appeal to my audience? ❏ Have I included enough information? ❏ Is my style appropriate for my audience?

How my writing addresses what's most significant for my purpose and audience:

....
....
....
....

What I plan to add, change, or delete:

....
....
....
....

	Questions To Ask as You Edit
Focus on grammar, spelling, and punctuation	❏ Have I used verb tenses consistently? ❏ Are there sentence fragments or run-on sentences? ❏ Have I introduced and punctuated quotations correctly? ❏ Are all of my pronoun references clear? ❏ Have I checked for other errors in grammar, spelling, and punctuation?

Do I need to rewrite or try a new approach to what I've written?   ❏ Yes   ❏ No

If "yes," describe how you will rewrite or try a new approach.

....
....
....
....
....

B

For use with Writing 5

Strengthening Your Writing

Revise first and then edit, putting a checkmark beside each question as you address it.

Your Purpose for Writing: ....

Your Audience: ....

	Questions To Ask as You Revise
Focus on addressing your purpose	❑ Do the ideas in my writing help to achieve my purpose? ❑ Do I need to develop new ideas? ❑ Does the information in my writing help to achieve my purpose? ❑ Do I need more information or details?
Focus on addressing your audience	❑ Will my claim, topic, or subject be clear to my audience? ❑ Will my ideas appeal to my audience? ❑ Have I included enough information? ❑ Is my style appropriate for my audience?

How my writing addresses what's most significant for my purpose and audience:

....
....
....
....

What I plan to add, change, or delete:

....
....
....
....

	Questions To Ask as You Edit
Focus on grammar, spelling, and punctuation	❑ Have I used verb tenses consistently? ❑ Are there sentence fragments or run-on sentences? ❑ Have I introduced and punctuated quotations correctly? ❑ Are all of my pronoun references clear? ❑ Have I checked for other errors in grammar, spelling, and punctuation?

Do I need to rewrite or try a new approach to what I've written? ❑ Yes ❑ No

If "yes," describe how you will rewrite or try a new approach.

....
....
....
....
....

C

For use with Writing 5

Strengthening Your Writing

Revise first and then edit, putting a checkmark beside each question as you address it.

Your Purpose for Writing: ....

Your Audience: ....

	Questions To Ask as You Revise
Focus on addressing your purpose	❑ Do the ideas in my writing help to achieve my purpose? ❑ Do I need to develop new ideas? ❑ Does the information in my writing help to achieve my purpose? ❑ Do I need more information or details?
Focus on addressing your audience	❑ Will my claim, topic, or subject be clear to my audience? ❑ Will my ideas appeal to my audience? ❑ Have I included enough information? ❑ Is my style appropriate for my audience?

How my writing addresses what's most significant for my purpose and audience:

....
....
....
....

What I plan to add, change, or delete:

....
....
....
....

	Questions To Ask as You Edit
Focus on grammar, spelling, and punctuation	❑ Have I used verb tenses consistently? ❑ Are there sentence fragments or run-on sentences? ❑ Have I introduced and punctuated quotations correctly? ❑ Are all of my pronoun references clear? ❑ Have I checked for other errors in grammar, spelling, and punctuation?

Do I need to rewrite or try a new approach to what I've written? ❑ Yes ❑ No

If "yes," describe how you will rewrite or try a new approach.

....
....
....
....
....

D

For use with Writing 5

Strengthening Your Writing

Revise first and then edit, putting a checkmark beside each question as you address it.

Your Purpose for Writing: ....

Your Audience: ....

	Questions To Ask as You Revise
Focus on addressing your purpose	❏ Do the ideas in my writing help to achieve my purpose? ❏ Do I need to develop new ideas? ❏ Does the information in my writing help to achieve my purpose? ❏ Do I need more information or details?
Focus on addressing your audience	❏ Will my claim, topic, or subject be clear to my audience? ❏ Will my ideas appeal to my audience? ❏ Have I included enough information? ❏ Is my style appropriate for my audience?

How my writing addresses what's most significant for my purpose and audience:

....
....
....
....

What I plan to add, change, or delete:

....
....
....

	Questions To Ask as You Edit
Focus on grammar, spelling, and punctuation	❏ Have I used verb tenses consistently? ❏ Are there sentence fragments or run-on sentences? ❏ Have I introduced and punctuated quotations correctly? ❏ Are all of my pronoun references clear? ❏ Have I checked for other errors in grammar, spelling, and punctuation?

Do I need to rewrite or try a new approach to what I've written? ❏ Yes ❏ No

If "yes," describe how you will rewrite or try a new approach.

....
....
....
....

E

For use with Writing 5

Strengthening Your Writing

Revise first and then edit, putting a checkmark beside each question as you address it.

Your Purpose for Writing: ....

Your Audience: ....

	Questions To Ask as You Revise
Focus on addressing your purpose	❏ Do the ideas in my writing help to achieve my purpose? ❏ Do I need to develop new ideas? ❏ Does the information in my writing help to achieve my purpose? ❏ Do I need more information or details?
Focus on addressing your audience	❏ Will my claim, topic, or subject be clear to my audience? ❏ Will my ideas appeal to my audience? ❏ Have I included enough information? ❏ Is my style appropriate for my audience?

How my writing addresses what's most significant for my purpose and audience:

....
....
....
....

What I plan to add, change, or delete:

....
....
....
....

	Questions To Ask as You Edit
Focus on grammar, spelling, and punctuation	❏ Have I used verb tenses consistently? ❏ Are there sentence fragments or run-on sentences? ❏ Have I introduced and punctuated quotations correctly? ❏ Are all of my pronoun references clear? ❏ Have I checked for other errors in grammar, spelling, and punctuation?

Do I need to rewrite or try a new approach to what I've written? ❏ Yes ❏ No

If "yes," describe how you will rewrite or try a new approach.

....
....
....
....
....

F

Writing 6

> **6. Use technology, including the Internet, to produce, publish, and update individual or shared writing products in response to ongoing feedback, including new arguments or information.**

Explanation

Using technology and the Internet, you can update your writing in response to **ongoing feedback** from readers. To ensure that you are able to receive and respond to feedback, create a **blog** where your audience can read and offer comments on your writing. A blog that can be accessed only by your class is an ideal environment for responding to ongoing feedback.

- **Respond to ongoing feedback: Post** your writing on a blog for your class and check frequently to read any comments. For example, you could write a blog post urging your fellow students to volunteer in their communities. A reader might respond that one part of your argument—volunteer work looks good on college applications—is especially persuasive. Respond to this feedback by placing greater emphasis on this point.

- **Respond to new arguments or information:** Look for new arguments and information in readers' comments on your blog posts or in posts on related topics. For example, another writer on your class blog might argue that students should not be expected to volunteer in their communities. This writer's post might include evidence that students already have too many responsibilities. Respond to the new argument and information by posting a comment or by updating your original post.

- **Develop new arguments and information:** As you respond to feedback, generate new ideas and gather new information on your topic. For example, you might respond to the argument that students should not be expected to volunteer by developing a counterargument. Gather evidence that committing just a few hours each month to volunteering in the community can benefit students. Use your new argument and information to update your original post or to write a new post.

Academic Vocabulary

blog short for "Web log," a popular online format that generally includes entries from writers as well as comments from readers.

ongoing feedback responses you continue to receive as you produce, publish, and update your writing

post to publish a piece of writing online; also, an entry on a blog

Apply the Standard

Use the worksheet that follows to help you apply the standard as you write. Several copies of the worksheet have been provided for you to use with different assignments.

- Using Technology

Name _____ Date _____ Assignment _____

Using Technology

Use the organizer below to describe ongoing feedback to your blog post, including new arguments and new information, and to plan how you will respond.

Name/URL of blog: _____

Who has access to this blog? _____

Subject/date of original post: _____

ONGOING FEEDBACK	
Date:	Number of comments/related posts:

Summarize feedback:
_____
_____
_____

Describe new arguments:
_____
_____
_____

List new information:
_____
_____
_____
_____

RESPONDING TO FEEDBACK	
❏ Respond in a comment	❏ Respond in a new post

Summarize your response:
_____
_____
_____

New arguments you will develop:
_____
_____
_____

New information you will gather:
_____
_____
_____

A

Name _____ Date _____ Assignment _____

Using Technology

Use the organizer below to describe ongoing feedback to your blog post, including new arguments and new information, and to plan how you will respond.

Name/URL of blog: _____

Who has access to this blog? _____

Subject/date of original post: _____

ONGOING FEEDBACK	
Date:	Number of comments/related posts:

Summarize feedback:
_____
_____
_____

Describe new arguments:
_____
_____
_____

List new information:
_____
_____
_____

RESPONDING TO FEEDBACK	
❑ Respond in a comment	❑ Respond in a new post

Summarize your response:
_____
_____
_____

New arguments you will develop:
_____
_____
_____

New information you will gather:
_____
_____
_____

B

For use with Writing 6

Name _____ Date _____ Assignment _____

Using Technology

Use the organizer below to describe ongoing feedback to your blog post, including new arguments and new information, and to plan how you will respond.

Name/URL of blog: _____

Who has access to this blog? _____

Subject/date of original post: _____

ONGOING FEEDBACK	
Date:	Number of comments/related posts:

Summarize feedback:

_____
_____
_____

Describe new arguments:

_____
_____
_____

List new information:

_____
_____
_____

RESPONDING TO FEEDBACK	
❏ Respond in a comment	❏ Respond in a new post

Summarize your response:

_____
_____
_____

New arguments you will develop:

_____
_____
_____

New information you will gather:

_____
_____
_____

C

For use with Writing 6

Name _____ Date _____ Assignment _____

Using Technology

Use the organizer below to describe ongoing feedback to your blog post, including new arguments and new information, and to plan how you will respond.

Name/URL of blog: _____

Who has access to this blog? _____

Subject/date of original post: _____

ONGOING FEEDBACK	
Date:	Number of comments/related posts:

Summarize feedback:
_____
_____
_____

Describe new arguments:
_____
_____
_____

List new information:
_____
_____
_____

RESPONDING TO FEEDBACK	
❏ Respond in a comment	❏ Respond in a new post

Summarize your response:
_____
_____

New arguments you will develop:
_____
_____

New information you will gather:
_____
_____
_____

D

For use with Writing 6

Name _____ Date _____ Assignment _____

Using Technology

Use the organizer below to describe ongoing feedback to your blog post, including new arguments and new information, and to plan how you will respond.

Name/URL of blog: _____

Who has access to this blog? _____

Subject/date of original post: _____

ONGOING FEEDBACK	
Date:	Number of comments/related posts:

Summarize feedback:
_____
_____
_____

Describe new arguments:
_____
_____
_____

List new information:
_____
_____
_____

RESPONDING TO FEEDBACK	
❑ Respond in a comment	❑ Respond in a new post

Summarize your response:
_____
_____
_____

New arguments you will develop:
_____
_____

New information you will gather:
_____
_____
_____

For use with Writing 6

Name _____ Date _____ Assignment _____

Using Technology

Use the organizer below to describe ongoing feedback to your blog post, including new arguments and new information, and to plan how you will respond.

Name/URL of blog: _____

Who has access to this blog? _____

Subject/date of original post: _____

ONGOING FEEDBACK	
Date:	Number of comments/related posts:

Summarize feedback:

_____
_____
_____

Describe new arguments:

_____
_____
_____

List new information:

_____
_____
_____

RESPONDING TO FEEDBACK	
❑ Respond in a comment	❑ Respond in a new post

Summarize your response:

_____
_____
_____

New arguments you will develop:

_____
_____
_____

New information you will gather:

_____
_____
_____

F

Writing 7

7. **Conduct short as well as more sustained research projects to answer a question (including a self-generated question) or solve a problem; narrow or broaden the inquiry when appropriate; synthesize multiple sources on the subject, demonstrating understanding of the subject under investigation.**

Explanation

Research projects vary in scope. Short research projects focus on narrow topics, while complex subjects require more **sustained research** involving in-depth investigation and multiple sources. You may need to narrow or broaden your **inquiry** based on the scope of your project. Be prepared to narrow your inquiry for a short research project or broaden it for a more sustained one.

Narrowing an Inquiry: Narrow a broad question or problem for a short research project. For example, if you are researching health problems faced by teenagers in the United States, narrow your inquiry to focus on strategies for improving teen health in your state. If this is still too broad, narrow your inquiry again, focusing on developing a fitness program for your high school.

Broadening an Inquiry: Broaden a narrow question or problem for a more sustained research project. For example, if you begin a research project by generating the question "How did nineteenth-century readers react to Whitman's *Song of Myself*?" broaden your inquiry to focus on the question "How did Whitman's *Leaves of Grass* change American poetry?"

Develop an understanding of your subject by gathering ideas and information from multiple sources, rather than only one or two. Then **synthesize** information from your sources and draw your own conclusions. When you present the results of your research, demonstrate your understanding of the subject under investigation by supporting your answer or solution with information from several different sources.

Academic Vocabulary

inquiry the process of looking for information to answer questions about a topic or to solve a problem

sustained research in-depth investigation or inquiry involving multiple sources

synthesize merge information from different sources to present a new answer or solution

Apply the Standard

Use the worksheets that follow to help you apply the standard as you write. Several copies of each worksheet have been provided for you to use with different assignments.

- Researching to Answer Questions or Solve Problems

- Synthesizing Information from Different Sources

Name _____ Date _____ Assignment _____

Researching to Answer Questions or Solve Problems

Narrow or broaden your inquiry before gathering ideas and information from multiple sources. In the box at the bottom of the page, write your answer or solution.

Subject: ....

Scope of Research Project: ....

```
┌──────────────────────────────────────────────────────────────────┐
│ Initial Question or Problem:                                        │
└──────────────────────────────────────────────────────────────────┘
```

❏ **Narrow Inquiry**　　　　　　　　❏ **Broaden Inquiry**

```
┌──────────────────────────────────────────────────────────────────┐
│ Narrowed/Broadened Question or Problem:                             │
└──────────────────────────────────────────────────────────────────┘
```

List your sources: ....

Ideas and information from Source 1: ....

....

Ideas and information from Source 2: ....

....

Ideas and information from Source 3: ....

....

Ideas and information from Source 4: ....

....

....

```
┌──────────────────────────────────────────────────────────────────┐
│ Your Answer or Solution:                                            │
│                                                                     │
└──────────────────────────────────────────────────────────────────┘
```

A

For use with Writing 7

Name _____ Date _____ Assignment _____

Researching to Answer Questions or Solve Problems

Narrow or broaden your inquiry before gathering ideas and information from multiple sources. In the box at the bottom of the page, write your answer or solution.

Subject: ....

Scope of Research Project: ....

Initial Question or Problem:

❏ **Narrow Inquiry**   ❏ **Broaden Inquiry**

Narrowed/Broadened Question or Problem:

List your sources: ....

....

Ideas and information from Source 1: ....

....

Ideas and information from Source 2: ....

....

Ideas and information from Source 3: ....

....

Ideas and information from Source 4: ....

....

Your Answer or Solution:

B

For use with Writing 7

Name _____ Date _____ Assignment _____

Researching to Answer Questions or Solve Problems

Narrow or broaden your inquiry before gathering ideas and information from multiple sources. In the box at the bottom of the page, write your answer or solution.

Subject: ....

Scope of Research Project: ....

Initial Question or Problem:

❏ **Narrow Inquiry**   ❏ **Broaden Inquiry**

Narrowed/Broadened Question or Problem:

List your sources: ....

....

Ideas and information from Source 1: ....

....

Ideas and information from Source 2: ....

....

Ideas and information from Source 3: ....

....

Ideas and information from Source 4: ....

....

....

Your Answer or Solution:

C

For use with Writing 7

Name _____ Date _____ Assignment _____

Synthesizing Information from Different Sources

Use the organizer below to synthesize information from your sources. Support your answer or solution with information from multiple sources. Then answer the questions at the bottom of the page.

Subject: ....

INFORMATION FROM DIFFERENT SOURCES			
Source 1	**Source 2**	**Source 3**	**Source 4**

SYNTHESIS
Your Conclusion: ....   Support:

Have you demonstrated understanding of the subject under investigation?

❏ Yes   ❏ No

Explain why or why not: ....

....

....

....

Name _____ Date _____ Assignment _____

Synthesizing Information from Different Sources

Use the organizer below to synthesize information from your sources. Support your answer or solution with information from multiple sources. Then answer the questions at the bottom of the page.

Subject: ....

INFORMATION FROM DIFFERENT SOURCES			
Source 1	**Source 2**	**Source 3**	**Source 4**

SYNTHESIS
Your Conclusion: .... Support:

Have you demonstrated understanding of the subject under investigation?

❏ Yes   ❏ No

Explain why or why not: ....

....

....

....

B

For use with Writing 7

Name _____ Date _____ Assignment _____

Synthesizing Information from Different Sources

Use the organizer below to synthesize information from your sources. Support your answer or solution with information from multiple sources. Then answer the questions at the bottom of the page.

Subject: ....

INFORMATION FROM DIFFERENT SOURCES			
Source 1	**Source 2**	**Source 3**	**Source 4**

SYNTHESIS
Your Conclusion: .... Support:

Have you demonstrated understanding of the subject under investigation?

❏ Yes   ❏ No

Explain why or why not: ....

....

....

....

C

Writing 8

> **8. Gather relevant information from multiple authoritative print and digital sources, using advanced searches effectively; assess the strengths and limitations of each source in terms of the task, purpose, and audience; integrate information into the text selectively to maintain the flow of ideas, avoiding plagiarism and overreliance on any one source and following a standard format for citation.**

Writing Workshop: Research Report

When you write a **research report,** your task is to read and study a topic in depth in order to present a focused synthesis of information. If your research report is a historical investigation, you may be investigating the historical context in which a literary work was written. The process begins with deciding on a topic and gathering enough information about it to arrive at a thesis. Research and analysis then continue as you develop, refine, and support that thesis with authoritative information from multiple sources. During this process, you will also develop your own insights and perspectives, which you will merge with the thinking of others in your report. Beginning with the notetaking process and continuing throughout the process of writing, revising, and editing, you must also pay careful attention to the correct and honest citing of your source material, both within the body of the paper and in a Works Cited list or bibliography at the end.

Assignment

Write a historical investigation report about a literary work. That is, investigate an issue that helps to form the literary context of the work, such as the Dust Bowl or the Revolutionary War. Include these elements:

✓ a topic that you can explore in substantial detail

✓ a clear, specific thesis that provides an overview of your entire paper

✓ body paragraphs that explain and develop your thesis by smoothly integrating source material with your own insights

✓ substantial support from a variety of authoritative print and nonprint sources

✓ an effective of organization, including transitions between and within paragraphs

✓ complete, correct documentation within the paper and at the end

✓ correct manuscript conventions and correct use of language conventions

*Additional Standards

Language
1.d. Establish and maintain a formal style and objective tone while attending to the norms and conventions of the discipline in which students are writing.

2. Demonstrate command of the conventions of standard English

capitalization, punctuation, and spelling when writing.

7. Consult short as well as more sustained research projects to answer a question (including a self-generated question) or solve a problem; narrow or broaden inquiry when appropriate; synthesize multiple sources on the

subject, demonstrating understanding of the subject under investigation.

9. Draw evidence from literary or informational texts to support analysis, reflection, and research.

Name _____ Date _____ Selection line _____

Prewriting/Planning Strategies

Scan your textbooks and notebooks. Flip through your notebooks, literature and history textbooks, and writing journals, and list topics that attract your attention or pique your interest. Write down specific questions you have about a historical period or the historical context in which a literary work was written.

Ask a research question. Once you have a list of several topics, ask a question or two about each one. That is, try to narrow your focus just a bit or zero in on an aspect of your topic so that you can do a more productive search for information.

Do a research preview. Use your topics and questions to do a quick ten-to-fifteen-minute search of each topic. Seek out both primary and secondary sources. This quick search will help you spot possible subtopics or narrowed topics. It will also confirm the availability of information on each topic.

Choose one topic and narrow it down. Make sure your topic is substantial but not too ambitious for a short research paper. Narrow an overly broad topic by finding a more focused subject that fits within the larger area of interest. Use a flowchart like this one:

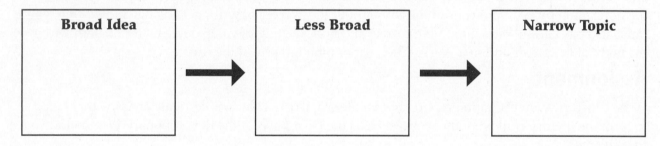

| Broad Idea | | Less Broad | | Narrow Topic |

Name _____ Date _____ Selection line _____

Propose a working thesis statement and an audience. Your research report should develop a coherent thesis statement or controlling idea. You will revisit and refine this statement as you research, draft, and revise your paper. Also decide who would be most interested by your topic or most likely to benefit by learning about it, and think about the characteristics and knowledge of your assigned audience.

What My Audience Already Knows About My Topic	What My Audience Might Like to Find Out
•	•
•	•
•	•

Researching from Print and Digital Sources

Research and read. Information is the basis of a successful research report, and the successful research report depends on systematic and careful research, reading, and note-taking. Throughout the research and reading process, you will be choosing and evaluating sources, taking notes from them, and documenting them.

Start with general sources. To develop an overview of your topic, as well as to learn new aspects of it, begin the research process with general reading in encyclopedias and reference books. Specialized encyclopedias or references, such as those that index topics in American literature, or eras in history, can be particularly useful. Many of these resources are available online with a public library card. You may have to visit a library to find others on the shelves of the reference section.

Name _____ Date _____ Selection line _____

Use primary sources. When you are writing about literature, the literary work or works on which you base your paper are the primary source; also, any sources on which the literary work was based are primary. So, for example, if T. S. Eliot quotes or refers to a line from Hesiod, that source is also primary. To investigate and analyze the historical context in which a work is set, or its specific historical references, consult other primary sources, which are original or firsthand accounts of events. These primary sources include interview transcripts, journals, letters, eyewitness accounts, and speeches. Also consult secondary sources, such as books, as other sources that look back on the event or era.

Use a variety of other sources. Use multiple sources to explore your topic. Among the most valuable sources for research are databases, which index magazines, newspapers, general and specialized encyclopedias, and scholarly journals. You can access databases from terminals in your local library. To access them from home, you usually need a library card number. Other sources you might consult include almanacs, atlases, microfiche, and even government documents such as records of proceedings in Parliament or Congress.

Do advanced searches. Advanced searches enable you to select a variety of options in order to limit your search to specific criteria. Learn how to use the "Advanced Search" function on the home page of your favorite search engine as well as in your library catalog and specific databases. Typically, your search engine will allow you to limit your search to documents with some words but not others, as well as by the domain. For example, you can limit your search to government publications only by specifying the domain .gov.

To use the advanced search function in a library catalog, look for a link on the catalog home page. An advanced search in a library catalog might allow you to limit your results to the material type (print book, e-book, DVD, periodical, software, and so on); to the collection type (adult or children's); to the language, and to the publication date. You might also be able to order your search results by relevance, by date, or by other criteria.

Re-evaluate your topic and thesis. After you have gathered a variety of sources and begun to read with a specific thesis in mind, stop to make sure the topic you have chosen is appropriate to your task, your purpose, and your audience. Refine your thesis as needed.

Name _____ Date _____ Selection line _____

Evaluating Credibility and Usefulness of Your Sources

Evaluate Web sites. You cannot use just any information in your paper; instead, you need reliable, credible, accurate information. For that reason, you cannot use just any Web site. Subject each and every Web site you use to a careful evaluation:

Web site name and URL:
Is this an authoritative site? *Use this box to record the author or sponsoring information, if given, and the author's qualifications or relationship to the subject matter and other publications on the same subject.*
Is this a reliable site? *Use this box to record the type of site. That is, is it personal, special interest, professional, business, government, or a news/e-zine site? Next, is there any evidence that the material has been reviewed or edited? What documentation appears, such as footnotes or Works Cited list?*
Is this a current site? *Use this box to record when the site was last updated and whether the links are current.*
Is this a biased site? *Use this box to record the background or affiliations of the author or sponsor. Note whether the site has a persuasive agenda or is trying to sell you anything.*

For use with Writing 8

Name _____ Date _____ Selection line _____

Evaluate other Sources. For each source you consider, print and nonprint, decide its worth—or limitations—relative to your task, purpose, and audience. To do so, decide whether the source is authoritative: that is, note the author's qualifications and whether he or she is an authority on the subject. Then decide if the source is timely. Apart from primary sources, up-to-date information is often best. Because scholarship builds up on a topic over time, the best information on, for example, the Great Depression may not be from the 1940s but from a book published a year ago. Finally, decide whether the source is respected. Many periodical articles are intended as much to entertain as to inform: they are not meant to be the basis for research. For example, an edited biography from a university press is much more likely to provide reliable, well-documented facts than a made-for-television biography.

Source Title and Type	Authoritative?	Timely?	Respected?

Name _____ Date _____ Selection line _____

Recording Information

Taking notes. As you gather information, use index cards to keep track of each of your sources. On the source card for a book, record the name of the author, editor, and or translator; the title of the work; the publisher and city of publication; and the copyright date. If the source is a Web site, your source card should list the name and Web address of the site, the author and sponsoring institution if available, and the date you accessed the site.

For other types of sources, refer to the style guide you are using, such as the Modern Language Association (MLA) handbook or the American Psychological Association (APA) style guide. Look for all the types of information required to cite the work in a list at the end of the paper, and record all those types of information on your source card. Label each source you create with a letter, beginning with A, or a number, beginning with 1.

Make notecards. Create a separate notecard for every bit of information you take from your sources. Number or letter each source card or listing in the upper right hand corner with the number or letter you assigned to the source on your source card. Then record any useful or interesting information.

Revisit your thesis. Your research paper should develop a coherent thesis statement or controlling idea. Review your earlier thesis; think about the information you have now acquired; and rework your thesis statement as needed so that is supported by the evidence you discovered in primary and secondary sources. Your thesis should make a claim that your report will support; it should not state a simple fact.

Avoid plagiarism. If you do not credit sources accurately, you commit the serious offense of plagiarism, presenting someone else's work as your own. Plagiarism is stealing someone else's ideas, so it is both illegal and dishonest. Avoiding this problem is a process that begins in the note-taking stage of writing a research report. There are several steps you can take to help ensure against inadvertent plagiarism:

- **Do not copy and paste.** Avoid copying and pasting information from a Web site. It is too easy to confuse someone else's ideas with your own.

- **Paraphrase and summarize as much as possible.** The more you use your own words during the note-taking process, the less likely you are to insert the exact words of the source into your paper without crediting them.

- **Note it when you quote it.** Be sure to enclose in quotation marks any and every word that you copy directly from a source as you take notes. If you leave words out of a quotation, insert an ellipsis to show the omission.

Name _____ Date _____ Selection line _____

Organizing and Drafting Your Report

Write an outline. After you have completed the note-taking process, write a formal or informal outline. Consider points at which you might include rhetorical strategies other than exposition. For example, use an anecdote, a form of narration, or include the description of a key place. Gather ideas for a conclusion in which you attain closure by summarizing your main points and presenting a final generalization.

Choose an effective organization. To choose the best pattern of organization for your report, consider your thesis and your findings. Then structure your report using one of the methods listed below. You may also chose an overall organizational strategy and use other methods to support it. For example, your report may follow a chronological organization, but an individual paragraph might evaluate the causes and effects of a single important event.

- **Chronological order.** Discuss events in the order in which they occurred.

- **Cause and effect.** Analyze the causes and/or effects of an event.

- **Problem and solution.** Identify a specific problem and present a solution.

- **Parts-to-whole order.** Relate elements of a single event or topic to a whole.

- **Order of importance.** Present your support from most to least important, or from least to most important.

- **Compare and contrast.** Discuss similarities and differences between two events or subjects.

Map out body paragraphs. Record your specific thesis. Then develop topic sentences that reflect your research and relate specifically back to your thesis:

Topic Sentence:

Method of Organization:

Facts and Other Support:

1.

2.

3.

Name _____   Date _____   Selection line _____

Providing Elaboration

Include a variety of sources. Sometimes a single source appears to have everything you require to support your thesis. Deriving ideas primarily from one source, however, does not result in a good research report. You must, instead, vary your sources as you write.

As you draft, use direct quotations, paraphrases, and visuals from sources that are reliable, valid, and varied. Referencing multiple sources gives your writing more validity because it takes into account a variety of perspectives.

Analyze relationships among sources. In your research, you may have encountered differences of opinion in secondary sources or conflicting accounts of the same events in primary sources. You may even have found differing "facts." Either resolve these differences, if possible, or provide analysis and explanation about the reasons for such differences. To do so, consider the biases of the writers or sources. Think, too, about the possible limits on knowledge or understanding that might have been in place at the time of publication. Give reasons for why you think one primary source might be more reliable or valid than another.

Integrate source material smoothly. A strong research report is not a choppy collection of facts and quotations. It presents a smooth flow of ideas that are supported by valid, researched information. Therefore, a central task in the drafting process is to integrate those ideas smoothly. One way to create links or coherence is to introduce quoted, summarized, and paraphrased material with phrases such as "[Author's name] notes," "According to...," or "In [title of work]."

Similarly, keep in mind that whatever you quote or paraphrase may not only need explanation to relate it to your topic sentence and thesis, but it may also need to be clearly connected to the ideas that follow it. In some cases, you may need to insert a sentence or more to explain the significance of the cited information. That is, you must smoothly merge your own thinking and analysis as you make the ideas you report clearer to your audience. Above all, you must be sure your audience follows how your source material supports the points you are making.

Create a serious tone and formal style. Your purpose and task require you to sound as reasonable and objective as you can. Therefore, throughout your paper, choose formal words and phrases and standard usages. It is best to avoid all contractions and exclamation points. Use fragments sparingly, if at all, and only if required for rhetorical effect.

For use with Writing 8

Name _____ Date _____ Selection line _____

Citing Sources

Cite sources in the body of your report. Within the body of your paper, you must supply information that gives a brief summary of where you got your information. Information given in parentheses right after the source material is known as parenthetical citation.

Giving proper credit to the people whose ideas and words you have borrowed ensures that you will meet key requirements of research report writing. It is also necessary to obey copyright law. Responsible writers are thorough and accurate in citing all of their sources. Follow these instructions for parenthetical citations:

- **Print works.** Provide the author's or editor's name followed by a page number. If the work does not have an author, use a key word or short phrase from the title.

- **Web sources.** Provide the author's name, if given, the title of the article, if any, or the title of the site.

- **Other works.** For variations within books and web sources, such as multiple authors, multivolume works, translations, and so on, do not guess. Consult your style manual. Similarly, use your style manual to find the correct way to cite sound recordings, interviews, or other less common sources.

Compile a Works Cited list or bibliography. As your audience reads your paper, they will want to know where your facts and ideas come from. The parenthetical citations within the paper direct your audience to a longer, more complete list of information about your sources, known as the Works Cited list, that should serve as the last page or pages of your paper. There you must provide complete publication information for each source you cite. Sources on the list should be arranged alphabetically by author's or editor's last name. If the author or editor's last name is not given, then alphabetize by the first word of the title.

- **Books.** Provide the author's name (last name first), the title of the work, the city of publication, the name of the publisher, and the year of publication.

- **Periodicals.** Provide the author's last name, first name, title of the article, the name of the magazine, the date of the issue, the volume and issue number, and the pages of the article. For any month with more than four letters, abbreviate the month by using the first three letters followed by a period.

- **Web sites.** Use this order, depending on available information: the author's name, the title of the page, the title of the site, the date of last update, and the name of the sponsoring organization. Give the date you accessed the Web site and its full URL, or Web address.

Name _____   Date _____   Selection line _____

Revising

Define specialized vocabulary. General readers may not be familiar with the specialized terms that you have encountered in your research. Some words may be familiar only to experts in the field and may present obstacles to your readers' appreciation of your ideas. To aid readers' understanding, you must carefully define jargon that is specific to your topic.

Original: Clemens famously took his pen name from navigational language; *twain* is a term that means "two fathoms."

Revised: Clemens famously took his pen name from navigational language; *twain* is a term that means "two fathoms," or twelve feet.

In some cases, when the use of jargon is not appropriate to your task, your purpose, or your audience, you will need to replace the jargon with simpler language.

Original: Having spotted the riffle, the steamboat pilot made an adjustment, but was too late.

Inappropriately revised: Having spotted the riffle, a swift-current shoal, of somewhat linear shape, composed of sand, pebbles, and silt, the steamboat pilot made an adjustment, but was too late.

Appropriately revised: Having spotted sandbar, the steamboat pilot made an adjustment, but was too late.

Revising for Word Choice

When you revise for word choice that is appropriate to your audience, follow these steps:

1. Review your work and identify jargon, or specialized words that may be familiar to experts or scholars but not to your intended audience.

2. Consider whether the use of the jargon is appropriate to your purpose and audience. If it is, be sure you have defined it clearly and as simply as possibly at its first point of use.

3. If the jargon is not appropriate to your purpose and audience, replace it with simpler, more accessible language.

Revision Checklist

❏ If I have used specialized vocabulary, is it necessary to my purpose?

❏ If I have used specialized vocabulary that is necessary, have I defined it clearly and simply where it first appears?

For use with Writing 8

Name _____ Date _____ Selection line _____

Revising Strategies

Put a checkmark beside each question as you address it in your revision.

	Questions To Ask as You Revise
Task	❑ Does my research report present a historical investigation? ❑ Is my research report based on a topic that answers or is appropriate to the assignment requirements? ❑ Have I given credit to every source I used? ❑ Have I consistently used one style manual for all citations? ❑ Have I formatted my paper according to the assignment specifications or according to standard conventions for a research report?
Purpose	❑ Have I set forth a clear, specific thesis that adequately summarizes the scope of my report? ❑ Have I fully developed that thesis by setting forth a relevant, in-depth information from a variety of valid sources? ❑ Have I fully and convincingly supported my thesis? ❑ What details, if any, do not relate to my purpose and should be deleted? ❑ Where do I need to add more support or explanation to achieve my purpose?
Audience	❑ Will my audience be interested in my topic? ❑ Will my audience be able to identify my thesis and follow its development throughout the paper? ❑ Have I provided enough information to support my thesis? ❑ Have I led smoothly into and out of my support and provided enough information to link my support to my thesis? ❑ Do I sound objective? ❑ Have I limited myself to formal and standard word choices? Have I defined or replaced any jargon? ❑ Can my audience follow the sources of all my ideas?

For use with Writing 8

Name _____ Date _____ Selection line _____

Editing and Proofreading

Review your draft to correct errors in format, capitalization, spelling, and punctuation.

Focus on Format: The final copy of your research report should be prepared according to your teacher's recommended style. Common preferences include the following:

- Double-space the body of the paper and the entries on the Works Cited list.

- Use 12-point type. (Prefer a professional looking font such as Times Roman or Courier.)

- Leave one-inch margins on all sides of every page.

Focus on Capitalization: Make sure you have capitalized all proper nouns and proper adjectives correctly. Capitalize the name of historical events and eras when used as nouns or adjectives, as in *Vietnam War* and *Vietnam War protester*.

Focus on Spelling: Follow this spelling rule: for adjectives that end in *-ent*, such as the words *independent, potent,* and *different,* use *c* in place of *t* to form parallel forms, as in *independence, potency,* and *difference.*

Focus on Punctuation: Colons to Introduce Lists and Long Quotations Proofread your writing to find places where you have introduced lists or long quotations.

Rule: Use a colon before a list of items following an independent clause: *The book is a collection of description and narrative: it physically describes the river, it narrates the adventures of others on the river, and it provides an autobiographical account of experiences on the river.*

Rule: Use a colon to introduce a formal quotation or a long quotation that follows an independent clause. *Twain provides some real history but also infuses his work with his characteristic humor:*

> *"In the space of one hundred and seventy-six years the Lower Mississippi has shortened itself two-hundred and forty-two miles. That is a trifle over one mile and a third per year. Therefore, any calm person, who is not blind or idiotic, can see that in Old Oolitic Silurian Period, just a million years ago next November, the Lower Mississippi River was upwards of one million three hundred thousand millions long and stuck out over the Gulf of Mexico like a fishing rod."*

Name _____ Date _____ Selection line _____

Publishing and Presenting

Consider one of the following ways to present your writing:

Present an oral historical investigation report. Deliver your paper as an oral report. Incorporate visual aids and images to illustrate specific information. Provide classmates with a handout listing your sources.

Submit your paper for publication. Submit your paper to a magazine or Web site that publishes student writing or that covers your research topic.

Rubric for Self-Assessment

Find evidence in your writing to address each category. Then, use the rating scale to grade your work. Circle the score that best applies for each category.

Evaluating Your Historical Investigation Report	not very very
Focus: How well have you maintained a focus on a clear, specific thesis throughout your report?	1 2 3 4 5 6
Organization: How clearly have you linked all your ideas to your thesis and to each other? How well have you organized your ideas using patterns that are appropriate to your information?	1 2 3 4 5 6
Support/Elaboration: How well have you gathered your support from multiple, credible, authoritative, and varied print and nonprint sources?	1 2 3 4 5 6
Style: How well have you used a formal style and a serious tone that are appropriate to your task, your purpose, and your audience? How effectively have you followed a single style manual for all your parenthetical citations, your Works Cited list, or bibliography?	1 2 3 4 5 6
Conventions: How free is your research report from errors in grammar, spelling, and punctuation?	1 2 3 4 5 6

For use with Writing 8

Writing 9a

> **9a. Draw evidence from literary or informational texts to support analysis, reflection, and research.**
>
> - Apply *grades 11–12 Reading standards* to literature (e.g., "Demonstrate knowledge of eighteenth-, nineteenth- and early-twentieth-century foundational works of American literature, including how two or more texts from the same period treat similar themes or topics").

Explanation

One way to demonstrate your understanding of literature is to compare how two works from the same period reflect similar topics, **themes,** styles, or other literary elements.

Works with similar topics may express different points of view, such as those of a European settler and a Native American, but their subject matter is the same. Works with similar themes present the same central message about the topic. For example, they may argue that westward expansion was a problematic chapter in our nation's history.

Works may also share similar settings (such as the inner city or the frontier), similar characters (such as loners), and similar conflicts (such as the individual against nature). To compare works, follow these steps:

- Choose the element you will compare (such as the topic, theme, style, characters, or other literary element).

- List key similarities in how each text treats the element.

- List any differences in treatment.

- Give evidence from both works that shows the similarities and differences.

- Develop paragraphs that fully analyze and explain each point of comparison by incorporating and explaining evidence.

Academic Vocabulary

theme a central message or insight into life revealed by a literary work

Apply the Standard

Use the worksheet that follows to help you apply the standard as you write. Several copies have been provided for you to use with different assignments.

- Comparing Literature

Name _____ Date _____ Assignment _____

Comparing Literature

Use the organizer to record evidence from literary works that you compare on the basis of their topics, styles, or a specific literary element, such as theme or main character.

Common Topic, Style, or Literary Element:

First Point of Comparison:

Evidence from Work 1:	Evidence from Work 2:

Second Point of Comparison:

Evidence from Work 1:	Evidence from Work 2:

Third Point of Comparison:

Evidence from Work 1:	Evidence from Work 2:

A

For use with Writing 9a

Name _____ Date _____ Assignment _____

Comparing Literature

Use the organizer to record evidence from literary works that you compare on the basis of their topics, styles, or a specific literary element, such as theme or main character.

Common Topic, Style, or Literary Element:

First Point of Comparison:

Evidence from Work 1:	Evidence from Work 2:

Second Point of Comparison:

Evidence from Work 1:	Evidence from Work 2:

Third Point of Comparison:

Evidence from Work 1:	Evidence from Work 2:

Name _____ Date _____ Assignment _____

Comparing Literature

Use the organizer to record evidence from literary works that you compare on the basis of their topics, styles, or a specific literary element, such as theme or main character.

Common Topic, Style, or Literary Element:

First Point of Comparison:	
Evidence from Work 1:	**Evidence from Work 2:**

Second Point of Comparison:	
Evidence from Work 1:	**Evidence from Work 2:**

Third Point of Comparison:	
Evidence from Work 1:	**Evidence from Work 2:**

C

For use with Writing 9a

Writing 9b

> 9. Draw evidence from literary or informational texts to support analysis, reflection, and research.
>
> - Apply *grades 11–12 Reading standards* to literary nonfiction (e.g., "Delineate and evaluate the reasoning in seminal U.S. texts, including the application of constitutional principles and use of legal reasoning [e.g., in U.S. Supreme Court Case majority opinions and dissents] and the premises, purposes, and arguments in works of public advocacy [e.g., *The Federalist,* presidential addresses]").

Explanation

Two main types of reasoning are used in argumentation. **Inductive reasoning** is based on observations. For example, a writer using inductive reasoning might note that cats are able to run quickly and have sharp teeth and claws. From these observations the writer might conclude that a cat has many ways to protect itself. In many cases, inductive reasoning leads to illogical conclusions. For example, a writer might note that it has rained two Fridays in a row. From these observations, the writer draws a faulty conclusion: "It will rain this Friday."

A writer using **deductive reasoning,** however, begins with a generalization, then presents a specific situation, and provides facts and evidence that leads to a logical conclusion. For example, a writer might argue: "Interesting teachers make learning fun. Mr. Ortega is an interesting teacher. He tells great stories and uses creative teaching strategies. Taking his class will be fun."

Thomas Jefferson uses deductive reasoning in the Declaration of Independence. He asserts that God gives people the right to be free and that people have an obligation to claim that right (by overthrowing a government that denies that freedom, if necessary). He concludes that people have a duty to overthrow the government of George III.

When you evaluate an argument, look not only at the reasoning but also at the quality of evidence or support. For example, in the Declaration of Independence, Jefferson lists the many tyrannies George III has visited on "these States" as support for his assertions.

Academic Vocabulary

deductive reasoning arriving at a conclusion by applying a general principle to a specific situation

inductive reasoning drawing a general or broad conclusion from specific observations

Apply the Standard

Use the worksheet that follows to help you apply the standard as you complete your writing assignments. Several copies of the worksheet have been provided for you.

- Evaluating Reasoning

Name _____ Date _____ Selection line _____

Evaluating Reasoning

Use the organizer to analyze the reasoning used in an argument. Does the writer draw a conclusion from facts and observations? If so, fill out the left column. If the writer instead begins with a generalization, fill out the right column. Then answer the question.

Inductive Reasoning	Deductive Reasoning
Fact/Observation:	Generalization:
Fact/Observation:	Specific Situation:
Fact/Observation:	Facts and Evidence:
Conclusion:	Conclusion:

Is the writer's reasoning sound and conclusion valid? Explain:

....

....

....

....

A

For use with Writing 9b

Name _____ Date _____ Selection line _____

Evaluating Reasoning

Use the organizer to analyze the reasoning used in an argument. Does the writer draw a conclusion from facts and observations? If so, fill out the left column. If the writer instead begins with a generalization, fill out the right column. Then answer the question.

Inductive Reasoning	Deductive Reasoning
Fact/Observation:	Generalization:
Fact/Observation:	Specific Situation:
Fact/Observation:	Facts and Evidence:
Conclusion:	Conclusion:

Is the writer's reasoning sound and conclusion valid? Explain:

....

....

....

....

Name _____ Date _____ Selection line _____

Evaluating Reasoning

Use the organizer to analyze the reasoning used in an argument. Does the writer draw a conclusion from facts and observations? If so, fill out the left column. If the writer instead begins with a generalization, fill out the right column. Then answer the question.

Inductive Reasoning	Deductive Reasoning
Fact/Observation:	Generalization:
Fact/Observation:	Specific Situation:
Fact/Observation:	Facts and Evidence:
Conclusion:	Conclusion:

Is the writer's reasoning sound and conclusion valid? Explain:

....

....

....

....

For use with Writing 9b

Writing 10

> **10. Write routinely over extended time frames (time for research, reflection, and revision) and shorter time frames (a single sitting or a day or two) for a range of tasks, purposes, and audiences.**

Explanation

Some writing assignments extend over a long period of time to allow time for the student to reflect on a topic, gather research, write, and revise. A research report is an example of a longer-term assignment. Other assignments are short term and require only a single class period or two to complete. A cover letter can be completed in a short time frame.

A cover letter is a formal letter in which the writer asks to be considered for a job. It usually accompanies or "covers" a completed job application, a résumé, or both. Follow these steps to plan, write, and revise your letter.

Prewriting:

- Review the job requirements.

- Jot down notes that show how your interests and experiences match those requirements.

Drafting:

- Create a consistent format such as block format or modified block format, making sure to include: the heading, inside address, salutation or greeting, body, closing, and signature. In the heading, include your phone number and e-mail address on separate lines after your city, state, and Zip code.

- State the position you are applying for in the first sentence.

- Create a formal yet clearly interested **voice.** Show confidence and personality. Express interest in the position, but avoid language that is too friendly or informal, including slang, contractions, and exclamation points.

- Explain what makes your qualifications a good fit for the job, but do not repeat your résumé or job application word for word.

Revising and Editing:

- Check that you have consistently and correctly formatted your letter.

- Evaluate your voice: Have you used formal language yet shown interest?

Academic Vocabulary

voice the writer's distinctive "sound" or way of "speaking" on the page

Apply the Standard

Use the worksheet that follows to help you apply the standard as you complete your writing assignments.

- Writing a Cover Letter

Name _____ Date _____ Selection line _____

Writing a Cover Letter

Use the organizer during prewriting to plan what you will say in your cover letter.

Key Words/Requirements in the Job Ad:
My Experiences, Interests, and Education: 1. 2. 3.
Ways I Can Match My Qualifications to the Job Requirements: 1. 2. 3.

Writing 10

> **10. Write routinely over extended time frames (time for research, reflection, and revision) and shorter time frames (a single sitting or a day or two) for a range of tasks, purposes, and audiences.**

Explanation

A memo is an example of writing that usually can be completed in one class period. A memo—short for *memorandum*—is a brief written message that focuses on policy changes, completing tasks, or other important updates. Memos are used in the workplace, but you might write a memo to your classmates about completing a group assignment. Effective memos are clear and focused, using a formal style and a professional tone.

Prewriting:

- Determine who the audience for your memo will be.

- Write a brief phrase that sums up your purpose.

- Jot down major points you want to share with your audience.

Drafting:

- Begin with a conventional memo heading, which features these elements, each on a separate line: TO, FROM, DATE, and **Re** or SUBJECT. For TO, identify your audience; for RE or SUBJECT, write the phrase that sums up your purpose.

- State your purpose and explain your major points. Specify any needed actions.

- Use **block format** with longer memos. Include bullet points as appropriate.

Revising and Editing:

- Check your heading: Is your subject line clear and accurate?

- Check your tone and style: Is your memo formal, polite, and businesslike?

Academic Vocabulary

block format each part of the memo begins at the left margin, and a double space is used between paragraphs

Re Latin for "about"; may be used instead of "Subject" in conventional memo heading

Apply the Standard

Use the worksheet that follows to help you apply the standard as you complete your writing assignments.

- Writing a Memo

Name _____ Date _____ Selection line _____

Writing a Memo

Use the organizer to plan a memo.

Audience:

Purpose:

Subject/Re Line:

Paragraphs or Bullet Points:

-

-

-

-

Writing 10

> 10. Write routinely over extended time frames (time for research, reflection, and revision) and shorter time frames (a single sitting or a day or two) for a range of tasks, purposes, and audiences.

Explanation

A reflective essay is an example of writing that can be completed in one or two class periods or over a day or two. A reflective essay makes connections between a writer's personal experiences and the larger world. Effective reflective essays are written in the first person and use concrete language, vivid imagery, and a personal style.

Prewriting:

- Choose a personal experience or event that you can interpret in a way that will be meaningful for your audience. List details and images related to your topic.

- Write a topic sentence that identifies the experience or event and suggests the insight that you gained from it.

Drafting:

- Begin your essay with a strong, surprising, or dramatic opening statement that will draw your audience in. Consider using a quotation or a question.

- Identify and describe your experience or event. **Elaborate** by including concrete details and sensory images that will make your writing vivid and interesting.

- Reflect on your experience or event by describing your thoughts and feelings at the time when it occurred.

- End with an insight that you learned from the event or experience.

Revising and Editing:

- Is there enough emphasis on your insight, as opposed to the experience itself?

- Check for word choice: Are the words precise, vivid, and interesting?

Academic Vocabulary

elaborate extending ideas and statements by adding explanation, details, or images

Apply the Standard

Use the worksheet that follows to help you apply the standard as you complete your writing assignments.

- Writing a Reflective Essay

Name _____ Date _____ Selection line _____

Writing a Reflective Essay

Use the organizer to plan a reflective essay.

Topic Sentence:

↓

Details of the Event/Experience	**Your Thoughts and Feelings**
1. 2. 3. 4.	

↓

Lesson or Insight You Learned:

For use with Writing 10c

Writing 10

> 10. Write routinely over extended time frames (time for research, reflection, and revision) and shorter time frames (a single sitting or a day or two) for a range of tasks, purposes, and audiences.

Explanation

A letter to the editor is an example of writing that can be completed in a shorter time frame. A letter to the editor is a type of persuasive writing that comments on an issue or responds to a news story or an editorial. For example, you might write a letter to the editor to express your opinion about a recent development at your school or to disagree with an editorial in your local newspaper. Effective letters to the editor are brief, clear, specific, and supported with evidence.

Prewriting:

- Choose an issue, news story, or editorial about which you have a strong opinion.

- Write a thesis that states your opinion clearly and confidently.

- Gather factual evidence to support your argument.

Drafting:

- Begin by clearly identifying the issue, story, or editorial to which you are responding. For stories or editorials, include the date and title in parentheses.

- Present your argument, supporting it with facts and other evidence.

- Establish and maintain a polite tone; don't attack people with whom you disagree.

- Remain focused on your topic, and keep your argument brief.

Revising and Editing:

- Check your word choice: replace weak words with words whose **connotations** will add power to your argument.

- Check your evidence: Do you need to add facts or other evidence?

Academic Vocabulary

connotation a meaning or sense implied by a word in addition to its definition

Apply the Standard

Use the worksheet that follows to help you apply the standard as you complete your writing assignments.

- Writing a Letter to the Editor

Name _____ Date _____ Selection line _____

Writing a Letter to the Editor

Use the organizer to plan a letter to the editor.

Issue, News Story, or Editorial: **My Opinion:**
Facts and Other Evidence to Support my Opinion   •   •   •   •

Powerful words to use in my letter to the editor:

....

....

....

....

....

....

....

....

A

For use with Writing 10d

Speaking and Listening Standards

Speaking and Listening 1

> **1. Initiate and participate effectively in a range of collaborative discussions (one-on-one, in groups, and teacher-led) with diverse partners on grades 11–12 topics, texts, and issues, building on others' ideas and expressing their own clearly and persuasively.***

Workshop: Present a Persuasive Speech

Persuasive speech is language designed to influence the way other people think or act. In daily life, persuasive speech is spontaneous. Perhaps you want to convince a friend to see a movie, or a prospective employer to hire you. Both situations require you to speak persuasively. However, in formal speaking situations, you must develop persuasive speech with forethought. An effective persuasive speech depends on strong evidence and a powerful delivery.

Assignment

Prepare a coherent argument to present to your class. In your persuasive speech, include these elements:

- ✓ a clear thesis statement that defines your position

- ✓ well-organized evidence from reliable sources to support your position

- ✓ a coherent, logical organization appropriate to your purpose, audience, and context

- ✓ specific rhetorical devices and persuasive appeals

- ✓ appropriate gestures, pauses, eye contact, volume, and clear enunciation

- ✓ persuasive language that is formal and precise and that follows the rules of Standard English

Additional Standards

*

Speaking and Listening
1. Initiate and participate effectively in a range of collaborative discussions (one-on-one, in groups, and teacher-led) with diverse partners on grades 11–12 topics, texts, and issues, building on others' ideas and expressing their own clearly and persuasively.

1.a. Come to discussions prepared, having read and researched material under study; explicitly draw on that preparation by referring to evidence from texts and other research on the topic or issue to stimulate a thoughtful, well-reasoned exchange of ideas.

1.b. Work with peers to promote civil, democratic discussions and decision-making, set clear goals and deadlines, and establish individual roles as needed.

1.c. Propel conversations by posing and responding to questions that probe reasoning and evidence; ensure a hearing for a full range of positions on a topic or issue; clarify, verify, or challenge ideas and conclusions; and promote divergent and creative perspectives.

1.d. Respond thoughtfully to diverse perspectives; synthesize comments, claims, and evidence made on all sides of an issue; resolve contradictions when possible; and determine what additional information or research is required to deepen the investigation or complete the task.

4. Present information, findings, and supporting evidence, conveying a clear and distinct perspective, such that listeners can follow the line of reasoning, alternative or opposing perspectives are addressed, and the organization, development, substance, and style are appropriate to purpose, audience, and a range of formal and informal tasks.

5. Make strategic use of digital media (e.g., textual, graphical, audio, visual, and interactive elements) in presentations to enhance understanding of findings, reasoning, and evidence and to add interest.

6. Adapt speech to a variety of contexts and tasks, demonstrating command of formal English when indicated or appropriate.

Language
1. Demonstrate command of the conventions of standard English grammar and usage when writing or speaking.

Name _____ Date _____ Assignment _____

Plan Your Speech

Before you begin writing, take the time to consider which issues provoke strong opinions in you. To speak persuasively, you must choose an issue you care about.

Choose your topic. Choose a topic on which you can express a well-thought-out position. Remember, your purpose is to persuade your audience, so people must hold varied opinions about the topic you choose.

To prompt ideas, read newspapers or listen to news programs to learn about current, controversial issues. Also, look at Internet message boards sponsored by local schools, government agencies, or media sources. Avoid issues to which your only opinion is "I like___" or "I dislike ___." To keep track of your search, use the chart below:

Source	Topic	My Opinion

Refine your topic. Consult with a small group to help make your choice. Listen for good suggestions about your topic, and offer your thoughts about other students' topics. Respond to and ask questions of the group to help clarify your main idea. Collaborative discussions can prove helpful as you plan your speech.

Develop your thesis. Determine your thesis, or position. It should be a statement with which reasonable people could agree or disagree. Write it on the line below.

Thesis statement: ....

....

Name _____ Date _____ Assignment _____

Gather Support and Use Persuasive Language

Support your position. Why do you think the way you do about your topic? What reasons are most persuasive? To help listeners understand your opinion, gather strong evidence to support your reasons. Strong evidence includes facts, statistics, expert testimony, and other details.

Draw from a variety of sources as you research your topic. Books, magazine articles, Web sites, and interviews only scratch the surface of all the content available for you to mine. Remember that not every source will be reliable, however, and evaluate each source as you research. Evaluating sources is especially important on the Internet. The most reliable Web sites tend to have URLs ending in **.edu** and **.gov**.

Take notes in the chart as you research. Be sure to include divergent views you come across, so you can state them accurately and prepare counter-arguments.

Reasons	Support	Other Viewpoints

Use persuasion. Effective reasoning includes persuasive appeals that a speaker uses to sway an audience, such as:

- **Logical appeals** based on facts and sound reasoning

- **Emotional appeals** that engage the audience's emotions

- **Ethical appeals** that cite evidence that establishes credibility

Build persuasive language into your speech. Some strategies may be more useful than others in certain situations. For example, a speaker asking for volunteers or for a donation to a worthy cause may use emotional appeals more than logical appeals.

Use rhetorical devices. Speakers also use rhetorical devices to persuade. Here are some effective devices:

- **Rhetorical questions:** questions not meant to be answered but to establish solidarity with an audience

- **Parallelism:** repetition of similar ideas in similar grammatical forms

- **restatement** repetition of an idea in a variety of ways

For example, a rhetorical question for a speech about increasing library funding could include "Shouldn't the library be a valuable resource for students?"

Name _____ Date _____ Assignment _____

Organize Your Persuasive Speech

Organize the body of your speech to defend your thesis with detailed evidence, keeping in mind your audience and purpose. Then, conclude your speech with a restatement of your thesis and with a call to action, or what you want done.

Introduction
Thesis statement:

Body		
Main Point 1:	Main Point 2:	Main Point 3:
Detailed Evidence: ❏ Persuasive Appeals 1) 2) 3) ❏ Rhetorical Devices 1) 2) 3)	Detailed Evidence: ❏ Persuasive Appeals 1) 2) 3) ❏ Rhetorical Devices 1) 2) 3)	Detailed Evidence: ❏ Persuasive Appeals 1) 2) 3) ❏ Rhetorical Devices 1) 2) 3)

Conclusion
Call to Action:

Name _____ Date _____ Assignment _____

Presentation Techniques

Your delivery is especially important when giving a persuasive speech. Remember, your purpose is to convince your audience to adopt your opinion on a subject. Sometimes speakers make the mistake of focusing on only the most receptive members of their audience, avoiding eye contact with those who most need persuading.

Use presentation techniques. Use these tips to ensure that your delivery will be persuasive.

- **Eye contact:** Hold your audience's attention by looking at your listeners and making eye contact with receptive listeners as well as those who may disagree with you.

- **Speaking rate:** Modify the speed with which you speak, pausing briefly before important points to emphasize them for your audience.

- **Volume:** Monitor and vary the volume with which you speak to create variety and to emphasize points to help your audience maintain interest.

- **Enunciation:** Careful and precise enunciation, or pronunciation of words, will help you to communicate ideas clearly.

- **Purposeful gestures:** Use gestures and movement to support a point, convey emotion, and show that you think your topic is important. Too many gestures, however, can be distracting.

- **Language conventions:** To ensure your ideas are clear, use the conventions of standard American English, the version of English taught in school. An occasional use of colloquial language, however, can help you dramatize a point.

Preview the listening rubric to anticipate how your audience will evaluate your speech.

Speaking Technique	Listening Rubric
Eye contact	❏ Did the speaker maintain eye contact? ❏ Did you feel the speaker was speaking directly to you?
Speaking rate	❏ Was the speaker's rate evenly-paced and deliberate? ❏ Did you feel the speaker used pauses effectively?
Volume	❏ Was the speaker loud enough for everyone to hear? ❏ Did the speaker vary his or her tone for dramatic effect?
Enunciation	❏ Was the speaker's delivery easy to understand? ❏ Did the speaker exhibit control over the language in his or her speech?
Gestures	❏ Did the speaker use effective gestures to emphasize important points in the speech?
Language conventions	❏ Did the speaker use standard English and avoid slang?

For use with Speaking and Listening 1

Name _____ Date _____ Assignment _____

Visuals and Multimedia

You can enhance your evidence and line of reasoning with the right visual displays, such as charts, graphs, diagrams, and multimedia elements.

Use visual displays and multimedia components. Presenting your evidence in visual displays, such as charts and diagrams, can be especially persuasive. Multimedia components can also improve your speech, if handled effectively.

Collaborate with a small group to brainstorm ideas for visuals and multimedia elements to use in your speech. Discuss the major points you make in your speech so the group can generate ideas for visuals and other media elements that might be appropriate. Then use the chart below to help you decide what you want to use and to help you plan and integrate the elements into your presentation.

Visual Display or Multimedia Element	Main Point It Supports	Where to Include It

Name _____ Date _____ Assignment _____

Discuss and Evaluate

After you have delivered your persuasive speech, participate with a small group in a discussion of the content and delivery of your speech.

Discuss and evaluate the persuasive speech. Survey the group to see if they found your speech to be persuasive. Ask them if they were able to identify your thesis. Ask whether or not your evidence helped to reinforce the thesis. Try to reach an agreement on the strengths of your speech and on aspects of it that should be improved. If a consensus cannot be reached, summarize the points of agreement and disagreement among group members. Refer to the guidelines below to ensure a productive discussion.

Guidelines for Discussion

In order to prepare for the discussion, review these guidelines:

- Help the group set goals for the discussion and assign the roles of leader and note-taker as applicable.

- Ask questions and answer group members' questions in a way that helps maintain focus and meet the goals of the group.

- Be receptive to new ideas suggested by group members and, when appropriate, change your perspective to take such ideas into account.

- Make sure all group members have a chance to express their views within the discussion.

Guidelines for Group Discussion

Discussion Rubric	Notes
❑ Did each member participate in the discussion? ❑ Did each member feel free to express his or her opinion?	
❑ Was someone serving as a leader to guide the discussion? ❑ Was someone taking notes to share with the group at the end of the discussion?	
❑ Did participants ask questions and answer those posed by others? ❑ Did participants' questions and answers focus on the topic?	
❑ Were members of the group accepting of comments from others? ❑ Were members of the group open to new ideas or perspectives suggested by others?	

For use with Speaking and Listening 1

Name _____ Date _____ Assignment _____

Self-Assessment

Take a few moments to reflect on your speech. Ask yourself how well you thought it went. Think about whether or not you effectively presented a clear thesis, strong support, and a logical organization. Consider how well you integrated visuals or multimedia elements into your presentation. Also consider how others reacted to your presentation.

Using a rubric for self-assessment. Think about what you learned from your classmates' response to your speech and apply those insights and your own thinking as you fill out the self-assessment rubric below. Use the rating scale to grade your work, and circle the score that best applies to each category.

Criteria	Rating Scale					
	not very				very	
Focus: How effectively did I present a clear thesis stating my position?	1	2	3	4	5	6
Organization: How well did I organize my arguments in a logical progression, using an appropriate structure and a range of perspectives?	1	2	3	4	5	6
Support/Elaboration: How effectively did I support my thesis with valid evidence from reliable sources?	1	2	3	4	5	6
Delivery: How effectively did I use purposeful gestures and pauses for effect, maintain eye contact, and speak clearly and at an adequate volume?	1	2	3	4	5	6
Conventions: How free was my presentation from errors in grammar, spelling, and punctuation?	1	2	3	4	5	6

For use with Speaking and Listening 1

Speaking and Listening 2

> **2. Integrate multiple sources of information presented in diverse formats and media (e.g., visually, quantitatively, orally) in order to make informed decisions and solve problems, evaluating the credibility and accuracy of each source and noting any discrepancies among the data.**

Explanation

Research is not only for school assignments. To make an informed decision or to solve a problem, you may need to refer to a wide variety of print and non-print media sources. These sources include television programs, newspapers, videos, Web sites, books, and interviews. As you research, you will encounter information in diverse formats, including:

- visual elements, such as photographs and video clips
- quantitative information, such as graphs and charts
- oral elements, such as interviews, narration, or song lyrics

However, not every source is useful or reliable. There are many factors that can influence the **credibility** and accuracy of a source, such as the personal interests and feelings of the source's author or sponsor, the method in which information was gathered, and the age of the source. As you **evaluate** each source, consider its intended audience and purpose. Evaluate the authority and objectivity of each source. Also, account for any discrepancies between sources, and look for bias that may distort how information is presented.

To share your findings, **integrate** information from all your sources to create a cohesive and convincing multimedia presentation. Be sure to select the appropriate medium for each section of your presentation.

Examples

- **Gather Information** To make a decision or solve a problem, search for information from a variety of sources. For example, suppose you would like to learn to play the guitar. You might look in the phone book for music schools, search the Internet for teachers in your area, and watch video clips to decide which teacher you prefer.
- **Evaluate Sources** You must evaluate the accuracy and credibility of each source. For example, you may come across a personal blog entry whose author praises a certain teacher excessively. In this case, ask yourself: Who wrote the blog? Does the writer know the teacher personally? If so, how might that have influenced his review?
- **Note Discrepancies** Sources often contradict one another. When they do, continue your research until you can resolve any discrepancies.

Academic Vocabulary

credibility the capacity to inspire belief; trustworthiness

evaluate to judge the value of something

integrate to bring parts together in order to create a cohesive whole

Apply the Standard

Use the worksheet that follows to help you apply the standard. Several copies of the worksheet have been provided for you to use with different assignments.

- Integrating Multiple Sources of Information

Name _____ Date _____ Selection _____

Integrating Multiple Sources of Information

Use the first column of this organizer to note information from each source you consulted. In the second column, evaluate each source. Finally, note and resolve any discrepancies among your sources.

Information from Sources	Evaluation of Sources
• Type of source: .... ❑ Visual ❑ Quantitative ❑ Oral • Author: .... • Important details:	This source: ❑ helps answer my research question. ❑ is credible and accurate. ❑ is useful.
• Type of source: .... ❑ Visual ❑ Quantitative ❑ Oral • Author: .... • Important details:	This source: ❑ helps answer my research question. ❑ is credible and accurate. ❑ is useful.
• Type of source: .... ❑ Visual ❑ Quantitative ❑ Oral • Author: .... • Important details:	This source: ❑ helps answer my research question. ❑ is credible and accurate. ❑ is useful.

Describe any discrepancies you found among your sources. How did you resolve them?

....

A For use with Speaking and Listening 2

Name _____ Date _____ Selection _____

Integrating Multiple Sources of Information

Use the first column of this organizer to note information from each source you consulted. In the second column, evaluate each source. Finally, note and resolve any discrepancies among your sources.

Information from Sources	Evaluation of Sources

• Type of source: ....
   ❏ Visual
   ❏ Quantitative
   ❏ Oral
• Author: ....
 	
• Important details: ....
 	
....
 	
....
	This source:
	
	❏ helps answer my research question.
	❏ is credible and accurate.
	❏ is useful.

• Type of source: ....
   ❏ Visual
   ❏ Quantitative
   ❏ Oral
• Author: ....
 	
• Important details: ....
 	
....
 	
....
	This source:
	
	❏ helps answer my research question.
	❏ is credible and accurate.
	❏ is useful.

• Type of source: ....
   ❏ Visual
   ❏ Quantitative
   ❏ Oral
• Author: ....
 	
• Important details: ....
 	
....
 	
....
	This source:
	
	❏ helps answer my research question.
	❏ is credible and accurate.
	❏ is useful.

Describe any discrepancies you found among your sources. How did you resolve them?

....

B

For use with Speaking and Listening 2

Name _____ Date _____ Selection _____

Integrating Multiple Sources of Information

Use the first column of this organizer to note information from each source you consulted. In the second column, evaluate each source. Finally, note and resolve any discrepancies among your sources.

Information from Sources	Evaluation of Sources

• Type of source: ....
   ❏ Visual
   ❏ Quantitative
   ❏ Oral
• Author: ....
 	
• Important details: ....
 	
....
 	
....
	This source:
	
	❏ helps answer my research question.
	❏ is credible and accurate.
	❏ is useful.

• Type of source: ....
   ❏ Visual
   ❏ Quantitative
   ❏ Oral
• Author: ....
 	
• Important details: ....
 	
....
 	
....
	This source:
	
	❏ helps answer my research question.
	❏ is credible and accurate.
	❏ is useful.

• Type of source: ....
   ❏ Visual
   ❏ Quantitative
   ❏ Oral
• Author: ....
 	
• Important details: ....
 	
....
 	
....
	This source:
	
	❏ helps answer my research question.
	❏ is credible and accurate.
	❏ is useful.

Describe any discrepancies you found among your sources. How did you resolve them?

....

C

For use with Speaking and Listening 2

Speaking and Listening 3

> 3. Evaluate a speaker's point of view, reasoning, and use of evidence and rhetoric, assessing the stance, premises, links among ideas, word choice, points of emphasis, and tone used.

Explanation

A careful evaluation of a speech or presentation involves identifying and assessing the following elements: point of view, the perspective on the subject, or stance, that the speaker takes; the speaker's expressed or implied **premises,** underlying beliefs or assumptions; the speaker's **tone,** or attitude toward the subject, which usually reflects the stance and influences the choice of words; and the speaker's reasoning, the logical connections between the evidence and the arguments and between the arguments themselves. In addition to appealing to logic, speakers can also

- appeal to emotion by arousing an audience's feelings, and
- appeal to authority by claiming that experts support an idea.

It is also important to assess a speaker's use of **rhetorical devices** like the following to persuade an audience:

- *parallelism:* repeating the same grammatical structure to express related ideas
- *restatement:* expressing the same idea in a variety of different ways
- *rhetorical questions:* asking a question that has a self-evident answer

Example

Following is an example of one listener's shorthand analysis of a political speech:

- point of view: against increasing taxes
- premise (implied): big government is bad government
- tone: indignant ("It is unfair for government to place this burden on us.")
- word choice: words with negative connotations to describe taxation (*wasteful, tyranny*)
- reasoning: little specific evidence used to support the argument
- appeal to emotion: fear ("Next, government will take your wallet out of your pocket.")
- appeal to authority ("This is what Ronald Reagan taught us.")
- rhetorical devices: parallelism ("Earn your own money, keep your own money, and spend your own money, free of interference.")

Academic Vocabulary

premise expressed or implied assumptions behind an argument

tone attitude toward a subject

rhetorical device specific use of language to persuade

Apply the Standard

Use the worksheets that follow to help you apply the standard. Several copies of each worksheet have been provided for you to use with different assignments.

- Evaluating Elements of a Speech
- Evaluating a Speaker's Use of Evidence

Name _____ Date _____ Assignment _____

Evaluating Elements of a Speech

Use the chart below to evaluate a speaker's point of view, reasoning, and persuasive appeals. Then, assess the speaker's word choice and tone and their effects on the audience.

Topic and speaker	
Audience	
Speaker's point of view	
Speaker's reasoning	
Persuasive appeals	❏ appeal to emotion Example: ❏ appeal to authority Example:
Rhetorical Devices and Word Choice	Examples: Effect on Audience:
Tone	Description of Tone: Effect on Audience:
How well did the presentation convey and support the argument? Explain.	

For use with Speaking and Listening 3

Name _____ Date _____ Assignment _____

Evaluating Elements of a Speech

Use the chart below to evaluate a speaker's point of view, reasoning, and persuasive appeals. Then, assess the speaker's word choice and tone and their effects on the audience.

Topic and speaker	
Audience	
Speaker's point of view	
Speaker's reasoning	
Persuasive appeals	❏ appeal to emotion Example: ❏ appeal to authority Example:
Rhetorical Devices and Word Choice	Examples: Effect on Audience:
Tone	Description of Tone: Effect on Audience:
How well did the presentation convey and support the argument? Explain.	

Name _____ Date _____ Assignment _____

Evaluating Elements of a Speech

Use the chart below to evaluate a speaker's point of view, reasoning, and persuasive appeals. Then, assess the speaker's word choice and tone and their effects on the audience.

Topic and speaker	
Audience	
Speaker's point of view	
Speaker's reasoning	
Persuasive appeals	❏ appeal to emotion Example: ❏ appeal to authority Example:
Rhetorical Devices and Word Choice	Examples: Effect on Audience:
Tone	Description of Tone: Effect on Audience:
How well did the presentation convey and support the argument? Explain.	

C

Name _____ Date _____ Assignment _____

Evaluating a Speaker's Use of Evidence

Use the chart, below, to evaluate the evidence a speaker uses.

Topic and speaker	
Speaker's Point of View	
Supporting Evidence	**Example:** **Was the evidence** ❑ relevant? ❑ of good quality? ❑ credible? ❑ persuasive? ❑ exaggerated or distorted? **Example:** **Was the evidence** ❑ relevant? ❑ of good quality? ❑ credible? ❑ persuasive? ❑ exaggerated or distorted? **Examples of exaggerated or distorted evidence:**
How well did the evidence support the speaker's reasoning? Explain.	

Name _____ Date _____ Assignment _____

Evaluating a Speaker's Use of Evidence

Use the chart, below, to evaluate the evidence a speaker uses.

Topic and speaker	
Speaker's Point of View	
Supporting Evidence	**Example:** **Was the evidence** ❏ relevant? ❏ of good quality? ❏ credible? ❏ persuasive? ❏ exaggerated or distorted? **Example:** **Was the evidence** ❏ relevant? ❏ of good quality? ❏ credible? ❏ persuasive? ❏ exaggerated or distorted? **Examples of exaggerated or distorted evidence:**
How well did the evidence support the speaker's reasoning? Explain.	

Name _____ Date _____ Assignment _____

Evaluating a Speaker's Use of Evidence

Use the chart, below, to evaluate the evidence a speaker uses.

Topic and speaker	
Speaker's Point of View	
Supporting Evidence	**Example:** **Was the evidence** ❏ relevant? ❏ of good quality? ❏ credible? ❏ persuasive? ❏ exaggerated or distorted? **Example:** **Was the evidence** ❏ relevant? ❏ of good quality? ❏ credible? ❏ persuasive? ❏ exaggerated or distorted? **Examples of exaggerated or distorted evidence:**
How well did the evidence support the speaker's reasoning? Explain.	

Speaking and Listening 4

4. Present information, findings, and supporting evidence, conveying a clear and distinct perspective, such that listeners can follow the line of reasoning, alternative or opposing perspectives are addressed, and the organization, development, substance, and style are appropriate to purpose, audience, and a range of formal and informal tasks.

Explanation

In order to present a speech effectively, first identify your purpose, audience, and task. Knowing these factors will help you determine what kind of **evidence,** or proof, to include and how to adapt your arguments to the audience and the occasion. Also, anticipate questions and objections listeners may have and address alternative or opposing **perspectives,** or viewpoints. You never want to leave audience members thinking you avoided a touchy subject. Fairly stating and then refuting opposing arguments will show that you are objective.

Make sure your line of reasoning is focused and coherent. To develop your ideas and present them clearly, consider using one of the following organizational patterns:

- *Order of Importance* Present ideas and evidence from most to least important, or vice versa.

- *Cause-and-Effect* Analyze the causes and effects of a particular event or problem.

- *Problem-and-Solution* Identify a specific problem and propose a solution to it.

Example

- One way to gain an audience's trust is to state opposing perspectives fairly and then address these other viewpoints. For example, in arguing that the public library should add several computer workstations, you might anticipate the counter-argument that the library cannot afford this expenditure. To refute this argument, you could say, "The concern of some library patrons, that adding computer workstations will be expensive, is legitimate and sensible. However, these patrons should also be aware that not providing computers will ultimately mean a drop in library usage and less usage, in turn, will reduce state funding for this essential institution."

- Consider which organizational structure will best highlight your ideas and make them clear and easy to follow. For example, if you were arguing for more computer workstations in the library, you might use a problem-and-solution organization.

Academic Vocabulary

evidence proof or support of an idea or claim

perspectives ways of regarding a situation or topic

Apply the Standard

Use the worksheets that follow to help you apply the standard. Several copies of each worksheet have been provided for you to use with different assignments.

- Presenting a Speech Effectively
- Addressing Alternative or Opposing Perspectives

Name _____ Date _____ Assignment _____

Presenting a Speech Effectively

Use the chart, below, to plan your speech and deliver it effectively.

Topic: ....
Intended Audience: ....
Task and Occasion: .... **Is the occasion** ❏ **formal?** ❏ **Informal?** **Explain:** ....
Supporting Evidence: ....
Presentation Checklist **The presentation** ❏ **conveys a clear perspective.** ❏ **uses effective supporting evidence.** ❏ **is organized logically.** ❏ **meets the needs of the audience.** ❏ **meets the needs of the occasion.**

A

Name _____ Date _____ Assignment _____

Presenting a Speech Effectively

Use the chart, below, to plan your speech and deliver it effectively.

Topic: ....
Intended audience: ....
Task and Occasion: .... **Is the occasion** ❏ **formal?** ❏ **formal?** **Explain:** ....
Supporting Evidence: ....
Presentation Checklist **The presentation** ❏ **conveys a clear perspective.** ❏ **uses effective supporting evidence.** ❏ **is organized logically.** ❏ **meets the needs of the audience.** ❏ **meets the needs of the occasion.**

Name _____ Date _____ Assignment _____

Presenting a Speech Effectively

Use the chart, below, to plan your speech and deliver it effectively.

Topic: ....
Intended audience: ....
Task and Occasion: ....   **Is the occasion**   ❏ formal?   ❏ formal?   **Explain:** ....
Supporting Evidence: ....
Presentation Checklist   **The presentation**   ❏ conveys a clear perspective.   ❏ uses effective supporting evidence.   ❏ is organized logically.   ❏ meets the needs of the audience.   ❏ meets the needs of the occasion.

For use with Speaking and Listening 4

Name _____ Date _____ Assignment _____

Addressing Alternative or Opposing Perspectives

After completing a draft of a speech, use the chart below to help you revise it and to make sure you anticipate questions and address alternative or opposing perspectives.

Topic:

My Perspective:

Audience:

What questions might listeners have?	How would you answer them?

What alternate or opposing perspectives might listeners have?	In what ways might you refute them?

Name _____ Date _____ Assignment _____

Addressing Alternative or Opposing Perspectives

After completing a draft of a speech, use the chart below to help you revise it and to make sure you anticipate questions and address alternative or opposing perspectives.

Topic:
My Perspective:
Audience:

What questions might listeners have?	How would you answer them?
What alternate or opposing perspectives might listeners have?	**In what ways might you refute them?**

Name _____ Date _____ Assignment _____

Addressing Alternative or Opposing Perspectives

After completing a draft of a speech, use the chart below to help you revise it and to make sure you anticipate questions and address alternative or opposing perspectives.

Topic:

My Perspective:

Audience:

What questions might listeners have?	How would you answer them?

What alternate or opposing perspectives might listeners have?	In what ways might you refute them?

C

For use with Speaking and Listening 4

Speaking and Listening 5

> **5. Make strategic use of digital media (e.g., textual, graphical, audio, visual, and interactive elements) in presentations to enhance understanding of findings, reasoning, and evidence and to add interest.**

Explanation

A good multimedia presentation makes **strategic** use of digital media. Digital media includes a variety of formats:

- **textual elements,** such as titles and captions

- **graphical elements,** such as charts, maps, and diagrams

- **audio elements,** such as music, recorded narration, and sound effects

- **visual elements,** such as still pictures and video clips

- **interactive elements,** such as message boards and games

Choose a few strong elements that have clear meanings and relevance to the presentation, instead of using many elements that are not clearly connected. Adding sounds, images, and other media will not disguise a weak presentation but can enhance a strong one. Strategic use of multimedia supports the main points of the presentation. It emphasizes and reinforces key points. Ask yourself how well the multimedia elements tell your story by themselves.

Examples

- Use media that complement one another. For example, in a presentation on national parks, use photographs of parks to support a recorded interview with a park ranger. Avoid repeating in words what other media are already communicating.

- Also avoid overuse of one form of media by replacing repetitive elements with different media elements. For example, including photographs and video footage of a national park may be repetitive. Provide variety by replacing some visual elements with a graph of visitors per year or an audio interview with a park ranger.

- Make sure that the media elements in your presentation flow logically and support your findings and evidence. For example, instead of a series of photographs showing the same park scene from different angles, use one photograph followed by a map.

Academic Vocabulary

strategic integral or essential to a carefully made plan

Apply the Standard

Use the worksheet that follows to help you apply the standard.

- Using Digital Media

Name _____ Date _____ Assignment _____

Using Digital Media

In the chart, describe the digital media elements you will include in your presentation. Then create an outline to plan where in the presentation you will include each element.

Digital Media Element	How This Element Enhances Understanding or Adds Interest
❏ Textual ❏ Graphical ❏ Audio ❏ Visual ❏ Interactive Description:	
❏ Textual ❏ Graphical ❏ Audio ❏ Visual ❏ Interactive Description:	
❏ Textual ❏ Graphical ❏ Audio ❏ Visual ❏ Interactive Description:	

Incorporating Digital Media Elements

Introduction: ....
I. ....
  A. ....
  B. ....
II. ....
  A. ....
  B. ....
III. ....
  A. ....
  B. ....

A

Speaking and Listening 6

> 6. Adapt speech to a variety of contexts and tasks, demonstrating command of formal English when indicated or appropriate.

Explanation

In order to effectively present a speech, first identify the **context** in which you will speak and the audience to whom you will be presenting. For example, you might be giving a formal presentation in class or giving an impromptu speech. Then, identify your task or purpose. Is it to persuade, to share information, to elicit information, to entertain, or to solve a problem? Keeping the context and task in mind, determine the best way to **adapt** your delivery to appeal to your audience. Enunciate, and speak at an appropriate volume and pace. Use gestures, facial expressions, and movement to emphasize your main ideas.

To ensure your ideas are clear, use the conventions of standard American English, the English taught in school. Use formal English. It shows that you respect both your subject and your audience. Avoid using casual, everyday language and slang when speaking. Use informal language only if the situation is casual.

Examples

- Remember to be mindful of the context of your presentation and your task when adapting your speech. For example, use formal speech for a classroom presentation and informal speech for a group discussion. Speak expressively and use pauses, gestures, and facial expressions when seeking to entertain, or vary your volume for emphasis when attempting to persuade.

- Avoid common usage problems, such as using *like* as a conjunction. "It's like he didn't care" is incorrect. *Like* should always be followed by an object. Do not use *like* before a subject and a verb. Use *as* or *that* instead.

- Although the use of slang terms may be acceptable in more informal presentations, look out for frequent use of temporizing words and phrases. This includes the repetitive use of *you know* and *I mean,* which interrupts the flow and pacing.

Academic Vocabulary

adapt change to suit a new purpose

context circumstances that determine interpretation

Apply the Standard

Use the worksheets that follow to help you apply the standard. Several copies of each worksheet have been provided for you.

- Adapting a Speech
- Using Appropriate Language

Name _____ Date _____ Selection line _____

Adapting a Speech

Use this chart to help you adapt a speech to the appropriate context, audience, and, task.

Topic: ....

What is the context, or situation?

Who is your audience?

What is your task, or purpose?

Adaptations I Will Make	**Reasons for Changes**
1.	
2.	
3.	

A

For use with Speaking and Listening 6

Name _____ Date _____ Selection line _____

Adapting a Speech

Use this chart to help you adapt a speech to the appropriate context, audience, and, task.

Topic: ....

What is the context, or situation?
Who is your audience?
What is your task, or purpose?

Adaptations I Will Make	Reasons for Changes
1.	
2.	
3.	

B

For use with Speaking and Listening 6

Name _____ Date _____ Selection line _____

Adapting a Speech

Use this chart to help you adapt a speech to the appropriate context, audience, and, task.

Topic: ....

What is the context, or situation?

Who is your audience?

What is your task, or purpose?

Adaptations I Will Make	Reasons for Changes
1.	
2.	
3.	

For use with Speaking and Listening 6

Name _____ Date _____ Selection line _____

Using Appropriate Language

Before you give a speech, use the checklist to evaluate your use of language.

Audience: ....

Context: ....

Speaking Task: ....

	Speech Checklist
Language	❑ Is my language appropriate for the context and speaking task? ❑ Do I avoid slang and temporizing words and phrases? ❑ Is my language and word choice precise and engaging enough to keep the listeners interested?
Sentences	❑ Are my sentences varied enough? ❑ Can I change sentence lengths to vary my pace and tempo? ❑ Do I use short sentences for dramatic effect or to emphasize important points?
Usage	❑ Are there too many pronouns in my speech? ❑ Is who or what my pronouns refer to absolutely clear? ❑ Do I use *like* only before an object?

A

Name _____ Date _____ Selection line _____

Using Appropriate Language

Before you give a speech, use the checklist to evaluate your use of language.

Audience: ....

Context: ....

Speaking Task: ....

	Speech Checklist
Language	❑ Is my language appropriate for the context and speaking task? ❑ Do I avoid slang and temporizing words and phrases? ❑ Is my language and word choice precise and engaging enough to keep the listeners interested?
Sentences	❑ Are my sentences varied enough? ❑ Can I change sentence lengths to vary my pace and tempo? ❑ Do I use short sentences for dramatic effect or to emphasize important points?
Usage	❑ Are there too many pronouns in my speech? ❑ Is who or what my pronouns refer to absolutely clear? ❑ Do I use *like* only before an object?

For use with Speaking and Listening 6

Name _____ Date _____ Selection line _____

Using Appropriate Language

Before you give a speech, use the checklist to evaluate your use of language.

Audience: ....

Context: ....

Speaking Task: ....

	Speech Checklist
Language	❑ Is my language appropriate for the context and speaking task? ❑ Do I avoid slang and temporizing words and phrases? ❑ Is my language and word choice precise and engaging enough to keep the listeners interested?
Sentences	❑ Are my sentences varied enough? ❑ Can I change sentence lengths to vary my pace and tempo? ❑ Do I use short sentences for dramatic effect or to emphasize important points?
Usage	❑ Are there too many pronouns in my speech? ❑ Is who or what my pronouns refer to absolutely clear? ❑ Do I use *like* only before an object?

Language Standards

Language 1a

> **1a.** Demonstrate command of the conventions of standard English grammar and usage when writing or speaking.
> - Apply the understanding that usage is a matter of convention, can change over time, and is sometimes contested.

Explanation

In school, you learn the rules of **standard English** grammar and usage. People are expected to follow them in their writing and speaking. Grammar and usage rules are **conventions,** or agreements, accepted by most speakers and writers. These conventions often change over time and are sometimes debated. To be taken seriously, however, you should understand and consistently apply the conventions of standard English that are accepted at any given time.

Examples

The conventions of standard English usage can change over time. For example, it was once the rule that future-tense verbs used with first-person pronouns required the helping verb *shall*, rather than *will*. That means the following sentences were once considered incorrect: *I will help you tomorrow. We will figure out what to do.* Gradually, however, the word *shall* fell from use, and today the helping verb *will* is considered correct for all future-tense verbs.

It is important to know the current conventions of standard English grammar and usage. The table below summarizes a few of the most important conventions.

Convention	Incorrect	Correct
A present-tense verb must agree with its subject.	One of the books are missing. The leaders of our class represents us. He study every night.	**One** of the books **is** missing. The **leaders** of our class **represent** us. **He studies** every night.
A pronoun must agree with its antecedent in person and gender.	One of the girls lost their jacket. Students need to do your homework.	One of the girls lost **her** jacket. Students need to do **their** homework.
Avoid shifting tenses when actions happen at the same time.	He ran to the door and opens it. She needs help and deserved it.	He **ran** to the door and **opened** it. She **needs** help and **deserves** it.
In your writing, avoid sentence fragments and run-ons.	My dad is waiting. Outside in the parking lot. I like to play basketball, it's fast and exciting.	My dad is waiting **outside in the parking lot.** I like to play basketball. **It's fast and exciting.**

Name _____ Date _____ Assignment _____

Apply the Standard

A. Circle the correct word in parentheses to complete each sentence.

1. The issues leading to the Civil War (was, were) bitterly divisive.

2. The North had an advantage in population and (is, was) more industrial.

3. The South was fighting for (its, their) very survival.

4. Many scholars still spend (his, their) careers studying the Civil War.

5. Today, the Civil War remains the bloodiest war that Americans have ever fought, and we (continue, continued) to feel its lingering effects.

6. One of the most famous Civil War generals (was, were) Ulysses S. Grant.

7. Of the leaders in the Civil War (he were, he was) one of the most controversial.

8. He knew that many fierce battles lied ahead a (accepts, accepted) the challenge facing the North anyway.

9. Many scholars (dispute, disputes) Grant's role winning the war and focus on his many personal flaws.

10. Each of the generals (remain, remains) a hero to people from the North and the South who admire their courageous leadership during that m horrible war.

B. Each sentence contains one or more error standard English grammar and usage. Circle each error, and write the sentence correctly on the ne.

1. The stories of Mark Twain is known for i umor.

....

2. Twain celebrated American English. And often uses dialect in his writing.

....

3. He was the most famous American writer of the 1800s, he wrote about the Mississippi River and the American West, he chooses themes that reflect a changing America.

....

4. He was also a journalist, and the audience for his newspaper stories were huge.

....

5. I predict that people will still enjoy Twain's humor and read their stories a hundred years from now.

....

Language 1b

> **1b. Demonstrate command of the conventions of standard English grammar and usage when writing or speaking.**
>
> - **Resolve issues of complex or contested usage, consulting references (e.g., *Merriam-Webster's Dictionary of English Usage, Garner's Modern American Usage*) as needed.**

Explanation

Because usage conventions can change over time and are sometimes contested, you may need to consult a dictionary or reliable reference book as you edit your writing. An up-to-date dictionary or usage handbook is your best guide to whether you are using a word correctly, according to current conventions.

Examples

To compare two people, places, or things, you use the **comparative** form of an adjective or adverb. To compare three or more things, you use the **superlative** form. The comparative form is made by adding *–er* to the modifier or using the word *more* before the modifier. The superlative form is made by adding *–est* to the modifier or using the word *most* before it.

Modifier	Comparative Form	Superlative Form
fast	faster	fastest
early	earlier	earliest
narrow	narrower	narrowest
lonely	lonelier	loneliest
loyal	more loyal	most loyal
difficult	more difficult	most difficult
suddenly	more suddenly	most suddenly

In the past, usage rules required using *more* and *most* with modifiers of two or more syllables. Today, however, many two-syllable modifiers have correct forms that end in *–er* and *–est*. For example, the comparative and superlative forms of *narrow* are *narrower* and *narrowest*. If you look up *narrow* in an up-to-date dictionary, you will find these forms listed after the entry word. If you look up two-syllable adjectives such as *shallow, useful,* and *modern,* you will not find any comparative or superlative forms listed. Their absence tells you that you must use *more* and *most* with these modifiers. Whenever you are in doubt about the correct comparative and superlative forms of a modifier, look up the word in a recently published dictionary. Consult an authoritative usage handbook for any other complex or contested usage issues in your writing.

Name _____ Date _____ Assignment _____

Apply the Standard

A. Circle the correct modifier in parentheses to complete each sentence.

1. *The Red Pony* is a (shorter, shortest) novel than *The Grapes of Wrath.*

2. *The Grapes of Wrath* is the (longer, longest) novel I've ever read.

3. It describes the (more unforgettable, most unforgettable) characters you'll ever meet.

4. The Joad family's farmland blows away in the (biggest, most big) dust storm of the century.

5. As the family travels west, they become (hungrier, more hungry) and (desperater, more desperate) than they were before they left home.

6. Steinbeck's fans are (loyaler, more loyal) than those of almost any other author I have read.

7. One of Steinbeck's (more earliest, earliest) novels is his classic *Of Mice and Men.*

8. That novel tells the story of two of my (favoritest, most favorite) characters, George Milton and Lenny Small, who go to work on a ranch.

9. Steinbeck's novels are (most admirable, more admirable) than his short stories.

10. Among American writers, few can challenge Steinbeck's position as the (popularest, most popular) author of the twentieth century.

B. Write the correct comparative or superlative form of the modifier to complete each sentence. Use an up-to-date college dictionary to check that you are using the currently accepted form.

1. Which of the two actors do you think is ....? (handsome)

2. Which of the three math problems is the ....? (simple)

3. Gold is a .... metal than copper. (precious)

4. I arrived .... than he did. (early)

5. He is the .... person I know. (generous)

6. This remote control is .... to use than that one. (easy)

7. The cello has a .... sound than the violin. (mellow)

8. What is the .... movie you've ever seen? (inspiring)

9. I think my lemonade is .... than yours. (sour)

10. She is the .... ballerina in the company. (graceful)

Language 2a

2a. Demonstrate command of the conventions of standard English capitalization, punctuation, and spelling when writing.

• Observe hyphenation conventions.

Explanation

In current standard American English, hyphens are often used in compound adjectives and compound nouns. They are occasionally used to separate a prefix from the word that follows it. When in doubt about using a hyphen, consult an up-to-date college dictionary or an authoritative usage guide.

Examples

The following table summarizes a few of the current standard American English conventions for using hyphens.

Use a hyphen...	...Rule	Examples
after a prefix	when the second word is capitalized.	un-American
	when the second word is a number.	pre-1914
	when more than one word follows it.	pre-nineteenth-century
	to distinguish a word from its homophone.	*recover* from an illness, but *re-cover* a chair
	when the prefix *ex-* means "former."	ex-president
in compound adjectives	when they come before a noun, unless the first word ends in *-ly*.	bright-eyed child widely known author
in compound nouns	when they name numbers.	twenty-one
	when they name equally important functions.	author-linguist
	when they include a prepositional phrase.	sister-in-law
	for *great* relatives and with *year-old*.	great-grandmother
	when they begin with *self* or *vice*.	six-year-old self-confidence vice-president

Name _____ Date _____ Assignment _____

Apply the Standard

A. Circle the words in each sentence that require a hyphen. Then write each hyphenated word correctly.

1. There are fifty two weeks in a year. ....

2. This part of town has many buildings of pre 1940 construction. ....

3. My little cousin is an active blue eyed three year old. ....

4. The vice president shows great self restraint in his speeches. ....

5. My brother in law is visiting his great grandfather. ....

6. His ex wife is the noted painter sculptor Sheila Brown. ....

7. A large scale project has just begun in that mineral rich nation. ....

8. Most of the world's population lives in non English speaking countries. ....

B. Rewrite the paragraph below, adding hyphens where they are needed.

    Inventor politician Benjamin Franklin lived a remarkable life. Born in 1709, Franklin grew up in pre Revolutionary War Boston. He was just a quick thinking twelve year old when he began working in his brother's print shop. In 1723, he ran away to Philadelphia, and by 1729, he was publishing his own highly regarded newspaper. In 1730, he began a common law marriage with Deborah Reed, a union that lasted forty four years, until her death. A self taught man, Franklin had only two years of formal education. His well known experiment with electricity was first described in his widely translated book *Experiments and Observations on Electricity.* Franklin helped draft the Declaration of Independence and was one of its fifty six signers. He also helped write the United States Constitution.

....

....

....

....

....

....

....

....

Language 2b

> **2b. Demonstrate command of the conventions of standard English capitalization, punctuation, and spelling when writing.**
> - **Spell correctly.**

Explanation

As a writer, you hope to capture your readers' interest—to sweep them away with your story or argument. You do not want readers tripping over misspelled words that can slow them down, confuse them, or cloud their opinion of you. Learning spelling rules, consulting a dictionary, and using a computer spell-checker can help you avoid making distracting spelling errors.

Examples

Some of the most common spelling errors occur when forming plurals or when adding prefixes and suffixes to words. The tables below explain important spelling rules you can apply in these situations.

FORMING PLURALS

Rule	Examples
For words ending in *s, ss, x, z, sh, and ch,* add *–es.*	dresses, waltzes, pouches
For words ending in *y* preceded by a consonant, change the *y* to *i* and add *–es.*	parties, luxuries, queries
For most words ending in *o* preceded by a consonant, add *–es.*	potatoes, tomatoes, heroes
For some words ending in *f* or *fe,* change the ending to *v* and add *–es.* For others, just add *–s.*	leaves, knives, wives beliefs, safes

ADDING PREFIXES

Rule	Examples
When a prefix is added to a root word, the spelling of the root word remains the same. This will sometimes result in a double letter.	un + happy = unhappy un + noticed = unnoticed im + patient = impatient im + moral = immoral

ADDING SUFFIXES

Rule	Examples
For a root word ending in *e,* drop the *e* when adding a suffix beginning with a vowel.	nature + al = natural care + ful = careful
For a root word ending in a consonant + *y,* change *y* to *i* unless the suffix begins with *i.*	funny + er = funnier modify + ing = modifying
The shus sound can be spelled with the suffix *-cious* or *-tious.* Check a dictionary to be sure.	gracious, suspicious infectious, cautious
The *shun* sound is usually spelled with the suffix *-tion.* The *zhun* sound is usually the suffix *-sion.*	caution, mention confusion, decision

Name _____ Date _____ Assignment _____

Apply the Standard

A. Follow the instructions to form new words. Be sure to spell them correctly. Check a dictionary if you are unsure of the correct spelling.

1. Write the plural of the word *shelf*. ....

2. Write the plural of the word *torpedo*. ....

3. Write the plural of the word *injury*. ....

4. Add the prefix *un-* to *usual*. ....

5. Add the prefix *un-* to *natural*. ....

6. Add the suffix *–ish* to *style*. ....

7. Add the suffix *–ful* to *pity*. ....

8. Add the suffix *–able* to *enjoy*. ....

9. Add the *shun* sound to the end of *prevent*. ....

10. Add the *zhun* sound to the end of *revise*. ....

B. Each sentence contains one or more misspelled words. Circle them, and write the correct spellings on the line.

1. The teacher was disatisfied with the explanasion I gave for my tardiness.

....

2. Joe is trying to be more relyable and less impatient.

....

3. Many countries have policys to reduce pollutants.

....

4. Hospitals take precausions to prevent the transmission of infecious diseases.

....

5. The number of tomatos in our garden was unbelieveable.

....

Language 3a

3a. Apply knowledge of language to understand how language functions in different contexts, to make effective choices for meaning or style, and to comprehend more fully when reading or listening.

- **Vary syntax for effect, consulting references (e.g., Tufte's *Artful Sentences*) for guidance as needed; apply an understanding of syntax to the study of complex texts when reading.**

Explanation

Good writers are experts in syntax, or the different ways of arranging words in sentences. They vary the syntax, or structure, of their sentences to create certain effects, such as suspense, surprise, or humor. You can expand your understanding of syntax to become a better writer and a better reader.

Examples

By using a variety of sentence structures, you can create dramatic effects and prevent your writing from becoming monotonous. For example, short sentences create a sense of speed and drama, while longer sentences cause the reader to slow down and reflect. Simple sentences focus the reader's attention on a single idea, while compound and complex sentences emphasize the relationships between ideas.

SENTENCE TYPES

Simple: A single independent clause	*I like playing baseball.*
Compound: Two or more independent clauses, joined by a comma and coordinating conjunction (*and, but, or*) or a semicolon	*I like playing baseball, but I prefer shooting hoops.*
Complex: One independent clause and one or more subordinate clauses	*I like to stop at the local pizza place when I play an away game.*
Compound-Complex: Two or more independent clauses and one or more subordinate clauses	*When I play basketball, I enjoy the speed of the game, and I find the teamwork very rewarding.*

SENTENCE BEGINNINGS

Notice how you can express the same idea in five different ways, just by changing the beginning of a sentence.

Subject	*Eli, determined to win, desperately took a shot in the game's final second.*
Prepositional Phrase	*In the game's final second, a determined Eli desperately took a shot.*
Participle	*Taking a desperate shot in the game's final second, Eli was determined to win.*
Adverb	*Desperately, a determined Eli took a shot in the game's final second.*
Subordinate Clause	*As the final second of the game ticked off, a determined Eli desperately took a shot.*

Name _____ Date _____ Assignment _____

Apply the Standard

A. Combine each group of sentences, using the sentence type indicated in parentheses.

1. Mariah fakes to the left and passes the ball. Jenna shoots. (compound)

   ....

2. Mariah likes basketball. Jenna prefers soccer. (compound)

   ....

3. Brandon scored the final goal. He did it after Avi passed him the ball. (complex)

   ....

4. Brandon is reading a book. He borrowed it from me. (complex)

   ....

5. Mom cut the vegetables. Dad stir-fried them. I was doing my homework at the time.
   (compound-complex)

   ....

B. Rewrite each sentence to begin as indicated in parentheses.

1. The guests honored the bride and groom with applause and gifts. (prepositional phrase)

   ....

2. The young couple, smiling and shaking hands, greeted their guests. (participial phrase)

   ....

3. The band began to play suddenly. (adverb)

   ....

4. The guests began to dance when they heard the music. (subordinate clause)

   ....

5. After the reception, I took home a piece of cake. (subject)

   ....

C. Write an example of each of the following sentence types.

1. Begin with a subordinate clause and write a complex sentence.

   ....

2. Begin with a prepositional phrase and write a compound-complex sentence.

   ....

For use with Language 3a

Language 4a

> **4a.** Determine or clarify the meaning of unknown and multiple-meaning words and phrases based on grades 11–12 reading and content, choosing flexibly from a range of strategies.
>
> - Use context (e.g., the overall meaning of a sentence or paragraph; a word's position or function in a sentence) as a clue to the meaning of a word or phrase.

Explanation

While reading, you have probably used **context clues**—or nearby words, phrases, and sentences—to figure out the meaning of an unfamiliar word or a word with multiple meanings. Improving your strategies for clarifying the meaning of words in context will help you read complex texts more proficiently.

Examples

You can use several types of context clues to identify the meaning of unknown words and phrases.

Clues in Nearby Words Look for a nearby word or phrase that may have a meaning similar to, or the opposite of, the unknown word. Look also for examples that may clarify the meaning of a word.

> **Similar meaning:** *We need to be <u>in total agreement</u> on this issue, so the vote must be **unanimous**.*
> (The clue suggests that *unanimous* means "in total agreement.")

> **Opposite meaning:** *We want to achieve **salutary** effects, <u>not destructive</u> ones.*
> (The clue suggests that *salutary* means the opposite of *destructive*, so it must mean "beneficial.")

> **Examples:** *Great Britain assembled a **martial** array of <u>naval ships, heavy artillery, and British soldiers</u> in the colonies.*
> (The examples suggest that *martial* means "warlike" or "prepared for war.")

Clues in the Meaning of the Sentence Look for the main idea of the sentence. You can often use it to figure out the meaning of an unknown word.

> *An army of three million who are committed to the cause of liberty are <u>invincible</u>.*
> (The general meaning of the sentence suggests that *invincible* means "unable to be defeated.")

Clues in the Word's Function in the Sentence Look at the position of the word in the sentence. Think about the job, or function, of the word. Does it follow an article or an adjective? Does it serve as a subject or as an object of a preposition? If so, it is probably a noun. Does it express action? If so, it is probably a verb. Use that information, plus any of the first two types of clues, to figure out the meaning of an unknown word.

> *As Patrick Henry pointed out, the question of whether or not to join the colonists in revolution against the British was one of awful **moment** for such a young country.*

(*Moment* is the object of a preposition, so it is a noun. However, it does not seem to have the familiar meaning of "a small amount of time." The sentence seems to suggest that the question is very important. *Moment,* in this context, seems to mean "importance": "The question is one of awful *importance* to this young country.")

Name _____ Date _____ Assignment _____

Apply the Standard

A. Use context clues in each passage to determine or clarify the meaning of each underlined word. Write the probable meanings on the lines provided.

1. The British thought the colonists were weak and not able to defeat a <u>formidable</u> adversary.

....

2. The woman soldier was a <u>termagant</u>, loud and often angry, with a fierce temper and real strength.

....

3. Some colonists acted in a most friendly and <u>conciliatory</u> manner toward the British to appease them.

....

4. In the early years of the war, the colonist soldiers acted with great <u>perseverance</u> in fighting the British because they were convinced in the rightness of their cause and committed to preserving their freedom. ....

5. In the Declaration of Independence, Thomas Jefferson declared that only a grievous wrong would <u>impel</u> the colonists to take such action as to separate themselves from England.

....

B. Think about the function and position of the underlined word in each sentence. Use that information, plus any other context clues, to define the underlined word. Write the meanings on the lines.

1. The colonists tried to <u>avert</u> war by negotiating with the British on the issue of taxation.

....

2. The colonists finally concluded, after all of their efforts to negotiate, that war was <u>inevitable</u>.

....

3. The British had an <u>infallible</u> belief that America did not have a right or the ability to rule itself.

....

4. The colonists were <u>constrained</u> by the force of their beliefs: no taxation without representation.

....

5. They would, if need be, <u>shirk</u> their responsibilities to their own family and farms to take up arms

to fight. ....

For use with Language 4a

Language 4b

> **4b. Determine or clarify the meaning of unknown and multiple-meaning words and phrases based on grades 11–12 reading and content, choosing flexibly from a range of strategies.**
>
> • **Identify and correctly use patterns of word changes that indicate different meanings or parts of speech (e.g., *conceive, conception, conceivable.*)**

Explanation

When you add a suffix to a root word, you change its meaning and part of speech. Many root words change their parts of speech in predictable ways. Once you learn these patterns of word changes, you can easily identify a word's part of speech. You can also understand the meaning of related words by analyzing their root words and suffixes.

Examples

Many adjectives end in *–ent* or *–ant.* You can usually transform them into nouns by changing *–ent* to *–ence* and *–ant* to *–ance*:

- **adjectives:** prudent, benevolent, vigilant, resistant

- **nouns:** prudence, benevolence, vigilance, resistance

One word family of verbs all include the Latin root *scribe.* These verbs can be changed into nouns, following a predictable pattern. Some also follow the same pattern to form adjectives:

- **verbs:** prescribe, describe, proscribe, inscribe, transcribe

- **nouns:** prescription, description, proscription, inscription, transcription

- **adjectives:** prescriptive, descriptive, proscriptive

A number of verbs end in *–ate.* These verbs can be changed into nouns ending in *–ation*, and many can also be formed into adjectives ending in *–ative.*

- **verbs:** speculate, degenerate, create, vegetate, fluctuate, retaliate

- **nouns:** speculation, degeneration, creation, vegetation, fluctuation, retaliation

- **adjectives:** speculative, degenerative, creative, vegetative

Finally, you will find many nouns that end in *–y.* Many of these nouns can be changed into adjectives ending in *–ic* and verbs ending in *–ize*:

- **nouns:** sympathy, democracy, harmony, energy

- **adjectives:** sympathetic, democratic, harmonic, energetic

- **verbs:** sympathize, democratize, harmonize, energize

Name _____ Date _____ Assignment _____

Apply the Standard

A. Look at the suffix in each word. Then write the word's part of speech.

1. evacuation ....

2. tolerate ....

3. persistence ....

4. persistent ....

5. sympathize ....

6. creative ....

7. vigilant ....

8. vigilance ....

9. vegetate ....

10. demonstrative ....

11. inspection ....

12. insolence ....

13. allowance ....

14. restive ....

15. randomize ....

16. theocracy ....

17. benevolence ....

18. defection ....

19. presumptive ....

20. pathetic ....

B. Fill in each blank with the correct form of the word in italics.

1. When the doctor *prescribes* a medication, she writes a ....

2. When you *describe* something, you write a .... paragraph.

3. When people are *reluctant* to do something, they show their ....

4. *Tolerant* people are able to .... the differences among people.

5. A *sympathetic* person shows his or her .... for other people.

6. A *democratic* nation has a form of government called a ....

7. When you add *energy* to a discussion, you .... it.

8. An *empathetic* person is able to .... with other people.

9. A person who shows *prudence* is a .... person.

10. A *vigilant* person demonstrates the quality of ....

Language 4c

> **4c.** Determine or clarify the meaning of unknown and multiple-meaning words and phrases based on grades 11–12 reading and content, choosing flexibly from a range of strategies.
>
> - Consult general and specialized reference materials (e.g., dictionaries, glossaries, thesauruses), both print and digital, to find the pronunciation of a word or determine or clarify its precise meaning, its parts of speech, its etymology, or its standard usage.

Explanation

Reference materials such as dictionaries, glossaries, and thesauruses are indispensable resources for readers and writers. In a **dictionary,** you can determine or clarify a word's precise meaning and part of speech. You can also learn a word's **etymology,** or history, as well as whether it is considered standard English, colloquial (conversational English), or slang. A **glossary** is an alphabetical list of terms that are used in a particular text. It provides a handy way to clarify the meaning of a word in a textbook you are reading.

A **thesaurus** is a book of synonyms, words that have the same surface meaning, but often have different connotations. When you write, you can use a thesaurus to vary your word choice. Before you use a listed synonym, however, look up the word in a dictionary to make sure that its connotations express exactly what you want to say.

Examples

> **de vout** (di vout') *adj.* **–er, est   1.** very religious; pious
> See synonyms at **religious.   2.** showing reverence
> **3.** sincere; earnest [Midle English *devouren*, from Old
> French, from Latin *devotus*, past participle of *devovere*,
> to vow. See DEVOTE.] —**de vout' ly** *adj.* —*devoutness n.*

Usage Indicators: There are no usage indicators in the dictionary entry for *devout*, because the word is considered standard English. For words that are not considered standard English, the dictionary entry will include a label before the definition, such as **colloq:** colloquial, conversational English; **slang:** informal, nonstardard English; **dial:** dialect, part of the special language of a particular region or group of people; and **archaic:** outdated English.

> **de vout** *adj.* deeply concerned with religion: devotional, godly,
> holy, pious, prayerful, religious, saintly, reverent, fervent. *See*
> RELIGION. *Ant.* See IRRELIGION.

Name _____ Date _____ Assignment _____

Apply the Standard

A. Use a print or electronic dictionary to answer these questions.

1. Which syllable of the word *clandestine* is accented when you pronounce the word?

....

2. What different parts of speech can the word *right* function as? ....

3. Trace the path by which the word *January* entered the English language. What god was it named

after, and why? ....

4. Which definition of the word *cool* is not considered standard English usage?

....

5. How do the words *strong* and *stalwart* differ in their connotative meanings?

....

B. Use a thesaurus to find five synonyms for each underlined word. Then use a dictionary to choose the best synonym to replace the underlined word in the context of the sentence.

1. The evidence for his claim was <u>thin</u>.

synonyms: .... best synonym: ....

2. It's time for us to make some <u>tough</u> choices.

synonyms: .... best synonym: ....

3. The peasants lived in a <u>mean</u>, ramshackle cottage.

synonyms: .... best synonym: ....

4. The background music played at a smooth, <u>even</u> tempo.

synonyms: .... best synonym: ....

5. An exciting new technology company is beginning an <u>aggressive</u> sales campaign.

synonyms: .... best synonym: ....

COMMON CORE COMPANION • COMMON CORE COMPANION • COMMON CORE COMPANION

Language 4d

> **4d. Determine or clarify the meaning of unknown and multiple-meaning words and phrases based on grades 11–12 reading and content, choosing flexibly from a range of strategies.**
>
> • **Verify the preliminary determination of the meaning of a word or phrase (e.g., by checking the inferred meaning in context or in a dictionary.)**

Explanation

You have learned how to infer the meaning of an unfamiliar word by analyzing its word parts—prefix, root, or suffix—and by using **context clues**—other nearby words or phrases and sentences. Sometimes the first inference you make about a word's meaning won't be correct. As you read on, you can use more context clues to verify the meaning of the word. If you require further assistance, consult a dictionary.

Examples

Unfamiliar terms In the passage below about Frederick Douglass's experiences as a slave, you may not be familiar with the word *chattel*.

> On entering upon the career of a slaveholding mistress, Mrs. Auld was singularly deficient; nature, which fits nobody for such an office, had done less for her than any lady I had known. It was no easy matter to induce her to think and to feel that the curly-headed boy, who stood by her side, and even leaned on her lap; who was loved by little Tommy, and who loved little Tommy in turn; sustained to her only the relation of a <u>chattel.</u>

Since Mrs. Auld is a slaveholder and Douglass, "the curly-headed boy," is a slave, you may infer that *chattel* refers to a servant who is less than human. To verify if that meaning is correct, look up *chattel* in a dictionary.

Multiple-meaning words Some of the puzzling words you encounter in your reading will be familiar, multiple-meaning words that are used in unfamiliar ways. When you infer their meaning in context, try replacing the word with the inferred meaning to see if it makes sense. For example, Douglass writes, "If my condition <u>waxed</u> bad, that of the family <u>waxed</u> not better." You can infer that, in this context, the word *waxed* means "grew." When you replace the word *waxed* with the word *grew* in the sentence, it makes sense.

Name _____ Date _____ Assignment _____

Apply the Standard

Read each sentence, paying special attention to the underlined word. As you read, try to infer the meaning of the underlined word, using word analysis and context clues. Use additional context clues to verify whether your preliminary determination was correct. Then look up each word in a dictionary to confirm its meaning.

1. The builders had their food and daily rations <u>commingled</u> with the pikes, saws, and hammers, all of it in one large canvas bag.

   Preliminary inferred meaning: ....

   Dictionary meaning: .... Inferred meaning: ....

2. Everyone was working when, with a sudden <u>arrest</u> of his motion, one of the workers dropped all of his tools on the ground and sat down.

   Preliminary inferred meaning: ....

   Dictionary meaning: .... Inferred meaning: ....

3. The others in the group could tell something was wrong because the worker was <u>audibly</u> distressed, mumbling and grumbling as if to himself.

   Preliminary inferred meaning: ....

   Dictionary meaning: .... Inferred meaning: ....

4. After lifting up his heavy shirt, the others could see the deep, red <u>abrasion</u> on the worker's back, the result no doubt from some unfortunate accident while building the cellar.

   Preliminary inferred meaning: ....

   Dictionary meaning: .... Inferred meaning: ....

5. One man on the roof stood <u>petrified</u>, knowing that his difficulty in transporting a load of heavy stones resulted in his companion's injury and worried sick that he would be fired as a result.

   Preliminary inferred meaning: ....

   Dictionary meaning: .... Inferred meaning: ....

Language 5a

5a. **Demonstrate understanding of figurative language, word relationships, and nuances in word meanings.**

- **Interpret figures of speech (e.g., hyperbole, paradox) in context and analyze their role in the text.**

Explanation

Figurative language is writing or speech that is used imaginatively. Its meaning must be interpreted, rather than taken literally. All of the many types of figurative language are known as **figures of speech.** Writers use figures of speech to state ideas in vivid and imaginative ways.

Examples

Figure of Speech	Definition	Example
simile	compares two unlike things, using *like* or *as*	My love is like a blooming rose.
metaphor	compares two unlike things; does **not** use *like* or *as*	Before the party, our house was a beehive of activity.
synecdoche	uses part of something to stand for the whole	Dozens of willing hands made the bake sale a success.
paradox	states an idea that seems contradictory or impossible, but is actually true in some way	A coded message both increases communication and decreases communication.
personification	gives human qualities to a nonhuman thing	A gentle breeze played happily through the trees.
hyperbole	exaggerates; overstates the truth	It seemed like everyone in the state of Virginia was at the game.
understatement	says less than is really meant	I guess it was a little crowded; there were two people sitting on my lap.
verbal irony	says the opposite of what is really meant	Say that a little louder. The neighbors across the street might not have heard you.
idiom	the literal meanings of the words do not add up to the actual meaning of the expression	I was sitting on top of the world after I won the contest.

Name _____ Date _____ Assignment _____

Apply the Standard

A. Identify the type of figurative language used in each sentence.

1. The hearts of a grateful nation welcomed the soldiers home. ....

2. My uncle felt like he was living on borrowed time after his heart surgery. ....

3. In his poem "To Althea, from Prison" Richard Lovelace says: "Stone walls do not a prison make, / Nor iron bars a cage." ....

4. The sea pounded the shore angrily. ....

5. The diver got a little nervous when his oxygen began to run out. ....

6. Can you move a little slower? We're only half an hour late! ....

7. It rained so hard and so long that I thought I might have to build an ark. ....

8. Eric wants to buy a new set of wheels before the dance. ....

9. Her smile was a ray of sunshine on a cloudy day. ....

10. Elderly people often say, "Youth is wasted on the young." ....

B. Read the passage below. Identify examples of figurative language. Then explain how the figures of speech affect your understanding of the text and your emotional response to it.

> *I have always been regretting that I was not as wise as the day I was born. The intellect is a cleaver; it discerns and rifts its way into the secret of things.*

> –Henry David Thoreau

....

....

....

Language 5b

5b. **Demonstrate understanding of figurative language, word relationships, and nuances in word meanings.**

• **Analyze nuances in the meaning of words with similar denotations.**

Explanation

Words have **denotations,** which are their basic meanings, as well as **connotations,** which are the feelings or ideas associated with them. Many words with similar denotations convey different **nuances,** or slight differences in meaning. When you read, it is important to notice word choices that convey different shades of meaning. When you write, it is important to choose words that have the exact meaning and connotations you want to convey.

Examples

This chart shows words that are synonyms for *look.* They all share the same basic denotation. Notice the different connotations and shades of meaning that each word conveys.

Word	Connotation/Nuance	Example Sentence
1. *glance*	to take a quick, casual look	*I glanced at the TV as I walked through the family room.*
2. *peek*	to take a quick, secret look at a thing you're not supposed to see	*I peeked at the presents that were hidden in the closet.*
3. *gaze*	to look intently and steadily, in wonder or delight	*Dan gazed into Sara's eyes as he asked her to marry him.*
4. *glare*	to stare at someone in anger	*When I came home late, my mother glared at me and asked where I'd been.*
5. *peer*	to look at something closely and searchingly	*The chemist peered through the microscope to examine the rare isotope.*

Name _____ Date _____ Assignment _____

Apply the Standard

A. Use a synonym for *looked* to complete each sentence. Keep in mind the nuance each word conveys.

1. The store owner .... at me when I picked up the expensive vase and almost dropped it.

2. I .... at my sister's diary while she was out of the room.

3. We .... through the fog, searching for the trail we'd lost.

4. We .... in wonder at the lunar eclipse.

5. I wasn't really interested in the pictures, so I just .... at them.

B. Look up each pair of synonyms in a dictionary. Think about the shades of meaning that each word conveys. Then use each word in a sentence that conveys its connotations.

1. illustrious/notorious

....

....

2. multitude/mob

....

....

3. requested/demanded

....

....

4. inquisitive/prying

....

....

5. declined/refused

....

....

For use with Language 5b

335

Language 6

> **6. Acquire and use accurately general academic and domain-specific words and phrases, sufficient for reading, writing, speaking, and listening at the college and career readiness level; demonstrate independence in gathering vocabulary knowledge when considering a word or phrase important to comprehension or expression.**

Explanation

In your high school career, you have learned many **academic** and **domain-specific** vocabulary words and phrases.

- **Academic words** include words that you use every day at school to solve problems, analyze a text, express your ideas, and so on.

  Examples include *infer, evaluate, classify, summarize,* and *predict.*

- **Domain-specific words** are words that are specific to a course of study. In a science course, examples include *invertebrate, stimulus,* and *oxidation.* In a social studies course, examples include *capitalism, society,* and *totalitarian.*

Learning the meanings of academic and domain-specific words and using them frequently will help you to complete school assignments effectively and express yourself clearly.

Examples

In many of your courses, you are asked to complete tasks based on specific academic words and phrases. On many tests, you are asked to write essays that fulfill directions containing academic words and phrases. Here are examples:

Defend your ***opinion*** of. . .	***Evaluate*** the ***argument*** that . . .
Assess the ***validity*** of . . .	***Describe*** the ***challenge*** that . . .
Summarize the causes of . . .	***Classify*** and ***differentiate*** between . . .

In a literature course, you learn and use many domain-specific words and phrases, as shown below. Make an effort to learn the domain-specific words in each of your courses.

archetype	*symbol*	*conceit*	*oratory*
rhetorical device	*heroic couplet*	*author's purpose*	*classical mythology*

Name _____ Date _____ Assignment _____

Apply the Standard

A. Match each domain-specific word or phrase with its definition. Write the letter of the correct definition on the line provided.

.... **1.** archetype   **a.** extended metaphor

.... **2.** rhetorical device   **b.** formal public speaking

.... **3.** symbol   **c.** technique used to emphasize ideas

.... **4.** couplet   **d.** pair of rhyming lines

.... **5.** conceit   **e.** pattern or symbol that repeats across cultures

.... **6.** author's purpose   **f.** person or thing that represents something else

.... **7.** oratory   **g.** stories of gods and heroes from ancient times

.... **8.** classical mythology **h.** reason that a writer has for writing

B. Each statement includes one or more academic words or phrases. Circle the letter of the phrase that completes each statement.

1. When you **classify** concepts, you ___.

    a. tell why they are important   **c.** provide support for them

    b. sort them into groups   **d.** explain them

2. When you **summarize** a story, you ___.

    a. compare its characters   **c.** briefly tell the main events

    b. describe the setting   **d.** explain the theme

3. When you **evaluate** an **argument,** you ___.

    a. decide how persuasive it is   **c.** synthesize the pros and cons

    b. summarize its main points   **d.** tell whether you agree with it

4. When you **defend** your **opinion,** you ___.

    a. offer a compromise   **c.** fight for your right to be heard

    b. refuse to listen to alternatives   **d.** support a belief with reasons and facts

For use with Language 6

Performance Tasks

Name _____ Date _____ Assignment _____

Performance Task 1A

Literature 1 Cite strong and thorough textual evidence to support analysis of what the text says explicitly as well as inferences drawn from the text, including determining where the text leaves matters uncertain.*

Task: Support Analysis of a Text

Write an essay in which you cite textual evidence to support your analysis of a literary text. In addition to analyzing what the text says explicitly, provide strong and thorough textual support for any inferences you make. Be sure to identify ambiguous passages—places where the text leaves matters uncertain—and provide textual evidence to support any conclusions you draw about them.

Tips for Success

Produce an analysis of a literary selection you have read. In your analysis, include these elements:

✓ a brief, objective summary of the work, including an identification of its theme

✓ a thesis statement that clearly and concisely conveys the main idea of your analysis

✓ evidence from the text that supports your interpretation and any inferences you make

✓ evidence from the text that supports conclusions you draw from ambiguous passages

✓ a formal style and objective tone appropriate for your audience and the genre

Rubric for Self-Assessment

Criteria for Success	not very					very
How well have you clearly and concisely summarized the work and stated its theme?	1	2	3	4	5	6
How well does the thesis state the main idea of your analysis?	1	2	3	4	5	6
To what extent have you provided an in-depth analysis of the text?	1	2	3	4	5	6
How well have you integrated relevant quotes, facts, or examples from the text to support your interpretation, inferences, and conclusions?	1	2	3	4	5	6
To what extent have you used a formal style and appropriate tone for your audience?	1	2	3	4	5	6

* Other standards covered include: Writing 2a, Writing 2b, Writing 2e, Writing 4, Writing 9, Speaking 4, Speaking 6, Language 3, Language 6

For use with Literature 1

Name _____ Date _____ Assignment _____

Performance Task 1B

> **Speaking and Listening 1** Initiate and participate effectively in a range of collaborative discussions (one-on-one, in groups, and teacher-led) with diverse partners on grade 11–12 topics, texts, and issues, building on others' ideas and expressing your own clearly and persuasively.

Task: Discuss the Responses to a Text

Participate in a group discussion in which you present an analysis of a literary text and respond thoughtfully to others' viewpoints. Build on the ideas of others to deepen the discussion.

Tips for Success

Participate in a discussion about an analysis of a literary text. As part of your participation, follow these tips for success:

✓ read or re-read the literary text and take notes on your interpretation

✓ with the group, develop discussion guidelines that ensure equal and full participation for each person

✓ prepare questions that will evoke further discussion from participants and propel the discussion forward

✓ formulate clear and full responses to questions asked by other group members

✓ find passages from the text that support the different points of view presented in the responses

✓ summarize the group's responses to the text

Rubric for Self-Assessment

Criteria for Discussion	not very					very
To what extent did you prepare for the discussion?	1	2	3	4	5	6
How effectively did the group establish guidelines for the discussion?	1	2	3	4	5	6
To what extent were the guidelines sufficient to ensure that everyone could participate fully and equally?	1	2	3	4	5	6
How successful were you at posing thoughtful questions that helped explore the points of view presented?	1	2	3	4	5	6
How effectively did you build on the responses of others?	1	2	3	4	5	6
How well did the discussion summarize the main perspectives of participants?	1	2	3	4	5	6

For use with Literature 1

Name _____ Date _____ Assignment _____

Performance Task 2A

> **Literature 2** Determine two or more themes or central ideas of a text and analyze their development over the course of the text, including how they interact and build on one another to produce a complex account; provide an objective summary of the text.*

Task: Analyze Themes

Write a literary analysis in which you identify and analyze two or more themes. Provide an objective summary of the text, and identify how the themes interact to produce a complex story.

Tips for Success

Develop a literary analysis of a selection in which you focus on theme. Include these elements:

✓ a brief and objective summary of the work

✓ a thesis statement that reveals your conclusion about the work's themes

✓ an analysis of how the themes interact

✓ evidence from the text that supports your interpretation of the themes

✓ a discussion of how the author integrates theme, style, and symbolism to produce a complex story

✓ a formal style and objective tone appropriate for your audience and the genre

Rubric for Self-Assessment

Criteria for Success	not very					very
How concise and objective is your summary of the work?	1	2	3	4	5	6
How clearly have you presented your thesis statement?	1	2	3	4	5	6
How effectively have you explained the way the themes relate to or interact with each other?	1	2	3	4	5	6
To what extent have you discussed the effect of this interaction on the overall impact of the work?	1	2	3	4	5	6
How effectively have you supported your analysis with strong and thorough textual support?	1	2	3	4	5	6
To what extent have you used a formal style and appropriate tone for your audience?	1	2	3	4	5	6

* Other standards covered include Writing 1, 1d, 1e, 2, 2b, 2c, 2f, 4, 9; Speaking 1a, 1b, 1c, 3, 4

For use with Literature 2

Name _____ Date _____ Assignment _____

Performance Task 2B

Speaking and Listening 1d Respond thoughtfully to diverse perspectives; synthesize comments, claims, and evidence made on all sides of an issue; resolve contradictions when possible; and determine what additional information or research is required to deepen the investigation or complete the task.

Task: Discuss the Themes in a Literary Work

With one or more partners who have analyzed the themes of a literary text, participate in a discussion to compare and contrast your interpretations of the themes and how the themes' interrelationship produces a complex work.

Tips for Success

Participate in a discussion about the themes of a literary text. Follow these tips for success:

- ✓ read or re-read the literary text and take notes to use in your discussion
- ✓ listen attentively to the points made by others and ask questions to deepen understanding
- ✓ analyze similarities and differences in the interpretations of group members
- ✓ identify further research to deepen understanding of the themes
- ✓ synthesize and evaluate conclusions reached by group members

Rubric for Self-Assessment

Criteria for Discussion	not very					very
To what extent did you come to the discussion prepared to discuss the themes of the literary work?	1	2	3	4	5	6
How attentively did you listen to points made by others?	1	2	3	4	5	6
To what extent did you ask probing questions that deepened understanding?	1	2	3	4	5	6
How successfully did you explore the similarities and differences in the interpretations of themes?	1	2	3	4	5	6
To what extent did you and others identify issues that were unclear and could be clarified by further research?	1	2	3	4	5	6
How well did your group synthesize and evaluate comments, claims, and evidence presented by individual members?	1	2	3	4	5	6

For use with Literature 2

Name _____ Date _____ Assignment _____

Performance Task 3A

> **Literature 3   Analyze the impact of the author's choices regarding how to develop and relate elements of a story or drama (e.g., where a story is set, how the action is ordered, how the characters are introduced and developed).**

Task: Analyze an Author's Choices

Write an analysis of a literary text in which you focus on the contribution of the author's choices, such as choice of setting, sequence of action, and methods of characterization.

Tips for Success

Produce an analysis of a literary selection you have read. In your analysis, include these elements:

- ✓ a brief, objective summary of the work

- ✓ an analysis of a particular setting choice and how that setting influences the work

- ✓ an analysis of how the introduction and development of characters affect the work

- ✓ an analysis of how the sequence of action affects the pacing or mood of the work

- ✓ a formal style and objective tone appropriate for your audience and the genre

Rubric for Self-Assessment

Criteria for Success	not very					very
How effectively have you summarized the work?	1	2	3	4	5	6
To what extent have you explained how the setting influences other elements of the work, such as the action and characters?	1	2	3	4	5	6
How effectively have you analyzed why the author chose to introduce characters in a particular sequence and the extent to which the characters were developed?	1	2	3	4	5	6
How well have you explained the effects of the sequence of action on the pacing and mood of the work?	1	2	3	4	5	6
How well have you supported your analysis with evidence from the text?	1	2	3	4	5	6
To what extent have you used a formal style and appropriate tone for your audience?	1	2	3	4	5	6

* Other standards covered include Writing 1, 1a, 1b, 1d, 1e, 2, 2b, 2e, 4, 9; Speaking 1a, 1b, 3, 4, 6

Name _____ Date _____ Assignment _____

Performance Task 3B

> **Speaking and Listening 1c Propel conversations by posing and responding to questions that probe reasoning and evidence; ensure a hearing for a full range of positions on a topic or issue; clarify, verify, or challenge ideas and conclusions; and promote divergent and creative perspectives.**

Task: Discuss the Analysis of Author's Choices

Participate in a group discussion in which you explain your analysis of a literary text and use probing questions to clarify, verify, or challenge the ideas and conclusions of other group members. Support your own conclusions by citing evidence from the text.

Tips for Success

Participate in a discussion in which you analyze a literary text. Follow these tips for success:

✓ prepare by reading or re-reading the literary text and taking notes

✓ develop guidelines with the group to ensure a hearing for a full range of divergent and creative perspectives

✓ prepare questions that probe reasoning and respectfully challenge speakers

✓ provide thoughtful and complete responses to questions

✓ listen actively to others, using nonverbal cues to convey your attention

Rubric for Self-Assessment

Criteria for Discussion	not very					very
To what extent did you come to the discussion prepared to discuss the work and engage in a thoughtful analysis?	1	2	3	4	5	6
How effectively did the group establish guidelines to ensure that everyone had an opportunity to fully explain their ideas?	1	2	3	4	5	6
To what extent did you and others ask thoughtful questions that probed the reasoning of the speaker?	1	2	3	4	5	6
To what extent did you challenge the speaker to clarify, verify, or defend conclusions?	1	2	3	4	5	6
How effectively did you respond to questions?	1	2	3	4	5	6
To what extent were you open to consideration of divergent and creative perspectives?	1	2	3	4	5	6
How effectively did you convey attention to the speaker?	1	2	3	4	5	6

For use with Literature 3

Name _____ Date _____ Assignment _____

Performance Task 4A

> **Literature 4** Determine the meaning of words and phrases as they are used in the text, including figurative and connotative meanings; analyze the impact of specific word choices on meaning and tone, including words with multiple meanings or language that is particularly fresh, engaging, or beautiful.*

Task: Analyze Word Choice

Write an essay in which you examine the influence of the author's word choice on the meaning and tone of the work. Support your thesis with evidence from the text.

Tips for Success

Produce an essay about a literary selection you have read. In your essay, include these elements:

✓ a brief, objective summary of the work

✓ an explanation of how words and phrases with denotations and connotations influenced the work

✓ analysis of specific word choices that contributed to the meaning and tone

✓ an analysis of how figurative language/literary devices contributed to the meaning and tone of the work

✓ a formal style and objective tone appropriate for your audience and the genre

Rubric for Self-Assessment

Criteria for Success	not very					very
To what extent does your summary provide the reader with the information needed to understand your essay?	1	2	3	4	5	6
How effectively have you focused on the denotations and connotations of particular words and phrases?	1	2	3	4	5	6
How effectively have you analyzed the influence of specific word choices on the meaning and tone of the work?	1	2	3	4	5	6
How effectively have you analyzed the influence of figurative language/literary devices on the meaning and tone of the work?	1	2	3	4	5	6
To what extent have you used a formal style and appropriate tone for your audience?	1	2	3	4	5	6

* Other standards covered include Writing 1, 1c, 1d, 2, 2b, 2c, 2d, 4, 5, 9; Speaking 1d, 4, 6

For use with Literature 4

Name _____ Date _____ Assignment _____

Performance Task 4B

Speaking and Listening 3 Evaluate a speaker's point of view, reasoning, and use of evidence and rhetoric, assessing the stance, premises, links among ideas, word choice, points of emphasis, and tone used.

Task: Evaluate a Speaker's Presentation

In small groups, take turns sharing your reflections on the word choices made by the author in a literary work. Focus on your own use of reasoning, evidence, word choice, and tone as you present your reflection. When listening to others present, evaluate the speaker's point of view, reasoning, and use of evidence and rhetoric.

Tips for Success

Participate in a discussion about an author's word choices in a literary text. As part of your participation, follow these tips for success:

✓ prepare by reading and reflecting on the literary text

✓ identify the point of view and major premises put forth by the speaker

✓ evaluate the extent to which the speaker supported ideas through reasoning and evidence

✓ evaluate the extent to which the speaker's word choice, organization, emphasis, and tone supported his or her ideas

✓ offer respectful and constructive criticism

Rubric for Self-Assessment

Criteria for Discussion	not very					very
How well prepared were you to discuss the literary work?	1	2	3	4	5	6
How effectively did you identify the speaker's point of view?	1	2	3	4	5	6
How well did you identify the speaker's main premises?	1	2	3	4	5	6
How objectively did you listen for reasoning and evidence as you evaluated the speaker's presentation?	1	2	3	4	5	6
To what extent did you take into account the effect of word choice, emphasis, and tone as you evaluated the presentation?	1	2	3	4	5	6
To what extent did you offer respectful, constructive criticism to the speaker?	1	2	3	4	5	6

For use with Literature 4

Name _____ Date _____ Assignment _____

Performance Task 5A

Literature 5 Analyze how an author's choices concerning how to structure specific parts of a text (e.g., the choice of where to begin or end a story, the choice to provide a comedic or tragic resolution) contribute to its overall structure and meaning as well as its aesthetic impact.*

Task: Analyze Structure

Write an essay on a work of fiction in which you examine the author's choices concerning how to structure and organize the work and how these choices contribute to the overall meaning and aesthetic impact of the work. Support your thesis with evidence from the text.

Tips for Success

Produce an essay about a work of fiction you have read. In your essay, include these elements:

✓ a brief, objective summary of the work

✓ a clear thesis statement that sums up your conclusions

✓ a discussion of the work's structure or pattern of organization

✓ an analysis of ways in which the author creates mood and tone

✓ a reflection on how the author's choices influence the overall meaning of the work, as well as its aesthetic impact

✓ a formal style and objective tone appropriate for your audience and the genre

Rubric for Self-Assessment

Criteria for Success	not very					very
To what extent does your summary help readers to understand your thesis and conclusions?	1	2	3	4	5	6
How effective is your analysis of the work's structure or pattern of organization?	1	2	3	4	5	6
How well have you analyzed the author's development of mood and tone?	1	2	3	4	5	6
How effectively have you reflected on the way the author's choices influence the meaning and aesthetic impact of the work?	1	2	3	4	5	6
To what extent have you used a formal style and appropriate tone for your audience?	1	2	3	4	5	6

* Other standards covered include Writing 1, 1a, 1b, 1c, 1d, 2, 2b, 2c, 2d, 9; Speaking 1d, 6

For use with Literature 5

Name _____ Date _____ Assignment _____

Performance Task 5B

> **Speaking and Listening 4** Present information, findings, and supporting evidence, conveying a clear and distinct perspective, such that listeners can follow the line of reasoning, alternative or opposing perspectives are addressed, and the organization, development, substance, and style are appropriate to purpose, audience, and a range of formal and informal tasks.

Task: Discuss Author's Choice of Structure

Present your essay on an author's choice of structure to a group of your peers. During your presentation, clearly convey and support your perspective, while comparing your ideas with opposing or alternative perspectives.

Tips for Success

Present your reflection about an author's choice of structure in a literary text. As part of your presentation, follow these tips for success:

- ✓ prepare by reading and taking notes on the literary text

- ✓ present your reflection in a clear and organized manner

- ✓ make effective use of reasoning, evidence, word choice, and tone

- ✓ explain alternative or opposing perspectives objectively, while arguing for your own interpretation

- ✓ make use of a tone and language that suit your purpose and audience

Rubric for Self-Assessment

Criteria for Discussion	not very					very
How well prepared were you to present your analysis of the literary work?	1	2	3	4	5	6
How clear and organized was your presentation?	1	2	3	4	5	6
To what extent did your presentation engage your audience and keep them interested?	1	2	3	4	5	6
How effectively did you use reasoning, evidence, word choice, and tone to persuade your audience?	1	2	3	4	5	6
How objectively did you present alternative or opposing perspectives?	1	2	3	4	5	6
How effectively did you counter opposing perspectives with evidence supporting your own conclusions?	1	2	3	4	5	6
How successfully did you use a tone and language appropriate to your purpose and audience?	1	2	3	4	5	6

For use with Literature 5

Name _____ Date _____ Assignment _____

Performance Task 6A

> **Literature 6** Analyze a case in which grasping point of view requires distinguishing what is directly stated in a text from what is really meant (e.g., satire, sarcasm, irony, or understatement).*

Task: Analyze a Text and Its Point of View

Write an analysis of a literary text in which you identify and discuss the author's use of literal and figurative meaning, as well as other literary devices, such as satire, sarcasm, and irony. Use your analysis to develop a thesis about the work's point of view. Provide textual evidence to support any conclusions you draw.

Tips for Success

Produce an analysis of a literary selection you have read. In your analysis, include these elements:

✓ a brief summary of the work to help the reader understand your analysis

✓ a thesis statement that describes the author's point of view

✓ appropriate examples from the text that support your thesis and any inferences you make

✓ appropriate examples from the text that support your conclusions about how the author's use of literary devices reveals point of view

✓ a clear and coherent analysis that leads to a strong and compelling conclusion

✓ a formal style and objective tone appropriate for your audience and the genre

Rubric for Self-Assessment

Criteria for Success	not very				very	
How effective is your summary of the work?	1	2	3	4	5	6
How accurately does your thesis statement describe the author's point of view?	1	2	3	4	5	6
To what extent have you provided examples from the work to support your thesis?	1	2	3	4	5	6
How effectively have you analyzed the relationship between the author's use of literary devices and the author's point of view?	1	2	3	4	5	6
How successfully have you concluded your analysis?	1	2	3	4	5	6
To what extent have you used a formal style and appropriate tone for your audience?	1	2	3	4	5	6

* Other standards covered include: Writing 1c, Writing 1d, Writing 1e, Writing 2b, Writing 2c, Writing 2f, Writing 4, Writing 9, Speaking 2, Speaking 4, Language 3, Language 4, Language 5

Name _____ Date _____ Assignment _____

Performance Task 6B

Speaking and Listening 6 Adapt speech to a variety of contexts and tasks, demonstrating a command of formal English when indicated or appropriate.

Task: Present an Analysis

Present to the class your analysis of the devices used in a literary text. Incorporate into your presentation readings of sections of the text that support your interpretation and conclusions. Allow time for the class to comment and ask questions.

Tips for Success

Present your analysis of a literary text. Follow these tips for success:

- ✓ prepare by revising your written analysis, adapting it for an oral presentation while maintaining a formal tone

- ✓ incorporate dramatic readings of supporting sections of text at appropriate points in your analysis

- ✓ assemble the analysis and readings into a coherent presentation

- ✓ rehearse your presentation, adapting your tone to suit your tasks

- ✓ demonstrate a command of English usage by avoiding incorrect tenses, and temporizing slang such as *you know* and *I mean*.

Rubric for Self-Assessment

Criteria for Discussion	not very					very
How clearly organized and professional was your presentation?	1	2	3	4	5	6
How effectively did you incorporate your analysis of the text with dramatic readings from the text?	1	2	3	4	5	6
How effectively did you adapt your presentation to the goals of the presentation?	1	2	3	4	5	6
To what extent did you demonstrate a command of correct English usage?	1	2	3	4	5	6
To what extent did you avoid slang and temporizing words?	1	2	3	4	5	6

Performance Task 7A

> **Literature 7** Analyze multiple interpretations of a story, drama, or poem (e.g., recorded or live production of a play or recorded novel or poetry), evaluating how each version interprets the source text. (Include at least one play by Shakespeare and one play by an American dramatist.).*

Task: Analyze Multiple Interpretations of a Drama

Write an evaluative analysis of two or more interpretations of a classic American drama, such as *Our Town, Death of a Salesman*, or *The Glass Menagerie*. Use recorded or live productions of the play and/or cinema or recorded versions with different actors in the leading roles. In your analysis, evaluate how effectively each version interprets the original play. Include analyses of whether any changes from the original were appropriate and effective.

Tips for Success

Read the original version of the play and then compare and contrast two or more different versions in a written, critical response. In your analysis, include the following:

- ✓ a synopsis of the play
- ✓ research on how literary scholars interpret the play
- ✓ an insightful account of each of the versions you watched or listened to
- ✓ an analysis of the relevance of changes in various versions
- ✓ a commentary on the strengths and weakness of each version
- ✓ a formal style and objective tone appropriate for your audience and the genre

Rubric for Self-Assessment

Criteria for Success	not very				very	
How well does your synopsis summarize the work?	1	2	3	4	5	6
How extensively have you researched analyses of the play by recognized literary scholars?	1	2	3	4	5	6
How effectively have you explained each of the versions you watched or listened to?	1	2	3	4	5	6
How effectively have you analyzed the changes between the original play and the selected versions?	1	2	3	4	5	6
How thoroughly have you analyzed the strengths and weaknesses of each version?	1	2	3	4	5	6
To what extent have you used a formal style and appropriate tone for your audience?	1	2	3	4	5	6

* Other standards covered include: Writing 1a, Writing 1b, Writing 1d, Writing 1e, Writing 2b, Writing 2c, Writing 2d, Writing 2f, Writing 4, Writing 8, Writing 9, Speaking 4, Speaking 5, Speaking 6, Language 3, Language 4, Language 5

Name _____ Date _____ Assignment _____

Performance Task 7B

Speaking and Listening 2 Integrate multiple sources of information presented in diverse formats and media (e.g., visually, quantitatively, orally) in order to make informed decisions and solve problems, evaluating the credibility and accuracy of each source and noting any discrepancies among the data.

Task: Present an Analysis Using Multiple Media

Present your analysis of various versions of a classic American drama, evaluating how well the versions adhered to the original. During your presentation, include video and audio clips from the selected versions combined with dramatic readings of the original play to support your evaluation.

Tips for Success

Prepare a multimedia presentation of your analysis. Follow these tips for success:

✓ perform an in-depth study of the original play as well as the selected versions

✓ identify sections of the play and of the selected versions that demonstrate their similarities and differences

✓ combine audio and video clips with oral interpretation into a multimedia presentation that supports your evaluation

✓ practice your presentation so that it is smooth, seamless, and effective

✓ prepare discussion questions to extend your analysis with your audience

Rubric for Self-Assessment

Criteria for Discussion	not very				very	
How well did you study the play and the chosen versions?	1	2	3	4	5	6
How successfully did you choose sections of the play and other versions to demonstrate their similarities and differences?	1	2	3	4	5	6
How effectively did you incorporate audio and video clips with oral interpretation in your evaluation?	1	2	3	4	5	6
How smooth, seamless, and effective was your presentation?	1	2	3	4	5	6
How effectively did you prepare questions to encourage your audience to extend the discussion?	1	2	3	4	5	6

For use with Speaking and Listening 2

Name _____ Date _____ Assignment _____

Performance Task 8A

> **Literature 9** Demonstrate knowledge of eighteenth-, nineteenth- and early twentieth-century foundational works of American literature, including how two or more texts from the same period treat similar themes or topics.*

Task: Write a Comparative Essay

Write an essay that compares and contrasts the way Nathaniel Hawthorne, Louisa May Alcott, and Ralph Waldo Emerson treat the topic of women in society in their literary works.

Tips for Success

Read works by all three authors and then write a comparative essay on the similarities and differences in their treatment of the topic of women in society. In your analysis, include the following:

✓ a thesis statement about the points of view of the three authors

✓ an analysis of the similarities between the works related to the topic

✓ an analysis of the differences between the works related to the topic

✓ an analysis of the views the authors support or oppose in their writing

✓ an effective organizational pattern

✓ a formal style and objective tone appropriate for your audience and the genre

Rubric for Self-Assessment

Criteria for Success	not very					very
How clear is your thesis statement?	1	2	3	4	5	6
How effective is your analysis of similarities in the works?	1	2	3	4	5	6
How effective is your analysis of differences in the works?	1	2	3	4	5	6
How well have you identified the fundamental point of view expressed by each author?	1	2	3	4	5	6
To what extent is your essay logically and effectively organized?	1	2	3	4	5	6
To what extent have you used a formal style and appropriate tone for your audience?	1	2	3	4	5	6

* Other standards covered include: Writing 1a, Writing 1c, Writing 1d, Writing 1e, Writing 2b, Writing 2c, Writing 2d, Writing 2f, Writing 4, Writing 9, Speaking 2, Speaking 4, Speaking 6, Language 2, Language 3, Language 4, Language 5, Language 6

For use with Literature 9

Name _____ Date _____ Assignment _____

Performance Task 8B

> **Speaking and Listening 5**   Make strategic use of digital media (e.g., textual, graphical, audio, visual, and interactive elements) in presentations to enhance understanding of findings, reasoning, and evidence and to add interest.

Task: Present an Analysis Using Digital Media

Convert your comparative analysis into a slide show presentation. Use graphic organizers and other visual techniques to compare the similarities and differences in the works and to summarize your analysis of the authors' treatment of the topic of women in society.

Tips for Success

Prepare a visual presentation of your analysis of the work of several authors. Follow these tips for success:

✓ select the most relevant and important points in your analysis

✓ prepare a slide on each point, while summarizing the content

✓ vary the look of your slides, including animation or other effects, where appropriate

✓ assemble your slides into a coherent presentation

✓ rehearse your presentation, seamlessly integrating commentary with the slides

Rubric for Self-Assessment

Criteria for Discussion	not very					very
How well did you identify significant points in your presentation?	1	2	3	4	5	6
How effectively did you prepare concise slides that summarized each point?	1	2	3	4	5	6
How effectively did you make your presentation visually appealing by varying the look of your slides?	1	2	3	4	5	6
How coherent was your presentation?	1	2	3	4	5	6
To what extent did you successfully integrate commentary with the content of the slides?	1	2	3	4	5	6

Name _____ Date _____ Assignment _____

Performance Task 9A

Literature 10 By the end of grade 11, read and comprehend literature, including stories, dramas, and poems, in the grades 11–CCR text complexity band proficiently, with scaffolding as needed at the high end of the range.*

Task: Write in the Style of an Author

Select a favorite author of stories, drama, or poetry. Demonstrate your comprehension of the author's unique style by writing a passage, scene, or poem in the style of the author, but on a different theme. Then, share your writing with the class.

Tips for Success

Write in the style of one of your favorite authors. Follow these tips for success:

✓ read several works by your chosen author and take notes on his or her style and the themes he or she explores

✓ in your writing, explore themes like those explored by the author

✓ in your writing create a mood and tone similar to those in works by the author

✓ in your writing use structures and syntax that reflect your author's style

✓ strive to evoke an emotional response in the reader similar to that evoked by your author

Rubric for Self-Assessment

Criteria for Success	not very					very
How closely have you analyzed the works of your chosen author?	1	2	3	4	5	6
How effectively have you explored themes like those explored by the author?	1	2	3	4	5	6
How well have you emulated the author's mood and tone?	1	2	3	4	5	6
How closely have you mirrored the author's style?	1	2	3	4	5	6
To what extent have you evoked an emotional response similar to those evoked by the author?	1	2	3	4	5	6

* Other standards covered include: Writing 3a, Writing 3b, Writing 3c, Writing 3d, Writing 3e, Writing 5, Writing 6, Speaking 1b, Speaking 1c, Speaking 1d, Speaking 3, Speaking 6, Language 1, Language 2, Language 3, Language 5

For use with Literature 10

Name _____ Date _____ Assignment _____

Performance Task 9B

> **Speaking and Listening 1a** Come to discussions prepared, having read and
> researched material under study; explicitly draw on that preparation by referring
> to evidence from texts and other research on the topic or issue to stimulate a
> thoughtful, well-reasoned exchange of ideas.

Task: Engage in a Discussion of an Author

Form a group with other students who have written in the style of a particular author. Prepare for a
discussion of each student's writing by reading a variety of selections from the author, making note
of particularly characteristic use of literary devices and other features of style. After each student's
presentation, contribute to a thoughtful, well-reasoned exchange of ideas.

Tips for Success

Prepare for a discussion of the style and point of view of a particular author. Follow these tips for
success:

✓ read selections by the author that clearly convey the author's unique style

✓ make note of word usage and literary devices that exemplify the author

✓ summarize the elements that make the author unique and memorable

✓ listen attentively to the passages, scenes, or poems written by others in the
group

✓ analyze the extent to which each piece of writing has successfully imitated
the author

✓ contribute to a thoughtful and courteous exchange of ideas

Rubric for Self-Assessment

Criteria for Discussion	not very					very
How thoroughly did you familiarize yourself with the author's unique style?	1	2	3	4	5	6
How thoroughly did you make note of textual examples of the author's style?	1	2	3	4	5	6
How well did you summarize the elements that make the author unique?	1	2	3	4	5	6
How attentively did you listen to the speaker?	1	2	3	4	5	6
How well did you evaluate the extent to which the speaker imitated the author?	1	2	3	4	5	6
How effectively did you contribute to a thoughtful and courteous exchange of ideas?	1	2	3	4	5	6

For use with Speaking and Listening 1a

Name _____ Date _____ Assignment _____

Performance Task 10A

> **Informational Text 1** Cite strong and thorough textual evidence to support analysis of what the text says explicitly as well as inferences drawn from the text, including determining where the text leaves matters uncertain.*

Task: Identify and Analyze Ambiguities in a Text

Write an essay about a work of informational nonfiction in which you cite textual evidence to support your analysis of explicit details in the text as well as passages that are left deliberately uncertain. Provide strong and thorough textual support for your analysis.

Tips for Success

Produce a response to an informational text you have read. In your essay, include these elements:

✓ a brief, objective summary of the text

✓ a thesis statement that clearly and concisely describes your conclusions

✓ evidence from the text that identifies both explicit details and ambiguities

✓ inferences and conclusions about the work

✓ evidence from the text that supports your conclusions, interpretation, and any inferences you make

✓ a formal style and objective tone appropriate for your audience and the genre

Rubric for Self-Assessment

Criteria for Success	not very					very
How clearly and objectively have you summarized the text?	1	2	3	4	5	6
How clearly does your thesis reveal your conclusions?	1	2	3	4	5	6
To what extent have you provided evidence from the text that identifies explicit details and ambiguities?	1	2	3	4	5	6
To what extent have you made inferences and drawn conclusions about the text?	1	2	3	4	5	6
To what extent have you provided textual evidence that supports your conclusions, interpretation, and inferences?	1	2	3	4	5	6
To what extent have you used a formal style and appropriate tone for your audience?	1	2	3	4	5	6

* Other standards covered include: Writing 1c, Writing 1d, Writing 1e, Writing 2b, Writing 2c, Writing 2d, Writing 2e, Writing 4, Writing 9, Speaking 4, Speaking 6, Language 3, Language 6

For use with Informational Text 1

Name _____ Date _____ Assignment _____

Performance Task 10B

> **Speaking and Listening 1** Initiate and participate effectively in a range of collaborative discussions (one-on-one, in groups, and teacher-led) with diverse partners on grade 11–12 topics, texts, and issues, building on others' ideas and expressing their own clearly and persuasively.

Task: Discuss the Responses to a Text

Participate in a group discussion in which you explain your analysis of an informational text and respond thoughtfully to the points of view of others. Build on the ideas of others in your discussion.

Tips for Success

Participate in a discussion in which you analyze a work of informational text. Follow these tips for success:

- ✓ prepare by reading or re-reading the work and identifying explicit details and ambiguities
- ✓ with group members, develop discussion guidelines that ensure equal and full participation for each person
- ✓ prepare questions that will evoke further discussion from participants and propel the discussion forward
- ✓ craft effective and convincing responses to questions asked by other group members
- ✓ summarize different points of view presented in the responses
- ✓ pay polite and respectful attention to speakers

Rubric for Self-Assessment

Criteria for Discussion	not very					very
How well had you prepared for the discussion?	1	2	3	4	5	6
How effectively did the group establish guidelines for the discussion?	1	2	3	4	5	6
To what extent were the guidelines sufficient to ensure that everyone participated fully and equally?	1	2	3	4	5	6
To what extent did you ask thoughtful questions that helped explore the points of view presented?	1	2	3	4	5	6
How effectively and convincingly did you respond to questions asked by others?	1	2	3	4	5	6
How well did the discussion summarize the main perspectives of the participants?	1	2	3	4	5	6
To what extent were you polite and respectful as you listened to other speakers?	1	2	3	4	5	6

For use with Speaking and Listening 1

Name _____ Date _____ Assignment _____

Performance Task 11A

Informational Text 2 Determine two or more central ideas of a text and analyze their development over the course of the text, including how they interact and build on one another to provide a complex analysis; provide an objective summary of the text.*

Task: Identify and Analyze Central Ideas

Write an analysis of an informational work of nonfiction in which you use textual support to identify two or more central ideas. Analyze how the ideas are developed through the work, how they interact, and how they build on one another to convey the author's point of view.

Tips for Success

Produce an analysis of an informational text. In your analysis, include these elements:

✓ an objective summary of the work

✓ identification of two or more central ideas from the work

✓ evidence from the text that illustrates the central ideas

✓ description of how the central ideas are developed

✓ analysis of how the central ideas work together to convey the author's point of view

✓ clear and coherent organization and a strong conclusion

✓ language that is formal, precise, and follows the rules of standard English

Rubric for Self-Assessment

Criteria for Success	not very					very
How clearly and objectively have you summarized the work?	1	2	3	4	5	6
How clearly have you identified two or more central ideas?	1	2	3	4	5	6
To what extent have you provided textual evidence to illustrate the central ideas?	1	2	3	4	5	6
To what extent have you described how the central ideas are developed?	1	2	3	4	5	6
How effectively have you analyzed how the central ideas work together to convey the author's point of view?	1	2	3	4	5	6
To what extent does your analysis have a clear and coherent organization and a strong conclusion?	1	2	3	4	5	6
How well have you succeeded in using a formal style and appropriate tone for your audience?	1	2	3	4	5	6

* Other standards covered include: Writing 1a, Writing 1c, Writing 1d, Writing 1e, Writing 2b, Writing 2c, Writing 2e, Writing 2f, Writing 4, Speaking 1b, Speaking 1d, Speaking 3, Speaking 4, Language 1, Language 6

For use with Informational Text 2

Name _____ Date _____ Assignment _____

Performance Task 11B

> **Speaking and Listening 1c** Propel conversations by posing and responding to questions that probe reasoning and evidence; ensure a hearing for a full range of positions on a topic or issue; clarify, verify, or challenge ideas and conclusions; and promote divergent and creative perspectives.

Task: Discuss Divergent Perspectives

Participate in a group discussion with other students who have analyzed the central ideas of the same work. After each student identifies the central ideas, discuss divergent ideas and creative perspectives by posing and responding to questions that probe reasoning and evidence.

Tips for Success

Participate in a discussion about an analysis of an informational text. Follow these tips for success:

- ✓ prepare by planning answers to questions about your analysis
- ✓ with group members, develop discussion guidelines that ensure equal and full participation for each person
- ✓ prepare questions that probe the reasoning of other students
- ✓ develop questions that require group members to clarify, verify, or challenge ideas and conclusions
- ✓ provide effective responses to questions about your conclusions
- ✓ pay polite and respectful attention to speakers

Rubric for Self-Assessment

Criteria for Discussion	not very					very
How thoroughly did you prepare to defend your ideas?	1	2	3	4	5	6
How effectively did the group establish guidelines for the discussion?	1	2	3	4	5	6
To what extent did you ask thoughtful questions that probed the reasoning of other students?	1	2	3	4	5	6
To what extent did you ask questions that required other students to clarify and verify their ideas and conclusions?	1	2	3	4	5	6
How effectively and convincingly did you respond to questions asked by others?	1	2	3	4	5	6
To what extent were you polite and respectful as you listened to other speakers?	1	2	3	4	5	6

For use with Speaking and Listening 1c

Name _____ Date _____ Assignment _____

Performance Task 12A

Informational Text 3   Analyze a complex set of ideas or sequence of events and explain how specific individuals, ideas, or events interact and develop over the course of the text.*

Task: Explain the Ideas or Events in an Informational Text

Write an essay in which you analyze the ideas and events in an informational text. In your essay, show the development and interaction of key ideas and events, along with an explanation of the strategies the author uses to develop them.

Tips for Success

Provide an analysis of an informational text. In your analysis, include these elements:

✓ a clear explanation of the events and ideas in the text and the relationships among them

✓ an explanation of the development of the ideas and events over the course of the work

✓ a description of how the ideas, events, and individuals interact

✓ sufficient information and details to support your explanation

✓ an appropriate tone and formal style that uses standard English

Rubric for Self-Assessment

Criteria for Success	not very				very	
How clearly have you explained the ideas and events in the work?	1	2	3	4	5	6
How well have you described the development of the ideas and events over the course of the work?	1	2	3	4	5	6
How effectively have you explained the interaction between the ideas, events, and individuals over the course of the work?	1	2	3	4	5	6
How well have you described the strategies the author uses to organize and develop the ideas and events in the work?	1	2	3	4	5	6
To what extent have you provided sufficient supporting details for your explanation?	1	2	3	4	5	6
To what extent have you employed an appropriate tone and formal style?	1	2	3	4	5	6

* Other standards covered include: Writing 2a, Writing 4, Writing 5, Writing 9b, Speaking 4, Speaking 6, Language 1, Language 2, Language 3, Language 6

For use with Informational Text 3

Name _____ Date _____ Assignment _____

Performance Task 12B

> **Speaking and Listening 5** Make strategic use of digital media (e.g. textual, graphical, audio, visual, and interactive elements) in presentations to enhance understanding of findings, reasoning, and evidence and to add interest.

Task: Develop a Media Presentation

Create a media presentation in which you show the development and interaction of ideas, events, and individuals in an informational text. Utilize strategic visual, audio, and interactive elements to enhance your audience's understanding of the work, your reasoning, and the evidence that supports your reasoning.

Tips for Success

Create a presentation in which you explain the development of ideas, events, and individuals in a work of nonfiction. In your presentation, include these elements:

✓ a description of the strategy used by the author to develop the ideas in the work

✓ visual, audio, and interactive elements that enhance the audience's understanding of the work, your reasoning, and the details that support your reasoning

✓ the use of gestures, eye contact, and varied tone and volume to maintain audience interest

✓ an appropriate tone and formal style

Rubric for Self-Assessment

Criteria for Discussion	not very					very
How effective was your presentation in explaining the development of the events, ideas, and individuals over the course of the work?	1	2	3	4	5	6
How well did you explain the author's strategy for presenting his or her ideas?	1	2	3	4	5	6
To what extent did you add text, graphics, audio, and multimedia to enhance the audience's understanding?	1	2	3	4	5	6
How effective were your use of eye contact, gestures, and varied tone and volume in maintaining audience interest?	1	2	3	4	5	6
To what extent did you maintain an appropriate tone and formal style in your presentation?	1	2	3	4	5	6

For use with Speaking and Listening 5

Name _____ Date _____ Assignment _____

Performance Task 13A

> **Informational Text 4** Determine the meaning of words and phrases as they are used in a text, including figurative, connotative, and technical meanings; analyze how an author uses and refines the meaning of a key term or terms over the course of a text (e.g., how Madison defines *faction* in Federalist No. 10).*

Task: Analyze the Literal and Figurative Language in a Speech

Write an analysis of a famous speech in which you identify and determine how words and phrases are used in a denotative, connotative, figurative, and/or technical way. In addition, analyze how an author uses and refines the meaning of key terms over the course of the speech.

Tips for Success

Produce a written analysis of a famous speech. In your analysis, include these elements:

- ✓ an analysis of key words or terms in each paragraph
- ✓ an analysis of the effect of figurative language in advancing the author's purpose
- ✓ an analysis of the author's word choices in producing a compelling message
- ✓ description of the extent to which the author's word choices provide new insights on the topic
- ✓ strong textual evidence to support your inferences and conclusions
- ✓ an appropriate tone and formal style that uses standard English

Rubric for Self-Assessment

Criteria for Success	not very					very
How well have you identified the key words or phrases in each paragraph?	1	2	3	4	5	6
How effectively have you analyzed the effect of figurative language in advancing the author's purpose?	1	2	3	4	5	6
To what extent have you analyzed the effectiveness of the author's word choices in producing a compelling message?	1	2	3	4	5	6
How effectively have you commented on the effect of the author's word choices?	1	2	3	4	5	6
To what extent have you cited strong textual evidence to support your inferences and conclusions?	1	2	3	4	5	6
To what extent have you maintained an appropriate tone and a formal style?	1	2	3	4	5	6

* Other standards covered include: Writing 1b , Writing 1c , Writing 1d, Writing 1e, Writing 2b, Writing 2c, Writing 2d, Writing 2f, Writing 4, Speaking 1a, Language 3, Language 4, Language 5, Language 6

For use with Informational Text 4

Name _____ Date _____ Assignment _____

Performance Task 13B

> **Speaking and Listening 3** Evaluate a speaker's point of view, reasoning, and use of evidence and rhetoric, assessing the stance, premises, links among ideas, word choice, points of emphasis, and tone used.

Task: Engage in a Discussion

Participate in a discussion in which you evaluate a speaker's point of view, reasoning, and use of evidence and rhetoric in a speech.

Tips for Success

Prepare an evaluation form and use it as you watch a speech. Follow these tips for success:

✓ with the group, agree on a videotaped speech to view and analyze

✓ list and evaluate the underlying assumptions in the speech

✓ list and evaluate the speaker's word choice, particularly emotionally-charged words and their effect

✓ list and evaluate the speaker's use of evidence and rhetoric in explaining key points

✓ list and evaluate the speaker's gestures, body language, and voice qualities

✓ list and evaluate the speaker's tone and attitude toward the subject and the audience

✓ summarize the overall effectiveness of the speaker's presentation

Rubric for Self-Assessment

Criteria for Discussion	not very					very
How thoroughly did you identify and evaluate the speaker's underlying assumptions?	1	2	3	4	5	6
How well did you list and evaluate word choice, particularly emotionally-charged words and their effect?	1	2	3	4	5	6
To what extent did you list and evaluate the speaker's use of evidence and rhetoric in explaining key points?	1	2	3	4	5	6
To what extent did you evaluate how the speaker's gestures, body language, and voice quality influenced the presentation?	1	2	3	4	5	6
How well did you evaluate the speaker's tone and attitude?	1	2	3	4	5	6
How well did you summarize the overall effectiveness of the speaker's presentation?	1	2	3	4	5	6

For use with Speaking and Listening 3

Name _____ Date _____ Assignment _____

Performance Task 14A

> **Informational Text 5** Analyze and evaluate the effectiveness of the structure an author uses in his or her exposition or argument, including whether the structure makes points clear, convincing, and engaging.*

Task: Compare the Effectiveness of Organizational Structure

Write an analysis in which you compare and contrast the effectiveness of the organizational structure of two informational texts. Make note of whether or not the structure of the writing has produced clear, convincing, or engaging texts.

Tips for Success

Produce a written comparison of the effectiveness of the organizational structure of two informational texts. In your comparison, include these elements:

- ✓ a discussion of the organizational structure of each work
- ✓ textual evidence to support your identification of the organization in each work
- ✓ an analysis of the strengths and weaknesses of each organizational structure
- ✓ an analysis of the effectiveness of each text's organizational structure
- ✓ a strong closing statement summarizing your conclusions
- ✓ an appropriate tone and formal style that uses standard English

Rubric for Self-Assessment

Criteria for Success	not very					very
How effectively have you identified the organizational structure of each work?	1	2	3	4	5	6
To what extent have you provided textual evidence to support your identification of the organizational structure?	1	2	3	4	5	6
How effectively have you analyzed the strengths and weakness of each text's organizational structure?	1	2	3	4	5	6
How thoroughly have you analyzed the effectiveness of each text's organizational structure?	1	2	3	4	5	6
How effectively does your closing statement summarize your conclusions?	1	2	3	4	5	6
To what extent have you maintained an appropriate tone and a formal style?	1	2	3	4	5	6

* Other standards covered include: Writing 1b , Writing 1d , Writing 1e, Writing 2b, Writing 2c, Writing 2d, Writing 2e, Writing 2f, Writing 4, Speaking 2, Speaking 4, Language 1, Language 3, Language 4a, Language 6

For use with Informational Text 5

Name _____ Date _____ Assignment _____

Performance Task 14B

> **Speaking and Listening 6** Adapt speech to a variety of contexts and tasks, demonstrating a command of formal English when indicated or appropriate.

Task: Give a Formal Oral Analysis of an Informative Text

Give a formal oral presentation of your comparison of the effectiveness of the organizational structure in two informational texts. Incorporate readings from the texts as part of your presentation. Invite questions from the audience at the conclusion of your presentation.

Tips for Success

Present a formal oral presentation of your comparison of organizational structure. Follow these tips for success:

- ✓ prepare by practicing your presentation until it is polished

- ✓ develop an organization that is interesting, appealing, and thought-provoking for your audience

- ✓ incorporate relevant excerpts from the works

- ✓ vary your tone, volume, and pacing to add interest to your presentation

- ✓ use formal English for your presentation; switch to a less formal tone when responding to questions

Rubric for Self-Assessment

Criteria for Discussion	not very				very	
How thoroughly did you prepare for your presentation?	1	2	3	4	5	6
How effectively did you organize your presentation to make it interesting, appealing, and thought-provoking for your audience?	1	2	3	4	5	6
How effectively did you incorporate relevant excerpts from the works that you compared?	1	2	3	4	5	6
How well did you vary your tone, volume, and pacing to add interest to your presentation?	1	2	3	4	5	6
To what extent did you adapt your presentation to suit the needs of your audience?	1	2	3	4	5	6

Name _____ Date _____ Assignment _____

Performance Task 15A

Informational Text 6 Determine an author's point of view or purpose in a text in which the rhetoric is particularly effective, analyzing how style and content contribute to the power, persuasiveness, or beauty of the text.*

Task: Identify and Analyze Author's Purpose or Point of View

Write an analysis of a chapter or section from an informational text in which you identify how the author's style and choice of content contribute to the power and persuasiveness of the text in advancing a particular purpose or point of view.

Tips for Success

Produce an analysis of a chapter or section from an informational text, such as an autobiography or biography you have read. In your analysis, include these elements:

- ✓ a clear, concise summary of the work
- ✓ identification of the author's purpose or point of view
- ✓ analysis of how at least three events in the work relate to the author's purpose
- ✓ examples of how the author expresses point of view through rhetoric or figurative language
- ✓ analysis of how the author's style and content contribute to the power and persuasiveness of the work
- ✓ a clear thesis and a strong conclusion

Rubric for Self-Assessment

Criteria for Success	not very					very
How clearly and concisely have you summarized the work?	1	2	3	4	5	6
How effectively have you identified the author's purpose or point of view?	1	2	3	4	5	6
To what extent have you analyzed the relationship between at least three events in the work and the author's purpose?	1	2	3	4	5	6
To what extent have you provided examples of the author's use of rhetoric or figurative language to express a point of view?	1	2	3	4	5	6
How effectively have you analyzed how the author's style and content contribute to the power and persuasiveness of the work?	1	2	3	4	5	6
To what extent does your analysis have a clear thesis and a strong conclusion?	1	2	3	4	5	6

*Other standards covered include: Writing 1, Writing 1c, Writing 1d, Writing 1e, Writing 2, Writing 2c, Writing 2d, Writing 2e, Writing 2f, Writing 4, Speaking 1a, Speaking 1d, Speaking 6, Language 1, Language 2, Language 3, Language 6

For use with Informational Text 6

Name _____ Date _____ Assignment _____

Performance Task 15B

> **Speaking and Listening 4** Present information, findings, and supporting evidence, conveying a clear and distinct perspective, such that listeners can follow the line of reasoning, alternative or opposing perspectives are addressed, and the organization, development, substance, and style are appropriate to purpose, audience, and a range of formal and informal tasks.

Task: Present a Clear and Distinct Perspective

Present your analysis of an author's point of view or purpose in an informational text, such as an autobiography, biography, or memoir. Your presentation should include your own line of reasoning as well as addressing alternative or opposing perspectives.

Tips for Success

In groups of four or five, take turns giving an oral presentation about an analysis of an informational text, followed by a discussion and questions from group members. As a part of your participation, include these elements:

- ✓ preparation for a smooth, informative, and interesting presentation
- ✓ supporting evidence for your line of reasoning
- ✓ inclusion of alternative or opposing perspectives
- ✓ questions that probe the reasoning of other group members
- ✓ effective responses to questions about your conclusions
- ✓ thoughtful responses to diverse perspectives

Rubric for Self-Assessment

Criteria for Discussion	not very					very
How thoroughly did you prepare a smooth, informative, and interesting presentation?	1	2	3	4	5	6
How effectively did you include evidence to support your line of reasoning?	1	2	3	4	5	6
To what extent did you include alternative perspectives?	1	2	3	4	5	6
To what extent did you ask questions that probed the reasoning of other group members?	1	2	3	4	5	6
How effectively did you respond to questions asked by others?	1	2	3	4	5	6
To what extent did you respond thoughtfully to diverse perspectives?	1	2	3	4	5	6

For use with Speaking and Listening 4

Name _____ Date _____ Assignment _____

Performance Task 16A

> **Informational Text 7** Integrate and evaluate multiple sources of information presented in different media or formats (e.g., visually, quantitatively) as well as in words in order to address a question or solve a problem.*

Task: Solve a Problem Using Multiple Sources of Information

Write a summary that draws on a variety of information sources to answer a complex question, such as "What were the causes and effects of regional population changes in the United States after the Civil War?" Integrate and evaluate information from statistical and governmental sources and historical commentary, as well as a variety of formats, in your summary.

Tips for Success

Write a response to a question that address, for example, the causes and effects of regional population changes in the United States after the Civil War. In your response, synthesize information from various informational texts and sources and include these elements:

- ✓ multiple sources of information in various sources and in different formats
- ✓ comparison and analysis of the types of information each source provides
- ✓ evaluation of the reliability of the information from each source
- ✓ information answering the question your response focuses on using cause-and-effect organization
- ✓ supporting textual evidence from each source
- ✓ convincing conclusion that summarizes the answer to the question

Rubric for Self-Assessment

Criteria for Success	not very very
How effectively have you incorporated multiple sources of information in various formats?	1 2 3 4 5 6
How effectively have you compared and analyze the types of information provided by each source?	1 2 3 4 5 6
To what extent have you analyzed the reliability of the information from each source?	1 2 3 4 5 6
How well do you integrated information from your research into a cause-and-effect organization?	1 2 3 4 5 6
To what extent do you include textual evidence from each source?	1 2 3 4 5 6
How convincing is your conclusion?	1 2 3 4 5 6

*Other standards covered include: Writing 1a, Writing 1b, Writing 1d, Writing 1e, Writing 2b, Writing 2c, Writing 2e, Writing 2f, Writing 4, Writing 6, Writing 7, Writing 8, Writing 9, Speaking 1d, Speaking 2, Speaking 4, Speaking 6, Language 1, Language 2, Language 3, Language 6

For use with Informational Text 7

Name _____ Date _____ Assignment _____

Performance Task 16B

> **Speaking and Listening 5** Make strategic use of digital media (e.g., textual, graphical, audio, visual, and interactive elements) in presentations to enhance understanding of findings, reasoning, and evidence and to add interest.

Task: Create a Presentation Using Digital Media

Present your response to a complex question, such as "What were the causes and effects of regional population growth in the United States after the Civil War?" as a digital multimedia presentation. As part of your presentation, integrate research from a variety of information formats into a well-organized, informative, and interesting presentation using digital media, such as graphics, audio, visual, or interactive elements.

Tips for Success

Prepare a brief presentation in response to a complex question and make use of digital media. As a part of your presentation, include these elements:

- ✓ opening that introduces the question and your thesis in an appealing way
- ✓ integration of some kind of digital elements, such as graphics, animations, slideshows, and text
- ✓ cause-and-effect organization that is easy to follow
- ✓ visual or auditory support from the sources to enhance understanding
- ✓ time for questions and answers after the presentation from others in the group

Rubric for Self-Assessment

Criteria for Discussion	not very					very
How effective was your opening in introducing the question and thesis?	1	2	3	4	5	6
How effectively did you integrate digital elements into your presentation?	1	2	3	4	5	6
How effectively did you produce an easy-to-follow cause-and-effect organization in response to your question?	1	2	3	4	5	6
To what extent did you include visual and/or auditory support from the sources to enhance understanding?	1	2	3	4	5	6
To what extent did you provide an opportunity for questions and answers after the presentation?	1	2	3	4	5	6

Name _____ Date _____ Assignment _____

Performance Task 17A

> **Informational Text 8** Delineate and evaluate the reasoning in seminal U.S. texts, including the application of constitutional principles and use of legal reasoning (e.g., in U.S. Supreme Court majority opinions and dissents) and the premises, purposes, and arguments in works of public advocacy (e.g., *The Federalist*, presidential addresses).*

Task: Analyze and Evaluate the Reasoning in a Speech

Write an analysis of a seminal speech, such as the address to Congress on Women's Suffrage by Carrie Chapman Catt in 1917. In your analysis, identify, analyze, and evaluate the effectiveness of rhetorical elements the speaker uses to persuade listeners.

Tips for Success

Write a brief analysis of a seminal U.S. speech in which you identify, analyze, and evaluate the speaker's rhetoric. In your analysis, include these elements:

- ✓ summary of the speaker's point of view and line of reasoning
- ✓ analysis and evaluation of appeals to reason, emotion, ethics, or authority
- ✓ identification, analysis, and evaluation of the speaker's use of such rhetorical devices as parallelism, rhetorical questions, and anecdotes
- ✓ evaluation of the evidence used to support the speaker's premises, purposes, arguments, and legal reasoning
- ✓ editing and revising to strengthen your analysis

Rubric for Self-Assessment

Criteria for Success	not very					very
How clearly have you identified the speaker's point of view and line of reasoning?	1	2	3	4	5	6
How effectively have you analyzed and evaluated appeals to reason, emotion, ethics, and authority?	1	2	3	4	5	6
To what extent do you identify, analyze, and evaluate the speaker's use of rhetorical devices?	1	2	3	4	5	6
How effectively have you evaluated the evidence used to support the speaker's premises, purposes, arguments, and legal reasoning?	1	2	3	4	5	6
To what extent have you edited and revised your analysis to make it stronger?	1	2	3	4	5	6

*Other standards covered include: Writing 1, Writing 2b, Writing 2c, Writing 2e, Writing 2f, Writing 4, Writing 5, Writing 7, Writing 8, Writing 9, Speaking 1b, Speaking 1c, Speaking 1d, Speaking 3, Speaking 4, Language 1, Language 2, Language 3, Language 5

For use with Informational Text 8

Name _____ Date _____ Assignment _____

Performance Task 17B

Speaking and Listening 6 Adapt speech to a variety of contexts and tasks, demonstrating a command of formal English when indicated or appropriate.

Task: Take Part in a Panel Discussion

Hold a conversation with a partner and participate in a panel discussion in which you discuss the rhetorical devices used in a famous speech. Each member of the panel should address a different aspect of the speech, such as persuasive appeals; word choice, connotation, and emotion; and rhetorical questions, parallelism, and analogies.

Tips for Success

Start by having a brief conversation with a partner about the assignment and the speech you selected. Then prepare for participation in a panel discussion by deciding which topic each speaker will present. As a part of your participation, include these elements:

✓ conversation with your partner about what the assignment requires and which speech you will focus on

✓ selection of a single, more focused topic to be your subject in the panel discussion

✓ examples from the speech to illustrate the points you make

✓ evaluation of the effectiveness of rhetorical elements of the speech

✓ analysis of how effectively elements were used to elicit emotion or persuade the listener

✓ discussion among panel members regarding how well the speech achieved the speaker's purpose

Rubric for Self-Assessment

Criteria for Discussion	not very					very
How productive was your conversation with your partner?	1	2	3	4	5	6
How well did you focus on one aspect of the speech as your part in the panel discussion?	1	2	3	4	5	6
How effectively did you give examples to illustrate the rhetorical element you were assigned?	1	2	3	4	5	6
To what extent did you analyze the effectiveness of elements in eliciting emotion or persuading the listener?	1	2	3	4	5	6
To what extent did you discuss how the elements worked together to achieve the speaker's purpose?	1	2	3	4	5	6

For use with Speaking and Listening 6

Name _____ Date _____ Assignment _____

Performance Task 18A

> **Informational Text 9** Analyze seventeenth-, eighteenth-, and nineteenth-century
> foundational U.S. documents of historical and literary significance (including
> The Declaration of Independence, the Preamble to the Constitution, the Bill of
> Rights, and Lincoln's Second Inaugural Address) for their themes, purposes, and
> rhetorical features.*

Task: Analyze a Foundational U.S. Document

Write an analysis of a major U.S. document, such as the essay on *Civil Disobedience* by Henry David
Thoreau or the Bill of Rights. Identify and analyze the theme, purpose, and the rhetorical devices
used to persuade the reader.

Tips for Success

Write an analysis of an important U.S. document, such as *Civil Disobedience* by Henry David
Thoreau. In your analysis, identify and analyze the theme, purpose, and rhetorical features, and
include these elements:

- ✓ identification and description of the theme and purpose of the document
- ✓ analysis of appeals to reason, emotion, ethics, or authority
- ✓ identification, analysis, and evaluation of the use of such rhetorical devices as
  parallelism, rhetorical questions, and anecdotes
- ✓ textual examples to support your analysis
- ✓ conclusions about the effectiveness of the essay

Rubric for Self-Assessment

Criteria for Success	not very					very
How clearly have you identified and described the theme and purpose of the document you chose to analyze?	1	2	3	4	5	6
How thoroughly have you analyzed its appeals to reason, emotion, ethics, and authority?	1	2	3	4	5	6
To what extent have you identified, analyzed, and evaluated the author's use of rhetorical devices?	1	2	3	4	5	6
To what extent do you provide textual examples to support your analysis?	1	2	3	4	5	6
How effectively do you draw conclusions about what makes the document of historical significance?	1	2	3	4	5	6

*Other standards covered include: Writing 1, Writing 2b, Writing 2c, Writing 2e, Writing 2f, Writing 4, Writing 9, Speaking 1a,
Speaking 1b, Speaking 1c, Speaking 3, Speaking 4, Language 1, Language 2, Language 3, Language 5

For use with Informational Text 9

Name _____ Date _____ Assignment _____

Performance Task 18B

> **Speaking and Listening 1d.** Respond thoughtfully to diverse perspectives; synthesize comments, claims, and evidence made on all sides of an issue; resolve contradictions when possible; and determine what additional information or research is required to deepen the investigation or complete the task.

Task: Compare and Contrast Perspectives

Participate in a group discussion designed to compare and contrast group member's analyses of a major U.S. document or literary work. Discuss diverse perspectives in your analyses as a group, and ask probing questions to elicit deeper thinking. Finally, determine what other information may be needed to enrich the investigation and resolve contradictions.

Tips for Success

Participate in a group discussion on a major U.S. document, such as Thoreau's *Civil Disobedience*. As a part of your participation, include these elements:

✓ present your own individual analysis of the work

✓ listen attentively to the different analyses of other group members

✓ identify diverse perspectives

✓ probe and clarify differences through thoughtful questions

✓ resolve contradictions through discussion or additional research

✓ use an appropriate, respectful tone and standard English

Rubric for Self-Assessment

Criteria for Discussion	not very					very
How well did you present and support your analysis?	1	2	3	4	5	6
How attentively did you listen to the analyses of other group members?	1	2	3	4	5	6
How accurately did you identify differences in perspectives?	1	2	3	4	5	6
To what extent did you ask thoughtful questions designed to probe and clarify differences?	1	2	3	4	5	6
To what extent did you resolve contradictions through discussion or additional research?	1	2	3	4	5	6
How well were you able to maintain an appropriate, respectful tone and use standard English throughout?	1	2	3	4	5	6

For use with Speaking and Listening 1d

Name _____ Date _____ Assignment _____

Performance Task 19A

Informational Text 10 By the end of grade 11, read and comprehend literary nonfiction in the grades 11–CCR text complexity band proficiently, with scaffolding as needed at the high end of the range.*

Task: Write a Critical Response to a Work

Write a critical response to a work of literary nonfiction. In your response, demonstrate your comprehension by discussing the elements of the writing, such as the quality of content, clarity of the thesis, organization, sentence variety, word choice, and use of rhetorical devices.

Tips for Success

Write a critical response to a work of literary nonfiction you have read. In your analysis, include these elements:

- ✓ summary of the work, including identification and description of the thesis
- ✓ analysis of the quality and clarity of content with supporting textual examples
- ✓ analysis of the author's use of word choice, sentence variety, and style to advance the thesis
- ✓ analysis and commentary on the author's use of rhetorical and literary devices, such as metaphor, hyperbole, and appeals to emotion or reason
- ✓ personal response to the work
- ✓ editing and revising where necessary

Rubric for Self-Assessment

Criteria for Success	not very					very
How clearly do you summarize the work and identify the thesis?	1	2	3	4	5	6
How effectively do you analyze the quality and clarity of the work?	1	2	3	4	5	6
To what extent do you support your analysis with textual examples?	1	2	3	4	5	6
To what extent have you analyzed the effect of the author's sentence structure, word choice, and style?	1	2	3	4	5	6
How well have you analyzed and commented on the author's use of rhetorical and literary devices?	1	2	3	4	5	6
How thoughtfully do you develop your own response to the work?	1	2	3	4	5	6
How effectively have you edited and revised your critical response?	1	2	3	4	5	6

*Other standards covered include: Writing 1, Writing 2b, Writing 2c, Writing 2e, Writing 2f, Writing 4, Writing 5, Speaking 1a, Speaking 1b, Speaking 1c, Speaking 3, Speaking 4, Language 1, Language 2, Language 3, Language 5

For use with Informational Text 10

Name _____ Date _____ Assignment _____

Performance Task 19B

Speaking and Listening 6 Adapt speech to a variety of contexts and tasks, demonstrating a command of formal English when indicated or appropriate.

Task: Take Part in a Literature Circle

Participate in a literature circle in which you discuss a work of literary nonfiction with others who have read the same work. Before beginning, discuss a format, the topics you will discuss, and any roles that group members will play.

Tips for Success

Participate in a literature circle with others who have written a critical response to the same work of literary nonfiction. As a part of your participation, include these elements:

✓ present your own response clearly and succinctly

✓ compare and contrast your response with those of others

✓ listen attentively to the responses of other group members

✓ ask thoughtful questions to clarify the responses of others

✓ convincingly answer questions about your own response

✓ summarize the responses of group members regarding the work

Rubric for Self-Assessment

Criteria for Discussion	not very					very
How clearly did you present your own response?	1	2	3	4	5	6
To what extent did you compare and contrast your own response with those of others?	1	2	3	4	5	6
How attentively did you listen to the responses of other group members?	1	2	3	4	5	6
To what extent did you ask thoughtful questions designed to clarify the responses of others?	1	2	3	4	5	6
How convincingly did you answer questions about your own response?	1	2	3	4	5	6
To what extent did you and other group members summarize responses?	1	2	3	4	5	6

For use with Speaking and Listening 6